THE
POWER
TO ACT

The development
of Scots law
for mentally
handicapped
people

Adrian D. Ward, LL.B.

 SSMH

Scottish Society for the Mentally Handicapped

Published by SSMH, 13 Elmbank Street, Glasgow, Scotland.

First published 1990

© Adrian D. Ward

British Library Cataloguing in Publication Data
Ward, Adrian D.
    The power to act: the development of Scots law for mentally handicapped people.
    1. Scotland. Mentally handicapped persons. Law
    I. Title   II. Scottish Society for the Mentally Handicapped
    344.110444

ISBN 0 9506697 7 6

Printed in Scotland by L.& S. Litho, 27 Arrol Place, London Road, Glasgow.

FOREWORD

The publication in 1984 of *Scots Law and the Mentally Handicapped*, Adrian Ward's first book, aroused considerable interest amongst professionals working with people with mental handicaps, parents and lawyers. For the first time in Scotland there was a guide to the legal position of mentally handicapped people – a difficult and complex area.

However, its careful explanation of complicated matters like guardianship, management of affairs, criminal law, special educational needs, and financial provision raised as many questions as it answered. Since then, Adrian Ward has opened out the debate in discussions with many organisations, lectures, talks, and in the media. It was obvious that a follow-up to *Scots Law and the Mentally Handicapped* was needed.

The Power to Act is the result of Adrian Ward's commitment to this challenging area of law. His enthusiasm for his subject is matched by a belief that debate and reform of certain areas of the law must be urgently encouraged if the legal rights of people with mental handicaps are to be improved.

Adrian Ward's passionate concern is SSMH's good fortune. We have benefitted from his legal expertise for some years and we are enormously grateful for the time and energy he has devoted to the preparation of this book, without charge. Few can appreciate what is involved: painstaking research, analytical insight, shaping and reshaping text, checking and rechecking. Most of this work has taken place at home and would not have been possible without the support of his family and the deferral at times of other interests. This foreword is an inadequate expression of our thanks to both Adrian Ward for his efforts and his family for their forbearance.

We hope that those who read this book will be informed and influenced by it; that some of Adrian Ward's commitment will spill over, and that others will be motivated to join him and SSMH in bringing about a better legislative support for people with mental handicaps.

William Learmonth
Chairman,
Scottish Society for the Mentally Handicapped

PREFACE

Any book which identifies and attempts to deal with the problems experienced by the mentally disordered and which provides guidance and possible solutions for them and for those who care for them is an important book.

Adrian Ward's previous book on *Scots Law and the Mentally Handicapped* has been widely acknowledged as a most useful commentary on the many and varied statutory provisions which affect the mentally handicapped in our society.

This, his second book, deals with the powers and limitations, the opportunities and the disadvantages, the rights and the wrongs which the mentally handicapped person has or experiences in taking his or her proper place in that society. *The Power to Act* is about legal capacity, the need to encourage this in someone who needs encouragement and to exercise it responsibly and effectively on behalf of someone who cannot do so himself or herself.

I welcome therefore Mr Ward's comprehensive study of guardianship and management of affairs. The Mental Welfare Commission said in its 1987 Annual Report that it is, in principle, neither for nor against guardianship but that it is only too aware of reservations expressed about its use and of criticisms made about its limited powers. As Mr Ward says, in the area of management of affairs, there is an urgent need for a comprehensive review and reform of the law by Parliament.

Such a review is long overdue and is about to be undertaken by the Scottish Law Commission. It will be assisted to a very significant extent by the author's interpretation of the existing provisions for statutory and personal guardianship and management of affairs; his most enlightening comparative study of guardianship codes in other legal systems, particularly the highly relevant Alberta and New Zealand Models; his assessment of the revival of the tutor-dative procedure (for which he was largely responsible) and of the partly implemented Disabled Persons Act; and his timely exhortation to participate in the inevitable reform of the law.

Mr Ward raises many other issues which are presently concerning the Mental Welfare Commission as well as lawyers, relatives and those who are involved with the mentally handicapped in hospitals and in the community. We need to ask why guardianship is so little used and how it might be improved or replaced. We should examine the enduring power of attorney, the making of a Will for a disabled person, the cost and rigidity of the curatory, the concept of advocacy. We should be making urgent enquiries into unfair discrimination, the need for greater individual choice, the provision of more multi-disciplinary services and joint planning.

If this book does no more than develop a greater awareness and understanding of mental disabilities, it will have achieved something, but not enough. It is essentially a challenge to respond to the compelling issues which are raised in these pages and which are the responsibility of a caring community.

Above all, it reminds us that we are required to treat the mentally handicapped in our community as individuals with unique and independent needs and characteristics.

Peter C. Millar
OBE, MA, LLB, DKS.
Chairman,
Mental Welfare Commission for Scotland

ACKNOWLEDGEMENTS

It would be impossible to name all those who have helped and encouraged my interest in mental handicap law, and who have assisted with this book. Without exception, the many lawyers at home and abroad from whom I have sought information, material and comment have responded with unstinting generosity. I have received similar help from countless members of other professions, members and workers of voluntary organisations, parents and relatives of mentally disabled people, and others. The omission of many implies no lack of appreciation for any. However, I do wish to mention some.

Dr David I. Nichols has been a source of much helpful information and stimulating comment, and I am greatly indebted to him for reading my first draft and suggesting many corrections and improvements. I have received helpful comment and information from Peter C. Millar, who has also kindly provided a Preface. Much help has been given by Sylvia Bell and Paul J. Treadwell in New Zealand, and by William Combes and Stanley S. Herr in the United States. Figure 2 on page 174 is reproduced from *The Balance of Care* by kind permission of ISD Publications and authors Nicki Baker and James Urquhart.

SSMH has become an invaluable national resource. The development of the Society's Legal and Information departments has been of major help in my work. The standing of mental handicap law was much enhanced by the appointment of Colin McKay as the Society's first Legal Adviser, and he has helped me greatly. The contribution of Linda Kerr, Information Officer, has been superb – providing me with material; reading, checking and editing; and bearing the brunt of the pressures, anxieties and sheer hard work of steering this book through to publication. Peter Bruce, Marcia Morris, Hugh Stewart and Douglas Webster of the Society all read the first draft and provided useful comment. And as ever Iain McMurray, the Society's Director, has guided this project as he has guided the development of the Society, with unrivalled knowledge and experience, balanced judgement, and unruffled good humour.

Those named above saw drafts at various stages, and bear no responsibility for any errors in the final text. Their help does not imply that they, or bodies with which they are associated, take any particular position in relation to the issues raised in this book: all opinions and comments are mine alone.

For practical help and general support, I thank colleagues and staff in my office, particularly Isobel Hannah, who typed most of the text on to word processor, then kept track of a host of alterations.

Finally, this book was written at home, in the evenings and at weekends. The task made large inroads into family time, and space. It could not have been written without the understanding tolerance of Dineke, Jennifer, Elizabeth and Carolyn.

Adrian D. Ward

CONTENTS

Personal decision-making and management of affairs
– curator bonis as manager – statutory guardian –
– the need for a "personal guardian" – tutor-dative as
"personal guardian" – historical summary.

Main features – tutors and curators in Roman law – tutors
and curators of children in Scots law – tutors and curators
of adults in Scots law – procedure for appointment of
tutors-at-law – curators bonis – tutors-dative – tutor as
personal guardian – the background to the introduction of
statutory guardianship – report of Royal Commission on the
Care and Control of the Feeble-Minded, 1908 – statutory
guardianship 1913-1984 – statutory guardianship under the
Mental Health (Scotland) Act 1984 – the tutor-dative returns.

UN Declaration on the Rights of Mentally Retarded Persons – tailoring
of guardianship powers to need – Report on Guardianship
of International League – general principles proposed by
American Association on Mental Deficiency – US Model
Statute – Dependent Adults Acts of Alberta – proposals of
English Law Society Group.

The *Morris Petition,* 1986 – tailoring of powers to need in Scots
law – comparison of powers of statutory guardians and

Diagrams etc.

I

INTRODUCTION

We are in the early stages of a quiet revolution. The law shows signs of evolving, as never before, towards a responsiveness to the needs of people with mental handicaps. Exciting developments have occurred, yet at the same time there is far greater awareness of the inadequacies and backwardness of existing provision for mentally handicapped people in our law. A few bright lights perhaps emphasise the blackness of the rest of the picture, but it is this awareness which is generating a great groundswell of demand for wider-reaching improvements.

Such awareness has increased remarkably. Demand for information is insatiable. On any miserable winter's evening, anywhere in Scotland, arrange a talk and question session on Scots law and the mentally handicapped, and an eager audience will assemble. Questions and debate will last until time runs out. Professionals concerned with social work, education, housing, psychology, the medical and paramedical professions, and perhaps others, will have given up their free time to come along. One or two lawyers or law students will be there, for the law itself is now seen as one of the professions with a significant role to play in relation to mentally handicapped people. There will be many voluntary workers, and some full time workers with voluntary organisations. And above all there will be parents and other carers – with their own hard-earned experience, and with their practical sense, anxieties, anger, certainties and uncertainties; and with their thoughtful questions, challenging those whose academic theories would cushion them from uncomfortable reality.

Awareness has spread into the country as a whole. A Private Member's Bill before Parliament to make certain improvements in provision for disabled people drew sympathy and support from individual MPs across the political spectrum, and acted as a catalyst for the public conscience. A series of English court cases about the sterilisation of mentally disabled women provoked national debate. We have seen outraged headlines about the living conditions of mentally handicapped residents in one particular hospital, followed by a stern and unequivocal expression of more general concern by the Mental Welfare Commission for Scotland. Likewise, there has been concern about the fate of those discharged into the community, if resources and support are insufficient. All of this has caused the man and woman in the street to question how our society provides for people with mental handicaps; what is their status; and what are their rights.

1

This book is mainly about specific developments which have taken place in Scots law. But those developments are a product of the broad trends which I describe, and must be considered in that context, rather than in academic isolation. And because we are looking at a dynamic situation, we must look at where existing trends could lead, and consider where perhaps they should lead.

Five years ago I wrote *Scots Law and the Mentally Handicapped*. That book described the law as it was in May 1984, but included the statutory changes which came into force on 30th September 1984 and which are now contained in the Mental Health (Scotland) Act 1984. Those changes did not represent significant progress towards meeting the needs of people with mental handicaps, and what I described was a largely static body of law which had shown little improvement in decades. Much of what I wrote then remains valid now – some specific changes are listed in Chapter XVI of this book. What has happened is that new areas have opened up; ideas identified in embryonic form five years ago are now fully fledged; concerns expressed briefly in passing five years ago have developed into major areas of debate. So instead of revising my first book and producing a new edition, I am able to leave it as it stands and to set this companion volume beside it.

This book assumes that readers have access to a copy of *Scots Law and the Mentally Handicapped*. This book also sets out to describe the law as clearly as possible for readers who are not lawyers. Unlike its predecessor, this book concentrates on specific areas of law: it is a survey of developments over the last five years, not a restatement of the whole area of law previously covered. In the areas which are covered, I have tried to respond to increasing demand for more detailed discussion of the principles of law involved, of why and how they have been developed, and of the form of legal provision which we should seek for the future.

My own awareness has developed too, in several directions – one being a greater awareness of how the law of other countries provides for people with mental handicaps. While it is disturbing to learn how backward are our own legal systems here in Britain, we do have in other countries ready-made models which we can study, and from whose experience we can learn. I have used some of this comparative material in this book.

Like *Scots Law and the Mentally Handicapped*, this book uses words with special legal meanings. Some of the terms which appear in this book are not mentioned in *Scots Law and the Mentally Handicapped*. These include terms of Scots law still in use, old terms no longer in use, and terms used in other legal systems. I have explained these terms in the course of the text, where they first appear, and I have included a glossary at the end.

The warning given in *Scots Law and the Mentally Handicapped* applies here also: several of these legal terms have wider areas of meaning, and the definitions which I have provided cover only what is necessary to understand these books. In relation to some key concepts, existing legal terminology is unacceptably inappropriate or imprecise, therefore I have used my own terms. These also appear in the glossary, in inverted commas.

"Mentally disabled" is not a term with special legal meaning. It is my own phrase to cover anyone whose legal capacity is limited because of some form of mental disability, including mental handicap. I would suggest that as a generic term it is more appropriate and more acceptable than terms which are found in our law, such as "mentally disordered", "mentally impaired" and "insane". Likewise, I prefer to refer to "mental disability law", where lawyers and legislators still tend to refer, misleadingly, to "mental health law". To informed laymen, "mental health" connotes mental illness, as opposed to mental handicap and other mental disabilities. By "mental disability law" I mean law which applies across the whole field of disabilities and conditions which are likely to result in any form of legal incapacity or special legal provision. Such disabilities and conditions include those resulting from mental handicap, mental illness, conditions associated with ageing, multiple sensory handicap and inability to communicate, and so forth – and also, of course, people with combinations of such conditions. See the panel on pages 4-5 for further information, including in particular definitions of mental handicap and mental illness, which are the most common causes of mental disability.

"Guardian" now has such a confusing range of meanings that I try to use more precise terms. I use "statutory guardian" for guardians under the Mental Health (Scotland) Act 1984, and "personal guardian" for true guardians empowered to provide help, make decisions, and exercise control in areas of personal decision-making. In relation to management of property and affairs, I use the terms "manager" and "management", rather than "guardian" and "guardianship".

I have sought to take account of all relevant developments in Scots law down to 31st August 1989. I mention provisions of the Self-Governing Schools etc. (Scotland) Bill which will only become law if the Bill is enacted with those provisions as they appeared in the Bill at 31st August 1989. In relation to other legal systems, I have used the most up-to-date information available to me at time of writing.

The long-awaited White Paper *Caring for People: Community Care in the Next Decade and Beyond* was published on 16th November 1989, as this book went to press. In view of the importance of the White Paper, I refer to particular proposals where relevant. In general terms, the regime

3

Mental handicap is characterised by (a) intellectual functioning which is significantly below average and (b) marked impairment in ability to adapt to the cultural demands of society. Both of these characteristics, not just one or the other, must be present before a person can be said to have a mental handicap. Mental handicap is not an illness or disease. It may be caused by an illness such as meningitis, or associated with a genetic condition such as Down's Syndrome. It may be caused by physical damage to the brain during pregnancy, during birth, or at any time during life. There may be complex social and psychological causes. In many cases the specific cause is unknown. Common consequences of mental handicap are poor concentration, poor short-term memory, learning difficulty, and difficulty in understanding complex or abstract ideas. There is great variation in degrees of handicap. More serious mental handicaps may be associated with degrees of difficulty in communicating, in performing everyday functions such as dressing and feeding, and in other areas of functioning. Mental handicap cannot be "cured", but with suitable education and training and a helpful environment a mentally handicapped person can learn to do much which he would not have learned unaided.

Some definitions of mental handicap require the intellectual impairment to have been present from an early age. Other definitions include people whose impairment occurred at any age, and this wider approach is used for the purposes of this book, as there is no need to distinguish those whose impairment occurred later in life.

Mental illness is a general term covering a variety of disturbances affecting emotional, social and cognitive functioning and behaviour. Understanding and communication are distorted rather than deficient. Behaviour is misdirected rather than inept. Emotional reactions are in various ways and degrees inappropriate. A broad definition of mental illness would include all of the following categories:

(a) Psychotic conditions, such as schizophrenia and manic depression.
(b) Disorders with organic causes, such as dementias and degenerative brain disorders.
(c) Psychoneurotic disorders, such as anxiety states and obsessional disorders.
(d) Disorders of conduct and personality.

> **Legal capacity** may be impaired by a mental handicap or by mental illness. The degree and nature of impairment may vary from one individual to another. In the case of mental illness, the impairment may be intermittent, or may vary rapidly. Legal capacity may also be impaired by other causes such as inability to communicate due to illness or serious multiple sensory handicap.
>
> **Mental disability** is proposed and used, in this book, as a generic term applied to all conditions and disabilities which are likely to result in any form of legal incapacity. **Mental disability law** is the whole body of law which applies to such disabilities. Excluded from this definition of mental disability are the legal incapacities of children, and legal incapacities and disqualifications unrelated to personal capability (such as those imposed on bankrupts, prisoners and some other offenders, aliens, and others).

envisaged by the White Paper will inevitably generate an additional and huge demand for clarification, improvement and reform of the law in all of the areas discussed in this book. It is inconceivable that the White Paper's proposals could fully achieve their stated objectives of independent living and achievement of full potential, in the absence of the development of private law described and advocated in this book. Any regime for the provision of services should be co-ordinated with the private law regime dealing with personal decision-making, guardianship, management of affairs, and so forth. I have often pointed out the possibility of using the same assessment procedures for both purposes. The proposals in the White Paper for multi-disciplinary assessment provide a splendid opportunity for achieving this, effectively and cost-efficiently.

Scots Law and the Mentally Handicapped was not intended to be a legal textbook. I made that clear in the first chapter, and avoided cluttering the text with references to legal authorities. In this book also I have refrained from decorating the text with copious references to footnotes, but I have listed some important references and sources of further information in Appendix I. While lawyers are likely to be the most frequent users of Appendix I, interested non-lawyers will also find much of the material referred to well worth reading.

Where case histories are given without reference to published authority, they are drawn from unpublished material in my possession. Identities and identifying features are obscured, and these case-histories are generally in simplified form. All of them are either drawn from my own experience, or have been reported to me from first-hand sources which I consider to be reliable. I have selected from a considerable amount of material reported to me personally, all of which has helped to shape this book. Non-selection of any particular material does not in any way imply doubts as to reliability.

Where "he or she" would be cumbersome, I have used "he" to cover both sexes. But where I describe law applicable to one sex only, I have sought to make that clear. In a historical context I have sometimes used older words such as "idiot" and "dumb", where they reflect the perceptions of the time more accurately than the preferred modern terms.

II

FUNDAMENTAL ISSUES

The dilemmas and debates which are receiving so much attention have origins in some quite simple propositions. People with mental handicaps, like some in other categories, may be less able than others to look after themselves, safeguard themselves and their interests, make decisions, and so forth. Special laws may be needed to protect such people. Across many areas of general law, special provisions, adaptations and exceptions may be needed to take account of their disabilities. To the extent that mentally handicapped people are considered unable to act or make decisions for themselves, they may be deemed not to have full "legal capacity". Their disability is reflected in their legal status in the form of some degree of "legal incapacity". Their acts may not have the same consequences as those of people with full legal capacity. Their legal incapacity may mean that they cannot validly make some decisions, take some actions, or enter some transactions. In consequence, other people may make decisions for them, and act and transact for them.

These general propositions may be easy to state. They lead to questions which are less easy to answer. What is the precise nature and extent of an individual's actual incapacity? For example, in the area of decision-making, does he simply require help in communicating his decisions; or does he require help in making them; or is he unable – even with such help – to make them? How should an individual's actual incapacity be assessed? Once assessed, how should it be translated into legal incapacity? Does our present law create or allow discrepancies between actual incapacity and legal incapacity? For example, does the law deprive an individual of the legal capacity to make for himself a decision of which he is in fact capable? Conversely, are there areas in which the law may thrust responsibility upon him unfairly?

Even if the law's special treatment of an individual is accurately matched to his actual needs and actual capacity, such differentiation is nevertheless a form of discrimination, with disadvantages as well as advantages. If we decree that certain actions and transactions of a handicapped individual should not have the usual legal consequences and effect, we may be protecting him, but we are also depriving him of rights and legal status which the rest of us have. It is difficult to protect without imposing restrictions on those protected. The restrictions upon the rights of the handicapped individual are obvious when the law appoints others to supervise him or to make decisions for him. In

7

practice the alternative to such appointment may be that others will assume such roles without any legal authority to do so, which is clearly an infringement of the rights of the handicapped person, no matter how well motivated or in fact beneficial.

At the heart of many of the dilemmas, debates and disputes is this step – taken by all legal systems – of conferring a supervisory or decision-making role on someone else. One person makes for another decisions which normally we all make for ourselves. Many questions arise, often difficult. Who should be appointed, when, and with what powers and duties? How, and by whom, should the exercise of powers and performance of duties be monitored? How should any changes in the nature or extent of the incapacity, or of the handicapped person's needs or circumstances, be monitored; and how and when should the appointment be reviewed, or the appointee's powers and duties adjusted? When different appointments are made for different purposes, how should they inter-relate and co-ordinate? How are the powers and duties of the appointee balanced against the rights of the handicapped person, and matched to his needs and capabilities? And what is the inter-relationship with the concerns, needs and legitimate interests of relatives, carers, and others?

These issues lead us into the more specific topics of the following chapters, but let us first pause and attempt to answer one fundamental question. Can we define, in general terms, the principles which should govern the special provision which the law makes for people with mental handicaps – the ideal towards which we would wish development of the law to lead us? I think that we can, and that the answers are valid for all those lacking full capacity, whether through mental handicap or from other causes. We can apply to the law the same fundamental principles as underlie the approach of other professions in their work with people with such disabilities. Ideally, for any handicapped individual, the same general law as applies to all of us should apply fully and without differentiation, except only to the minimum extent that special provision is necessary. Where special protection or special provisions are needed, they should be provided, but limited to the essential minimum. Where the price of protection is restriction, that price must be clearly worth paying, and the restrictions should be minimised. Decision-making should be taken away from the mentally disabled person to the minimum possible extent, and to that end he should if necessary be helped to make and communicate his own decisions. In areas of doubt, there should be a presumption of competence. When decision-making is transferred to others, they should still try to involve the mentally disabled person in decision-making as much as possible. Anyone appointed to a supervisory or decision-making role should be appointed by legal procedure entailing careful assessment of needs and circumstances; the appointment should be subject to periodic review; when appropriate the appointee's performance should be monitored. The total regime applying to the handicapped individual (made up of special rules and protections, and supervisory and decision-making appointments) should be co-ordinated to minimise doubt and conflict, and should be directed towards serving his best interests, enhancing his development and human dignity, and minimising the effects of his disability upon all areas of his life.

III

GUARDIANSHIP AND MANAGEMENT: AN OVERVIEW

Most legal systems, including Scots law, identify two broad areas of decision-making within which mentally disabled people may require special protection and help. Within each area, it may be necessary to appoint someone to act in a supervisory and decision-making role for the mentally disabled person.

The first area is the area of personal decision-making, where some form of personal guardianship may be required. The second is the area of management of affairs, including management of money and property, transaction of business, and so on, where some form of manager may be required.

In the last few years Scots law has seen substantial changes and developments in relation to personal decision-making and personal guardianship. These developments are still ongoing. We now have two persons who may be appointed to a supervisory and decision-making role in relation to mentally disabled adults. One is the statutory guardian: statutory guardianship has existed in its present form only since 1984. The other is the "tutor-dative": appointment of tutors-dative is one of our oldest procedures, which fell into disuse many decades ago, and was revived in its modern form in 1986. Shortly we shall explain these terms, and then we shall examine the whole subject of personal guardianship more closely in this and the next few chapters.

While the story of personal guardianship in Scots law has been one of recent and substantial development, which is ongoing, the position in relation to management of affairs is quite the opposite. While various management techniques are available, under current Scottish law and practice the only general manager of affairs who can be appointed to a mentally disabled adult is the "curator bonis". The curator bonis has been with us since the early eighteenth century, and the current regime governing curators bonis is substantially one laid down in 1849. We shall mention curators bonis again several times in this chapter and the next, and shall consider them in more detail and in their own right in Chapter X.

In both the area of personal decision-making and the area of management of affairs, there has been increasing pressure for change. In the area of personal decision-making, the law has responded as best it can. However, this rapid development has raised new concerns, and we have at best stop-gap solutions which are not ideal. In the area of management of affairs, the law has so far failed to respond to the ever

10

more urgent need for change and improvement. In both areas, albeit for contrasting reasons, the next development must be comprehensive review and reform of the law by Parliament.

At this point, let us look more closely at the major changes which have taken place in the area of personal decision-making, and at why we should now find in this territory both the statutory guardian and the tutor-dative.

Statutory Guardian

Since 1984, the statutory guardian has had no general role in the area of personal decision-making. A statutory guardian is usually appointed only as a last resort in unsatisfactory situations, when some form of intervention is required. The only powers of a statutory guardian are in relation to deciding place of residence; ensuring that a person attends for medical treatment, occupation, education or training; and ensuring that medical practitioners, mental health officers and others have access to the person. The modern statutory guardian is not a true "personal guardian", and does not meet the need for a form of personal guardianship in our law. "Personal guardian" is a descriptive term, not a technical term of Scots law. It is necessary to explain what the term means, and why there is a need for some form of personal guardianship.

The Need for a Personal Guardian

The law regards all young children as being under the complete supervision and control of their "tutors", who are normally their parents. The degree of parental control recognised by law usually lessens as they grow older. Once a person reaches adulthood at the age of 18, any remaining rights of supervision and control come to an end, even though that person may be mentally disabled. Neither the parents nor anyone else retains any automatic rights of supervision or control into adulthood, no matter how severe the disability or incapacity.

Some adults with mental handicaps do in fact need help and supervision. The extent will vary from individual to individual. For any one individual, the extent may vary as the years go by – it is not uncommon for the capabilities of people with mental handicaps to continue to develop for some time after reaching nominal adulthood at the age of 18.

The areas of decision-making in which help and guidance may be required range from mundane and everyday matters such as what to eat and what to wear, what to do and where to go, to major decisions such as where and with whom to live. There are decisions about taking part in work, training, and social activities; decisions about whom to associate with and whom not to associate with. Then there are decisions

11

about medical, dental and other health care. In these and many other matters individual handicapped people may be unable, at least without help, to make sound and reasonable judgements or decisions for themselves.

No-one has any automatic right to make such decisions for another adult, however handicapped. In every legal system, specific procedure is required in order to appoint someone to such a supervisory role. The essential elements of such procedure will include an assessment of whether such an appointment is needed, and a decision as to who should be appointed. Such an appointment does represent a diminution of the rights of the handicapped individual, but if the powers conferred are limited to those which are necessary, the only rights lost will be those which the handicapped person is unable to exercise for himself. There is greater risk of infringement of the rights of the handicapped person where there is no judicial determination that such an appointment is necessary, yet someone simply assumes such a role without any legal authority to do so.

Parents or other carers not greatly swayed by arguments about the rights and liberties of the handicapped person may nevertheless perceive a need for such an appointment on more practical grounds. For example, they may feel it important that they should be able to give medical consent. Or they may feel that, without such appointment, professionals and authorities treat them as having little or no standing in relation to decisions about the handicapped person.

As already mentioned "personal guardian" is not a technical term of Scots law. It is used in this book to describe someone legally appointed to exercise guidance, supervision and control in some or all of the areas which I have described.

Tutor-Dative

If we set the statutory guardian to one side as being an interventionist guardian with only limited specific powers of an interventionist nature, and as not being a true personal guardian, then the tutor-dative is the only true personal guardian of mentally disabled adults in Scots law.

"Tutor-dative" is a technical term of Scots law. "Tutor" is the legal label given to the parent of a young child. The same label is applied to someone else in the role of parent of a young child, or in a similar role in relation to a mentally disabled adult. "Dative" means appointed by a court. A "tutor-dative" is a person put by a court into a quasi-parental role in relation to a mentally disabled adult. The step of reviving this procedure was taken in a court case referred to as *Morris, Petitioner.*

The procedure of appointing tutors-dative disappeared from use early this century, but has now leapfrogged over decades of intervening legislation to reappear, clothed in new and more sophisticated detail, as a solution to modern needs. Those needs were for a personal guardian in the area of personal decision-making and personal care and supervision. They were not met by current legislative provision.

To understand the revival of this procedure, and the need for it, we need to look at the historical development of this area of law. For the sources of the new refinements, we have to look to the experience of other legal systems. The historical development is traced in Chapter IV, and the experience of some other legal systems is considered in Chapter V (and also, later, in Chapter XII).

This chapter concludes with a brief summary of the historical route by which we have arrived at the present-day trio of statutory guardian, tutor-dative, and curator bonis. This summary sets the scene for those interested in the more detailed history narrated in the next chapter; and it provides a sufficient basic historical background for those who wish to turn direct to Chapter V.

Historical Summary

This summary should be read in conjunction with the diagram on page 15.

1. In earliest Scots law the sovereign was guardian of people with serious mental illness, and the feudal lord was guardian of those with serious mental handicaps. Later the sovereign became guardian of both mentally ill and mentally handicapped people.

2. The sovereign delegated guardianship powers to curators-dative. They were a team of selected relatives. They were both personal guardians and managers of affairs.

3. The term "tutor-dative" gradually replaced "curator-dative". The meaning of both terms was the same.

4. From about the fourteenth century the Roman law of children was gradually introduced and applied to mentally disabled adults. The tutor-at-law, the nearest male relative, was introduced as both personal guardian and manager of affairs. This introduction of Roman law was confirmed by a statute of 1585.

5. The procedure to appoint a tutor-at-law continued in use through to the nineteenth century, and is still available, though no longer used. The procedure was cumbersome, rigid and expensive. Appointment was only possible when the mental disability was severe.

6. Tutors-dative survived despite the introduction of tutors-at-law.

13

Procedure to appoint tutors-dative as both personal guardians and managers of affairs remained in force. The procedure was used because it was quicker, less difficult and less expensive; and also because someone other than the nearest male relative could be appointed tutor-dative, but not as tutor-at-law.

7. Around 1700 the curator bonis was introduced as a manager of affairs only. This was also a response to the delays, difficulty and expense of procedure to appoint a tutor-at-law. The curator bonis was originally seen as a temporary appointment, and it is still the law that if a tutor-at-law should be appointed, then the appointment of the curator bonis terminates. An additional use of curators bonis was in cases of people who needed someone to manage their affairs, but whose mental disabilities were not sufficiently severe to permit appointment of a tutor-at-law.

8. In 1913 the statutory guardian was introduced. The definition of statutory guardian was the same as the tutor of young children – a full personal guardian.

9. Soon after 1913 the statutory guardian became the only personal guardian, and the curator bonis became the only general manager of affairs. Tutors to adults – both tutors-at-law and tutors-dative – dropped out of use. In the last reported case of appointment of a tutor-dative, reported in 1924, a tutor-dative was appointed as personal guardian only, so that an existing curator bonis continued to act as manager of affairs.

10. Statutory guardians were seen as having an interventionist role, rather than as being true personal guardians. In 1984 the definition of statutory guardian was changed to suit a purely interventionist role. This left a gap in legal provision for true personal guardianship at the very time when awareness of the importance of personal guardianship was increasing.

11. In 1986 the tutor-dative was brought back into use as a true personal guardian. In modern practice the tutor-dative is often given limited powers, tailored to the needs of the individual disabled person. Appointments so far have been limited to personal guardianship, and have not included management of affairs.

12. The current position is this:

    The statutory guardian has an interventionist role, with powers limited to deciding place of residence; ensuring that medical care, training, etc., is provided; and related powers.

    The tutor-dative is personal guardian, and can be appointed with

14

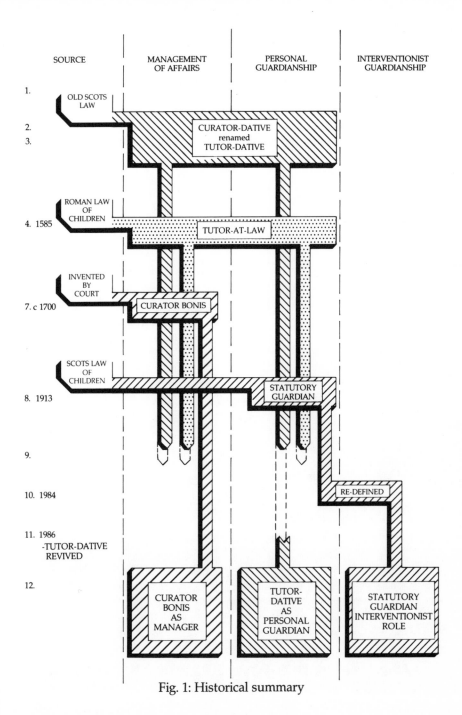

Fig. 1: Historical summary

limited powers. A tutor-dative could also be appointed to manage affairs, but that has not been done for many years.

The curator bonis is manager of affairs only.

Tutors-at-law have not been appointed for many years, but could be. A tutor-at-law would act as both personal guardian and manager of affairs, and would supersede any existing curator bonis.

IV

HISTORY OF PERSONAL GUARDIANSHIP IN SCOTS LAW

Some readers may wish to proceed directly to Chapter V, having read the summary at the end of the last chapter of the historical background to the modern position. This chapter tells the story in more detail. This story is the key to a full understanding of our present law, and some of the problems which we face. It also teaches lessons relevant to any discussion of reform and improvement of our law.

Before those still on board embark on this quick historical voyage, let me try to chart some of the main features and currents which we shall encounter. There have been three major influences on the development of Scots law of personal guardianship for mentally disabled people. The first is Roman law, which still forms the basis of our common law in this area. The second is the law of children, which has shared both concepts and terminology with the law concerning adults with mental disabilities. On occasions, the law of children seems to have been referred to and drawn upon in preference to the existing law concerning adults with mental disabilities. The third influence has been the law of management of property and affairs, which has of course always co-existed with the law of personal guardianship, and in the past has tended to be the dominant partner. More recently the trend has been for the two areas of law to diverge.

A recurring question is the relative weight to be given to claims of kinship, on the one hand, and to assessment of suitability, on the other, when determining who should be personal guardian.

Finally, watch out for tricky currents which have tended to cause terminology to shift its meaning and concepts to move from one side to the other! This has been true of the old terms "tutor" and "curator", and recently the definition of statutory "guardian" has changed substantially. Of course, these currents are not in fact either capricious or random. They generally represent a response to perceptions and social conditions at the time in question. This history not only explains where the law now stands, but encourages us to continue the process of adaptation to meet modern perceptions and social conditions.

Tutors and Curators: Roman Law

The two terms "tutor" and "curator" have a long history from early Roman law through to modern Scots law. Tutor is derived from the Latin for "defend", curator from the Latin for "care". Both terms involve

17

elements of both personal guardianship and management of affairs, but over the centuries their areas of meaning have altered and the boundary between them has shifted.

In Roman law the tutor had no role in relation to mentally disabled adults. The tutor was personal guardian and manager of the affairs of children up to the age of puberty. For this purpose the ages became fixed at 12 for girls and 14 for boys. These remain the relevant ages in modern Scots law, though this may soon change.

On the death of a father, a tutor to his children appointed in his Will took precedence over any other tutor. Failing a tutor appointed by Will, the tutor was a near relative – the heir who would succeed to the child's estate if the child died, or the nearest "agnate" (i.e. nearest male relative, related solely through males), or, in later Roman law, the next of kin, whether related through males or females. Failing any such tutor, a "tutor-dative" was appointed by a judicial official.

In Roman law there were two main types of curator. As Roman law developed, it was realised that older children required some degree of protection, so children up to the age of 25 had a curator. Dealings with such children required the concurrence of their curators. In modern Scots law the curator still advises and concurs in the dealings of children from 12/14 up to 18. In both Roman law and modern Scots law the curator's role is limited to management of affairs, and does not include personal guardianship.

The other main type of curator in Roman law was the curator to adults who were "furious" or "prodigal". This is the oldest use of the term "curator". The curator was both personal guardian and manager of property and affairs. The term "furious" can best be equated to "lunatic", though this form of curatory was extended to mental disability generally, including "persons of weak mind", and also to persons who were deaf, dumb, or chronically ill, on the grounds that they were not able to manage their own affairs. In early Roman law the nearest agnate became curator, but such appointment was subsequently superseded, in most cases, by appointment by a judicial official, who had a discretion as to whom he appointed. He could exclude the agnates if he thought fit. So even in Roman times, although appointment of a personal guardian to young children gave priority to a father's Will, or to close kinship, in the case of mentally disabled adults the emphasis shifted towards judicial appointment of someone best fitted for the role. Assessment of suitability tended to prevail over claims of kinship alone.

In Roman law there was an area of overlap between tutors and curators. A curator was appointed to over-ride the authority of an errant or incapable tutor, and likewise a curator was appointed in the event of litigation between a ward and the ward's own tutor.

Tutors and Curators of Children in Scots Law

In relation to "pupil" children (girls up to 12, boys up to 14), Scots law was substantially similar to Roman law right up to 1886, and in many respects is similar still. The tutor was, and still is, both personal guardian and the manager of affairs and property. Failing the father, the order of priority was (a) a tutor appointed by the father's Will; or (b) the nearest agnate (in Scots law, the nearest male on the father's side, even though related through females); and (c) a tutor-dative appointed by the court. There were two qualifications to the tutor's authority in the area of personal guardianship. Firstly, the mother, rather than the tutor, had custody until the child was 7. Secondly, if the nearest agnate would have been heir if the child died, he was not permitted to have custody.

The Guardianship of Infants Acts, of which the first was in 1886, altered the law to the present position in which the tutors are (a) both parents, or the surviving parent; or (b) appointed by Will; or (c) appointed by the court.

Curators to minor children had, and still have, a role in Scots law substantially similar to that in Roman law. They are not personal guardians. They advise and consent in the management of affairs. The child may have no curator, and act alone. Nowadays the curators are either the parents, or nominated by the parents, or chosen by the child. Minority ended at 21 until 1969, and now ends at 18.

Further change is on the way. The age of 16 has gradually gained increasing significance, and there is now a strong trend towards replacing the 12/14 threshold with a somewhat different one at 16. A report by the Scottish Law Commission (*The Legal Capacity and Responsibility of Minors and Pupils*, published December 1987) gives warning of impending redundancy in a section bluntly headed "Getting rid of tutors and curators". The Scottish Law Commission's proposals were embodied in a Private Member's Bill which was unsuccessful, but it would not be surprising if they were reintroduced in Parliament.

Tutors and Curators to Adults in Scots Law

It would appear that in early Scots law the sovereign was guardian of "the furious". Only the sovereign had power to have them physically restrained by being put in chains. The feudal lord was guardian of "his idiot and fatuous vassals".

Later, the sovereign was guardian of all those who were "insane", but always delegated guardianship – both personal guardianship and management of affairs – to selected kinsmen, usually a team of kinsmen from both father's and mother's side. Within the circle of kinship, those chosen required to be "men of judgement and discretion". The appointment followed a procedure called "cognition" – an inquest to ascertain whether the ward was "insane". The old definitions of insanity clearly included significant mental handicap.

From about the fourteenth century onwards the principles of Roman law were assimilated into many areas of Scots law. In this area of law, the result was a shift from the team of kinsmen acting as guardians to a single guardian who was the nearest male agnate. This was confirmed in a statute of 1585 which declared that, following Roman law, "the nearest agnates and kinsmen of natural fools, idiots and furious persons" should be appointed "to their tutory and curatory".

The terminology was shifting. In Roman law, the guardians of adults were called curators, and that appears to have been the term used in fifteenth-century Scotland. The statute of 1585 refers to "tutory and curatory", apparently as synonyms. Soon afterwards the shift in terminology was completed, and "tutor" took over from "curator" as the term for the personal guardian of mentally disabled adults. Curators were ousted from any role in relation to mentally disabled adults, and never again had any significant role as personal guardians, though they did return later in a role almost entirely limited to management of property and affairs.

Not only the label "tutor", but also much of the package to which it was attached, was taken from the Roman law concerning children and applied in Scots law to mentally disabled adults. Many legal texts simply relate that in this area Scots law follows Roman law: none, so far as I am aware, acknowledge that, although the Roman tutors and curators to children were given similar roles in Scots law, in the case of mentally disabled adults it was the Roman tutor to young children who entered Scots law, rather than the Roman curator to mentally disabled people. The most significant difference is that in appointing a tutor, kinship takes priority, whereas in appointing a curator to mentally disabled people, suitability took priority over kinship in Roman law. In this respect the earlier Scots law was closer to Roman law, in that a team of guardians was selected from the circle of kinsmen, appointment being based on suitability rather than closeness of relationship.

The nearest agnate, appointed as tutor in accordance with the statute of 1585, became known as the "tutor-at-law". The older Scots curator-dative did not disappear altogether, but by the same process of nameshift was rechristened "tutor-dative". These two tutors – the tutor-at-law and the tutor-dative – have remained the two available forms ever since.

In the seventeenth century the position was summarised as follows. Usually, the nearest male agnate was appointed the tutor-at-law. If the nearest male agnate did not have himself appointed, some other suitable person could be appointed tutor-dative. A tutor-dative could also be appointed as an interim measure, pending appointment of a tutor-at-law. But if a tutor-at-law was appointed, he always took over from the tutor-dative, no matter how long the tutor-dative had been acting. The tutor-at-law had to be at least 25 years old. In addition he had to be fit to administer the affairs of another, and he had to give security by producing a financial guarantee that he would administer the ward's affairs properly.

The tutor was manager of affairs and also personal guardian, but if the tutor-at-law would also have been heir in the event of the ward's death, custody was given to someone else. Apart from this proviso, there was no enquiry into the suitability of the tutor to act as personal guardian. Management of affairs was seen as the main role – hence the requirement that the tutor-at-law should be fit for that role, and able to find security for his actings in that role.

Originally the "nearest male agnate" rule applied to married women, but later it was held that the husband had prior claim to be appointed tutor-at-law to his wife.

In the seventeenth century tutors were customarily appointed to people who were deaf and dumb – they "had sufficient judgement, but could not act by it". However, that use of the procedure dwindled and disappeared in the eighteenth century.

If serious doubt arose as to the trustworthiness of a tutor, he could be removed by an "action of removing suspect tutors". Anyone could bring such an action.

Procedure for Appointment of Tutors-at-Law

It is worth looking at the old procedure. It gives a general indication of perceptions of the time. More particularly, the difficulties of that procedure were responsible for the survival of the tutor-dative and the creation of the modern curator bonis.

The procedure for appointing a tutor-at-law remained substantially the same for several centuries down to 1868. The procedure could be initiated by "any party having an interest", though in 1820 that was defined as meaning any relative. A writ called a brieve was obtained from Chancery, on payment of the appropriate fee. The brieve took one of two standard forms, the " brieve of furiosity" and the "brieve of idiotry". Applicants usually played safe by obtaining both.

The brieve was addressed to the appropriate judge, and directed him to summon an inquest – the cognition – to answer a list of standard questions. Was the person "incompos mentis" and either "fatuous and a natural idiot" or "prodigal and furious", and were there grounds for fear that he might alienate his lands and goods? When did that condition commence (any subsequent actings being deemed void)? Who was the nearest agnate aged over 25, was he fit to administer the affairs of another, and was he able to find security? Was the tutor the nearest heir (in which case someone else had to be nominated to take custody)?

A jury of fifteen was empanelled. Their duty was to answer these questions, their decision on each being by majority. The mental disability was proved by the depositions of acquaintances and the opinions of medical men. It was considered important that wherever possible the jury should actually see the person to whom the proceedings related. The jury were kept strictly to the terms of the brieve. In the case of mental handicap "fatuous" meant "entirely deprived of the faculty of reason", "a person without mind at all". Only if the handicapped person was held to come within these definitions could a tutor-at-law be appointed. It was not a question of deciding in general terms whether there was a significant mental disability "even though it be carried to that point that he cannot take care of himself, or manage his property".

Only the nearest agnate could be appointed tutor-at-law. If he declined appointment, the next nearest could not be appointed. As to fitness to administer, that was presumed unless the contrary was established.

Once the procedure had been completed, the Clerk of Court received the security for the due performance by the tutor-at-law of his duties, the papers were returned to Chancery, and the appointment of tutor-at-law completed.

While this procedure for appointment of tutors-at-law was still in force, an eminent legal writer described it as "very absurd, very cumbrous, and very expensive". The resulting creation of curators bonis and use of tutors-dative procedure are described in the next two sections.

The procedure for appointment of tutors-at-law was modified in 1868 by the Court of Session Act of that year. The procedure was transferred to the Court of Session. The terms of the brieve were altered to an enquiry as to whether the person was "insane". Insanity was defined as including not only the "fatuous" and "furious", but also unsoundness of mind rendering the person incapable of managing his affairs.

The Age of Majority (Scotland) Act 1969 has the effect of reducing to 18 the minimum age for tutors-at-law – should any now be appointed.

Curators Bonis

In the eighteenth century the term "curator" re-emerged in relation to mental disability, but the old term was applied to a new concept. This new curator – the "curator bonis" – was a manager of affairs only, not a personal guardian. The Court of Session started appointing curators bonis as a response to the delays and difficulties of procedure by cognition. Curators bonis were appointed as temporary managers until a tutor-at-law took over. They were also appointed to those unable to manage their affairs, but outwith the extreme definitions of the "fatuous" and "furious".

Curators bonis became, and remain, well established in our law. In this century curators bonis have taken over entirely from tutors in the management of the property and affairs of mentally disabled people. However, the appointment of a curator bonis was terminated by appointment of a tutor-at-law (and still could be). Early in the nineteenth century it became settled practice to require evidence of incapacity in the form of two medical certificates, and that remains the requirement. Since 1880 the Sheriff Courts have had jurisdiction to appoint curators bonis to smaller estates, and now the Sheriff Courts can appoint curators bonis to estates of any size. Some issues concerning curators bonis are discussed later, in Chapter X.

Tutors-Dative

As we have seen, the tutor-dative is the oldest form of guardian to mentally disabled people in Scots law. Originally called curator-dative, this was the guardian appointed by the sovereign in earliest times. The curator-dative was still the only form in 1476, according to records which survive of an appointment then.

Following the Act of 1585, which gave priority to tutors-at-law, appointment of tutors-dative became infrequent, but did not disappear. The sovereign's jurisdiction to appoint tutors-dative was exercised by the Court of Session until 1707, then by the Court of Exchequer until 1856, when jurisdiction of the Court of Exchequer was transferred back to the Court of Session, where it remains.

Originally, cognition – the judicial inquest – was a prerequisite for appointment of a tutor-dative, but in the seventeenth century a practice began of granting petitions for appointment of tutors-dative without cognition. Early in the eighteenth century cognition practically disappeared from tutor-dative cases, but not quite – as late as 1881, for example, a tutor-dative was appointed following cognition. By that date, however, it was generally regarded as sufficient to submit two medical certificates, as in petitions to appoint curators bonis. The nearest male agnate could, if he wished, opt to be appointed tutor-dative under this simpler procedure, as an alternative to appointment as tutor-at-law following cognition.

Tutors-dative accordingly survived because of various disadvantages which arose from the rules regarding tutors-at-law, and despite the precedence given to tutors-at-law as a result of the Act of 1585. Situations in which tutors-dative were appointed included the following:

1. Because of the length of time which it took to have a tutor-at-law appointed, a tutor-dative was sometimes appointed as a temporary measure, to act pending appointment of a tutor-at-law.

2. Only the nearest male agnate, and no-one else, could be appointed tutor-at-law. A tutor-dative would accordingly be appointed following cognition, if the nearest agnate declined office, or was shown to be unsuitable, or was unable to give security.

3. A tutor-dative was appointed when appointment of someone other than the nearest agnate was desired (for example, in one reported case the nearest agnate felt that he was too old and infirm to act as tutor, and he accordingly petitioned for someone else to be appointed tutor-dative).

4. Sometimes the nearest agnate opted to be appointed tutor-dative rather than tutor-at-law, because of the difficulties, delays and expense of procedure by cognition for appointment as tutor-at-law.

5. The appointment of a tutor-at-law automatically terminated any existing appointment of a curator bonis. If there was an existing curator bonis, and it was desired that the curatory should continue, this could be achieved by opting for appointment of a tutor-dative rather than a tutor-at-law. That was a factor in the very last reported case of appointment of a tutor-dative prior to revival of the procedure in 1986. The case was called *Dick -v- Douglas*, and was reported in 1924. A tutor-dative was appointed as personal guardian only, allowing the management of affairs by a curator bonis to continue.

Tutor as Personal Guardian

Until statutory guardianship was introduced in 1913, the only personal guardians of mentally disabled people were (a) tutors and (b) persons given custody in cases where a tutor-at-law was disqualified because he was heir. In practice, the disqualification applied when the disabled person owned heritage (land or buildings) to which the nearest agnate would fall heir on the death of the disabled person; but not otherwise.

The older legal writers were bluntly explicit about the reason for this disqualification. The nearest agnate was the best person to manage property, as he would take good care of that which he was likely to inherit. But the law had to "take away from him the temptation which the possession of the [ward's] person would give to accelerate his succession by sacrificing the [ward's] life"

The case of *Dick -v- Douglas,* mentioned above, is cited as indicating that latterly these fears were not regarded so seriously. In that case the nearest agnate was given personal guardianship, though he was appointed tutor-dative, not tutor-at-law.

When the tutor was personal guardian, he had complete control of the person and of personal decision-making – full and unqualified personal guardianship. In practice, however, the tutor's guardianship seems to have been seen simply as "possession of the ward's person". Normally the tutor was also the manager of property and affairs, and over the centuries the predominant interest and attention seems to have been given to property aspects of the role of the tutor, rather than to personal guardianship. It would appear that tutors were generally appointed only in cases where there were significant assets. At any one time, that must have represented only a small proportion of the mentally handicapped population. For the great majority of mentally handicapped people, there was probably no perception of a need for personal guardianship. Most mentally handicapped people would simply have been in the *de facto* guardianship of those who cared for them. Until the middle of last century many mentally handicapped people lived all their days in the communities into which they had been born. There was no statutory provision for them other than the poorhouse or workhouse. Some were placed in asylums or hospitals. Having a tutor as guardian probably, of itself, made little practical difference to their lives.

The Background to the Introduction of Statutory Guardianship

The most significant innovation for centuries in the area of personal guardianship came not as a development of the law relating to tutors, but as part of a change in general public policy towards care of the mentally handicapped population. Starting in 1857, the Lunacy Acts reflected a strong trend towards institutionalisation. The Lunacy Act of 1857 established the Lunacy Board, and contained the necessary legislative framework for "the erection of asylums for the reception and care of pauper lunatics".

The asylums were erected, or contracts were entered into to use existing premises as district asylums, and the "lunatics" were certified and put into them. The Lunacy Acts defined "lunatic" as meaning "every person certified by two medical persons to be a lunatic, an insane person, an idiot, or a person of unsound mind". These terms were not further defined. In practice there were large numbers of people with mental handicaps who did not qualify for certification as lunatics. The lack of legislative provision for such people caused increasing concern.

As a result the Royal Commission on the Care and Control of the Feeble-Minded was appointed in 1904, and published its report in 1908. The Commission summarised its findings as follows:

Of the gravity of the present state of things there is no doubt. The mass of facts that we have collected, the statements of our witnesses, and our own personal visits and investigations compel the conclusion that there are numbers of mentally defective persons whose training is neglected, over whom no sufficient control is exercised, and whose wayward and irresponsible lives are productive of crime and misery, of much injury and mischief to themselves and to others, and of much continuous expenditure, wasteful to the community and to individual families. We find a local and 'permissive' system of public education which is available here and there for a limited section of mentally defective children, and which, even if it be useful during the years of training, is supplemented by no subsequent supervision and control, and is in consequence often misdirected and unserviceable. We find large numbers of persons who are committed to prison for repeated offences which, being the manifestations of a permanent defect of mind, there is no hope of repressing, much less of stopping, by short, punitive sentences. We find lunatic asylums crowded with patients who do not require the careful hospital treatment that well-equipped asylums now afford, and who might be treated in many other ways more economically and as efficiently. We find, also, at large in the population many mentally defective persons, adults, young persons, and children who are, some in one way, some in another, incapable of self-control, and who are therefore exposed to constant moral danger themselves, and become the source of lasting injury to the community.

Statutory Guardianship 1913 - 1984

The Royal Commission's report led to the Mental Deficiency and Lunacy (Scotland) Act 1913. The main thrust of the Act was directed at remedying the perceived "lasting injury to the community" resulting from the presence of many people with mental handicaps "at large in the population" by establishing a regime under which they would be "placed" in institutions or in guardianship. Statutory guardianship thus arrived, and its legal characteristics remained substantially unaltered until 1984. Throughout that period the statutory guardian was a full personal guardian – defined in the 1913 Act as having the same powers as he would have had "if he had been the father of the defective and the defective had been under the age of fourteen, or, if a female, under the age of twelve". The guardian was equated with the tutor of a pupil child. The definition under the Mental Health (Scotland) Act 1960, which remained in force until 1984, was similar, giving the guardian the powers which he would have had if "he were the father of the patient and the patient were a pupil child".

It is interesting that this legislation chose to define statutory guardianship by reference to the law of parent and child, rather than achieving the same effect by referring to the legal relationship between tutor-dative and mentally disabled adult. Does this point to doubts about what were the powers of a tutor-dative in the area of personal guardianship, or at least to a situation in which the status of children was better known, and more clearly understood, than that of mentally disabled adults; or does it indicate an inherent paternalism? While it can be helpful to use the "parent-child" analogy, the analogy can be dangerous if used unthinkingly – some adults with mental handicaps may have some requirements similar in some respects to those of children, but they are not children. There are echoes of the Act of 1585 which, as we have seen, surreptitiously imported the Roman law of children into the Scottish provision for mentally disabled adults. The 1913 Act did not even recognise the existing law of personal guardianship of mentally handicapped adults to the extent of clarifying whether the powers of a statutory guardian should prevail over those of a tutor. The 1960 Act rectified this by conferring powers on the guardian "to the exclusion of any other person".

The 1913 Act enabled the Secretary for Scotland to qualify the powers of statutory guardian by regulation. Regulations the following year provided that guardians should have no power to administer estates, and prohibited them from administering corporal punishment. These qualifications were repeated in sections 29(5) and 29(6) of the 1960 Act.

Under the 1913 Act defined categories of mentally handicapped people under 21 could be placed in guardianship without any judicial procedure, but a petition to the Sheriff was required to keep or put them in guardianship after that age. Guardianship orders for adults were renewable after the first and second years, and thereafter at three-yearly intervals. All applications required two medical certificates. Under the 1960 Act guardianship applications, also accompanied by two medical certificates, for "patients" of all ages had to be submitted for approval to the Sheriff, and were renewable after the first and second years, and thereafter at two-yearly intervals.

The 1913 legislation clearly defines the categories of accommodation envisaged for persons detained or in guardianship under the Act. There were "state institutions", provided and maintained by the state; "certified institutions" provided by charities or district boards, where residents could be maintained at public expense; "certified houses" which were institutions for residents whose accommodation was paid for by private means; "licensed houses" for up to four people in guardianship, in which the person keeping the house would usually be the guardian; and ordinary "private dwellings", in which only one person in guardianship might be kept. So after the institutionalisation of the previous half-century there was at least legal provision for units similar in size to the modern concept of a group home; and for people in guardianship in normal dwelling-houses.

The tutor was displaced by the statutory guardian as personal guardian of people with mental handicaps. *Dick -v- Douglas,* reported in 1924, was the last case of appointment of a tutor of which I am aware, prior to recent revival. But, as I wrote in *Scots Law and the Mentally Handicapped,* the use of statutory guardianship itself dwindled in recent decades. Statutory guardianship never seems to have been treated as the normal way of regularising and legalising the relationship between people with mental handicaps and their carers. For long, statutory guardianship was seen primarily as a means of imposing control, similar in kind but lesser in degree to compulsory detention in institutions. Latterly, statutory guardianship was more and more seen as a method of intervention, imposed in situations considered to be unsatisfactory, and used as a last resort where persuasion had failed.

Statutory Guardianship under the Mental Health (Scotland) Act 1984

The 1960 Act was reviewed in a consultation paper issued by the Scottish Office in April 1982, which had the following to say on the subject of statutory guardianship:

> Guardianship was conceived as a method of ensuring satisfactory care for adult mentally disordered persons either in the family home or when boarded out with unrelated guardians. The number of persons under guardianship has fallen from 2,440 in 1960 to around 300 now, and few new guardianship orders have been made in recent years. However, it appears that guardianship may continue to have value as a means of ensuring that some mentally disordered people living in the community receive the protection and support they require, provided the system is adapted to current circumstances.
>
> It is proposed that guardianship powers should be limited to those which are considered essential, rather than, as at present, all the powers of a father of a child under 14; the aim being to achieve a reduction of detention and restriction and an emphasis of the protective function of guardianship.

The consultation paper suggested three specific "essential powers" which appeared in the ensuing amending legislation as the sole powers of a guardian. The consultation paper went on to suggest that the Sheriff should be able to approve additional powers where necessary, but the legislation did not contain scope for such extension of powers. The powers of the new statutory guardian, as now set out in section

41(2) of the Mental Health (Scotland) Act 1984, are

(a) power to require the patient to reside at a place specified by the authority or person named as guardian;

(b) power to require the patient to attend at places and times so specified for the purposes of medical treatment, occupation, education or training;

(c) power to require access to the patient to be given, at any place where the patient is residing, to any medical practitioner, mental health officer or other person so specified.

These are powers tailored to suit a concept of guardianship as a method of intervention – powers imposed as a last resort to remedy unsatisfactory situations. The definition of guardianship was thus narrowed down to fit more accurately the way in which statutory guardianship was being used. The official concept of statutory guardianship may have moved from "detention and restriction" to "protection", but the "protection" took the form of active intervention in an unsatisfactory situation. There are times when such interventionist powers may be needed, but to call a person with such a role a "guardian" is a misnomer. However, to avoid confusion I shall continue to use the description "statutory guardian". The modern statutory guardian has no authority to provide the day-to-day help, guidance and supervision required of a true personal guardian.

The 1984 Act retained the requirement for two medical certificates, but introduced an important social work element by giving a central role to the mental health officer. The renewal periods were halved, renewal now being required at six months, one year, and annually thereafter. The procedure is described in *Scots Law and the Mentally Handicapped,* pages 19-22. (The provisions introduced by the Mental Health (Amendment)(Scotland) Act 1983 are now embodied in the Mental Health (Scotland) Act 1984).

Originally, under the 1913 Act, the statutory guardian had to be an individual, but under the 1960 Act the statutory guardian could be an individual or the local authority itself. This idea of the local authority acting as a corporate guardian continues under the 1984 Act. It is an unhappy concept. If an individual local authority officer has established and can maintain a sufficiently close relationship with (and understanding of) the mentally handicapped person and that person's circumstances and environment to be able to exercise the powers of a statutory guardian beneficially, then the statutory guardian should be that individual, rather than the depersonalised corporate entity of the local authority itself. If no individual local authority officer has established such a relationship and is likely to be able to sustain it, then it is very doubtful whether statutory guardianship powers should be taken at all.

The Tutor-Dative Returns

From 1913 to 1984 the statutory guardian's powers – equated to those of a father of a young child – would have sufficed to provide a form of true personal guardianship, albeit somewhat rudimentary. It is ironic that at the same time that the trend in official thinking shifted the statutory definition to suit an interventionist role, the trend among many people actually living with and caring for mentally handicapped people was one of increasing awareness of the need for true personal guardianship. As explained in Chapter III (page 12), some were concerned that it was an infringement of the rights of a mentally handicapped person to exercise guardianship powers without legal authority to do so. Others were more concerned with establishing their status and role in relation to the mentally handicapped person, either generally or more specifically in areas such as giving medical consent.

In *Scots Law and the Mentally Handicapped* I briefly mentioned the procedure for appointment of a tutor, and suggested that the procedure might be resurrected following the change in definition of a statutory guardian, and with greater awareness of the need to provide a legal basis to the relationship between a mentally handicapped person and the person in fact exercising care and control. That suggestion was first taken up by a Mr and Mrs Morris, who, in a case which attracted quite a degree of publicity, successfully petitioned the Court of Session to appoint them joint tutors-dative to their adult handicapped son. Their petition set an important precedent by going further than just reviving the old procedure to appoint a tutor-dative. If the appointment of tutors were to be revived in an era of much greater concern for the status and rights of mentally disabled people, then it seemed reasonable that the court should be asked to limit the appointment in two ways. Firstly, the powers granted should be limited to those necessary in the particular case. Secondly, the appointment should be of limited duration, to ensure that it be reviewed. The court's order incorporated both of these refinements.

The revival of the tutor-dative was a logical consequence of the historical development of personal guardianship in Scots law which has been the main theme of this chapter. The refinements of specifically-tailored detailed powers, and of limited duration, were drawn from a different source – a comparative study of the more developed codes of personal guardianship in other countries. That comparative background is described in the next chapter.

V

PERSONAL GUARDIANSHIP: OTHER LEGAL SYSTEMS WHICH HAVE INFLUENCED THE DEVELOPMENT OF SCOTS LAW

"The mentally retarded person has a right to a qualified guardian when this is required to protect his personal wellbeing and interest". Thus runs Article 5 of the *United Nations Declaration on the Rights of Mentally Retarded Persons*, adopted by the United Nations General Assembly in 1971. Guardianship is recognised as something which some mentally handicapped people need, something to which they should have a right. Such a concept of guardianship is quite different from "detention and restriction" to avoid supposed "injury to the community" or from the interventionist "protection" imposed by modern British statutory guardianship. The equivalent ILSMH declaration (*Declaration of general and special rights of the mentally retarded*) goes on to rule out the authoritarian approach: "No person rendering direct services to the mentally retarded should also serve as his guardian"

We have to look to other legal systems for examples of the type of guardianship envisaged by the UN Declaration. Such modern guardianship codes are based on concepts similar to the "fundamental principles" which I have described in Chapter II (pages 8-9). When guardianship powers are needed, they should be provided, but limited to the minimum necessary in each individual case. Guardians should be appointed by legal procedure entailing careful assessment of needs and circumstances. The appointment, and the powers granted, should be subject to periodic review. Some codes go further, looking for example at the need to monitor performance, or the need to have a stand-by guardian ready to take over immediately if the appointed guardian dies or becomes incapacitated. Moreover, it is generally found necessary to have parallel provisions for management of affairs, and to co-ordinate personal guardianship and management of affairs.

The tailoring of guardianship powers, if granted, to the needs of each individual is of fundamental importance to any code of guardianship based not on control and restriction, but on enhancing the rights, interests and quality of life of the mentally handicapped person. The introduction of this concept into modern and enlightened legal systems has often been achieved by a campaign against the manifest unsuitability and injustice of an "everything or nothing" system under which every guardian has total guardianship powers. Tailoring of

31

guardianship powers to individual need is generally achieved by a form of "limited guardianship" or "partial guardianship"

Much of the impetus towards a more enlightened approach to guardianship can be traced back to the publication in 1969 of a Report on Guardianship by what is now the International League of Societies for Persons with Mental Handicap. A few brief quotations speak for themselves.

> ... serious difficulty arises because the law usually represents incompetence in simple black and white terms, with the result that most guardianships of the person are looked on as plenary guardianships.

> ... the idea that the person himself can properly retain and exercise some personal and even property rights, selectively, according to his individual capacity, is not adequately expressed in most existing statutes pertaining to guardianship.

> The retarded adult should be permitted to act for himself in those matters which he has competence. The limitations of legal capacity inherent in guardianship should not extend to these matters. It follows that a person whose mental retardation is characterised by impairments of social competence which are partial should enjoy a partial guardianship specifically adapted to his strengths and weaknesses.

There are as many different guardianship codes as there are legal systems, but it is possible to pick out some of the main elements often employed by systems which have adopted a "minimum necessary intervention" approach.

The first requirement is to have no guardianship order at all except when one is essential. This entails providing the necessary services and legal framework to ensure that wherever possible handicapped people can manage, and their interests can be adequately safeguarded, without formally transferring control and decision-making to someone else. If guardianship is thought to be necessary, a multi-disciplinary approach to assessment is generally found to be best. The next element frequently found is an independent judicial decision-making process, at which stage the results of the assessment are submitted, but in which other interests, particularly those of the mentally handicapped person, are independently represented.

The choice of guardianship powers takes several forms. One rather crude approach is similar to, and probably derived from, the "two tier" system of Roman child law (see page 18). One has the choice of a full form of guardianship, with total powers, or a secondary form of guardianship, with more limited powers. An increasingly common approach is to retain full or "plenary" guardianship when total powers are needed, but in other cases to have a form of partial or limited guardianship in which each individual guardian is given a detailed "package" of powers, tailored to individual need. A common way of doing this is for the legislation to contain a list of powers, from which a selection may be made in each case. Where such lists exist, their function is usually illustrative, in the sense that further refinement and adaptation is competent in each individual guardianship order.

An additional technique is to require the guardian to prepare a "guardianship plan" for approval. Here we are in the area of overlap between guardianship powers, and subsequent monitoring. The monitoring of performance, again, can take several forms. The most important is the review of the appointment. Generally speaking, a review procedure will repeat all or most of the original appointment procedure.

A comprehensive – or even representative – review of modern guardianship codes in other legal systems is beyond the scope of this book. We shall however look at some general principles and a suggested model statute, both published in the United States, as these give an introduction to the general trend of thinking in the United States. Then we shall look at the guardianship code in force in Alberta, Canada. The Alberta provisions were heavily drawn upon in formulating proposals for a guardianship code for England, which proposed code I shall also describe. The Alberta provisions and the English proposals in turn formed the basis of the refinements introduced into Scottish tutor-dative procedure. Later – in Chapter XII – I shall describe recent New Zealand legislation which probably now represents the "state of the art" in integrated legislative provision for the needs of adults lacking full legal capacity. I have deliberately left the New Zealand code until after we have considered some problems in the current Scottish provision for management of the property and affairs of mentally disabled people.

United States

The American Association on Mental Deficiency issued some position papers in 1973-75, in the course of which they offered guidance to parents and others involved in making guardianship decisions. In doing so they defined an enlightened concept of guardianship. They drew up the following list of general principles:

A Since guardianship necessarily denies an individual the right to exercise freely certain personal liberties, every effort should be made through the use of social counselling services to prevent the need for appointment of a guardian.

33

B No mentally retarded adult should have a guardian appointed unless (1) he or she is found to be significantly lacking the social competence necessary to make critical decisions respecting the conduct of his or her life; (2) the appointment of such guardian will be in the best interest of the person and the community; and (3) required procedures have been observed in reaching these findings.

C To the maximum extent of their capabilities, retarded persons, whether under guardianship or not, should be permitted to participate as fully as possible in all decisions which will affect them.

D Retarded children and adults who cannot assert their own rights should have individual guardians appointed, regardless of the setting in which they are living.

E The boundaries of a specific guardianship should be specified, taking full cognizance of the social competencies and limitations of the individual. In other words, the guardian's mandate should be prescriptive in nature permitting the retarded adult to act in his own behalf on all matters in which he is competent.

F Particular care should be taken that retarded adults are treated like adults, and not like children, even when they are under guardianship.

G All clinical judgments as to an individual's competence should be based on a careful evaluation conducted by a multi-disciplinary team. In no event should an evaluation of social competence be based on the judgment of a single professional.

A landmark in the development of improved legislative provision for people with mental handicaps in the United States was the Developmentally Disabled Assistance and Bill of Rights Act of 1975. It was a federal statute establishing an ambitious policy for improving services to developmentally disabled people, and enhancing their rights. It required "a massive adjustment of state legislation" for which there were "almost no up-to-date model laws or legislative guidelines". The American Bar Association's Commission on the Mentally Disabled set to work to fill the gap, supported by the US Department of Health and Human Services, Bureau of Developmental Disabilities. The results of these labours were published in 1982 in a major work entitled *Disabled Persons and the Law - State Legislative Issues*. The work on guardianship included a suggested model guardianship statute – or, to be precise, two model statutes, one more detailed, the other an optional short form.

The model statute covers both personal guardianship, providing for guardians and limited guardians, and also management of property and affairs, dealt with by "conservators" or "limited conservators". A characteristic of the American approach is the interdependence of the two elements of "rights" and "services", and this is reflected in the model statute. It envisages appointment of "disabilities resources officers" to advise on available services and resources, advise those contemplating guardianship petitions, help with preparation of guardianship plans, and so forth. An Oversight Commission has various duties including maintaining lists of people from whom multi-disciplinary evaluation teams are drawn, encouraging people to serve as volunteer public guardians, running training programmes for guardians and conservators, reviewing the working of public volunteer guardian programmes, and advising government.

Before any petition is commenced under the statute, the petitioner must consult with the disabilities resources officer. Procedure takes the form of a court petition. The petition must explain how the court order which is sought is the least restrictive alternative for meeting the needs of the disabled person. Anyone can intervene and have the petition dismissed if the order sought can be shown to be unnecessary.

The model statute envisages a swift timetable. Within ten days of the petition being lodged, the multi-disciplinary evaluation team is appointed. Within another ten days, it reports. A "pre-hearing conference" takes place within the next ten days, followed within another ten days by the hearing. In relation to personal guardianship, the purpose of the hearing is to determine the essential requirements for the disabled person's health and safety, the skills and knowledge necessary to meet those needs, the nature and extent of the person's disabilities, and whether the person comes within the statutory definition of "disabled" or "partially disabled".

If the person is "disabled" or "partially disabled", the court has various options. It may direct that the person should be provided with necessary services "on a non-custodial basis" or provided with residential services in a "small, licensed, community based residential home" (compare the licensed house in the Scottish Act of 1913, described on pages 27-28); or appoint a limited personal guardian or personal guardian.

If a guardian is appointed, the appointee must be an individual. The order of priority for appointment is: (a) someone chosen by the disabled person; (b) an existing guardian; (c) the disabled person's wife or husband; (d) an adult child; (e) a parent; (f) someone nominated in the Will of a deceased parent; (g) someone with whom the disabled person has been living for the last six months; (h) a sister or brother; (i) a volunteer public guardian.

Only a full guardian has custody. The limited guardian does not. The full guardian has all the powers in the following list, and each partial guardian has such powers from the list as are conferred in the guardianship order. The listed powers – paraphrased – are

1. To assure that the disabled person lives in the least restrictive and

most normal setting consistent with essential health and safety requirements.

2. To assure the care and comfort of the disabled person.

3. To assure that the disabled person receives services essential to physical health and safety, and services necessary to develop the maximum possible capacity to meet his or her own essential health and safety requirements.

4. To give any necessary consents or approvals.

Both full and limited guardians may be given other duties, including the duty of assisting the disabled person in fulfilling civil duties.

The powers of guardians (full and partial) are subject to specific limitations. There are strict limitations on powers to commit the disabled person to an institution, and on power to consent to abortion, sterilisation, psycho-surgery, removal of organs, and experiments. The guardian cannot consent to withholding of lifesaving medical procedures, cannot prohibit marriage or divorce, and cannot consent to termination of any parental rights of the disabled person.

The guardian has thirty days from appointment to submit an individual guardianship plan. The guardian must submit a report at least ten days before each review hearing. A review hearing is held one year after appointment of a limited guardian and reviews thereafter take place every two years. In the case of a full guardian, the first review is after six months, and subsequent reviews are at annual intervals.

There are provisions for appointment of emergency guardians, and the court has power to suspend and temporarily replace a guardian. The court can also designate a "stand-by guardian" to take over in the event of the resignation, incapacity or death of the guardian.

Alberta

We turn from a "model statute" to a statutory guardianship code actually in force, contained in the Dependent Adults Acts of Alberta. This statute also deals with both personal guardianship and management of property and affairs, the latter being termed "trusteeship". A full guardian is called a "plenary guardian", and a limited guardian is termed a "partial guardian".

Compared with the United States model, the list of guardianship powers is more detailed and extensive, but procedural and other provisions are expressed more simply. This guardianship code contains less emphasis on provision of services. There is no role similar to that of the disabilities resources officer, and no multi-disciplinary evaluation team.

Guardianship proceedings are brought before the Surrogate Court of Alberta. The guardianship application may be brought by the Public Trustee, the Public Guardian, or any other adult concerned for the welfare of the disabled person. A report by a doctor or psychologist must be submitted, and also the written consent of the proposed guardian. A copy of the application must be served on various people including the dependent person to whom it relates, the nearest relative (or next nearest, if the nearest is the applicant), the proposed guardian (if not the applicant), the person in charge of any institution where the disabled person resides, the Public Guardian, and any trustee. The court has a discretion to dispense with service on some of these people, but can only dispense with service on the disabled person if the Public Guardian consents.

The court enquires as to whether a plenary guardian, partial guardian, or any guardian at all is required. The court also enquires as to whether it is in the best interests of the disabled person for a guardian to be appointed. If the court is in doubt, it may appoint a person to report on all or any of the disabled person's physical, mental, social, vocational, residential, educational or other needs, present and future, and the disabled person's ability to care for himself and to make reasonable judgements in personal matters.

The court must not make a guardianship order unless it is satisfied that the order would be in the best interests of the disabled person. The court may make a guardianship order if satisfied that the disabled person is an adult, and is unable to care for himself (or herself), and is unable to make reasonable judgements in all or any personal matters, and is in need of a guardian. The court may not appoint a plenary guardian unless satisfied that partial guardianship would not meet the needs of the disabled person.

There is no list of priorities for appointment as guardian. Any adult person resident in Alberta may be appointed if the court is satisfied that he (or she) will act in the best interest of the disabled person, will not be in a position where his (or her) interests will conflict with those of the disabled person, and is a suitable person to act as guardian to that disabled person. The Act specifically declares that being a potential beneficiary, or being a relative, does not create a conflict of interest (in contrast with the former Scots rule prohibiting an heir from having custody - see pages 24-25).

When making or reviewing a guardianship order, the court can appoint an alternate guardian, to whom the same qualifications apply. The alternate guardian takes over automatically and immediately upon the death of the original guardian, with the same powers as the original guardian. The court can appoint the Public Guardian to be guardian in the absence of any other suitable candidate. On the death of a guardian, the Public Guardian automatically takes over if there is no alternate guardian.

The powers of a plenary guardian include power to make all decisions that (in Alberta) can be made by the father of a child under the age of 14. Allowing for the difference in the two legal systems, this is similar to the definition of the powers of the pre-1984 statutory guardian in Scotland. The plenary guardian also has a list of specific powers, similar to the list (given below) from which powers are selected for partial guardians.

In the case of partial guardianship, the court is directed to confer only such power and authority as the guardian needs to care for the disabled person or to make reasonable personal judgements for the disabled person, or to assist in such matters. The powers are selected from a list, but the court can impose conditions or restrictions, and can "restrict, modify, change or add to" anything in the list. The list is as follows:

(a) the right to decide where the dependent adult is to live, whether permanently or temporarily;

(b) the right to decide with whom the dependent adult is to live and with whom the dependent adult is to consort;

(c) the right to decide whether the dependent adult should (or should be permitted to) engage in social activities and, if so, the nature and extent thereof and matters related thereto;

(d) the right to decide whether the dependent adult should (or should be permitted to) work and, if so, the nature or type of work, for whom he is to work and matters related thereto;

(e) the right to decide whether the dependent adult should (or should be permitted to) take or participate in any educational, vocational or other training and, if so, the nature and extent thereof and matters related thereto;

(f) The power and authority to decide whether the dependent adult should apply or should be permitted to apply for any licence, permit, approval or other consent or authorization required by law;

(g) the right to commence, compromise or settle any legal proceeding that does not relate to the estate of the dependent adult and to compromise or settle any proceeding taken against the dependent adult that does not relate to his estate;

(h) the right to consent to any health care that is in the best interests of the dependent adult;

(i) the right to make normal day to day decisions on behalf of the dependent adult including the diet and dress of the dependent adult.

In the phrase "should (or should be permitted to)" I have added the brackets with a view to making the meaning clearer.

All guardians have the following duties. They must exercise their powers in the best interest of the disabled person. They must encourage the disabled person to become able to care for himself and to make reasonable judgements in personal matters. And they must exercise their powers in the least restrictive manner possible.

When the court makes a guardianship order, it must state when the order is to be reviewed. The maximum time between reviews is three years. An application for a review can however be made at any time by the disabled person or anyone concerned for the welfare of the disabled person (or by the Public Guardian or Public Trustee). At any review hearing the court must consider whether the guardian has acted in accordance with the guardianship order and the statutory requirements. The court may then amend the guardianship order, or cancel it, terminate it, continue it, vary it or replace it – subject to any appropriate conditions or requirements. There is a separate procedure for discharging (i.e. removing) a guardian, which may be initiated by the same people as may apply for review.

The guardianship part of the Alberta statute also contains provisions dealing with compulsory care, and with medical treatment of those unable to give consent.

Perhaps the most important lesson to be learned from Alberta is the extent to which the availability of this form of personal guardianship is taken up. The population of Alberta is less than half that of Scotland. In 1985 Alberta had over 6,200 guardianship orders in existence. While there are obvious hazards in crudely translating statistics from one country to another, these figures do tend to confirm the impression gained from experience that there is in Scotland a very large unmet need.

England

In England statutory guardianship was reformed and altered in 1983, and English statutory guardianship now has a similar restricted definition to Scottish statutory guardianship. However English law appears to have nothing akin to tutor-dative procedure. Astonishingly, English law is accordingly bereft of any provision for genuine personal guardianship. The gap can only be filled by legislation, and it is not surprising that there have been demands for such legislation. In 1985 the (English) Law Society's Group for the Welfare of People with a Mental Handicap produced a suggested guardianship code in the form of a draft *Dependent Adults Act*.

The draft is based on the guardianship provisions of the Alberta statute described above, and follows the Alberta provisions closely. The English draft uses the term "guardian" for "plenary guardian", but for the sake of clarity I have used the term "full guardian". The English draft uses "partial guardian" in the same way as the Alberta statute. The English draft is limited to personal guardianship, and does not cover management of property and affairs, or compulsory care, though it does have a section on medical consent (see Chapter VIII). There is no provision for a Public Guardian, or any other equivalent "fail-safe" mechanism.

The draft proposes that guardianship applications would be dealt with by the County Court. The guardianship application would be brought by any interested person. With the application would be submitted a certificate by a medical practitioner, and the written consent of the proposed guardian. The application would be served on the disabled person, unless the court decided that this would not be in the best interests of the disabled person. The application would also be served on the nearest relative (or next nearest, if the nearest is the applicant), the proposed guardian, the person in charge of any institution where the disabled person resides, and any receiver appointed by the Court of Protection. The court would have discretion to dispense with service on any of these people, and also to require the application to be served on any other person.

The court would enquire as to whether a guardian is needed by the disabled person, and would be in the best interests of the disabled person. If in doubt as to whether a guardian should be appointed, the court would be able to obtain such reports as the court considered necessary. These could include reports on present and future needs of a physical, mental, social, vocational, residential, educational or other nature. They could also include reports as to the disabled person's ability to care for himself and to make reasonable judgements in personal matters. Unlike the Alberta statute, the English draft does not require one person to report on all such matters. While the draft does not go so far as the multi-disciplinary evaluation team of the United States model, the court would certainly have scope to obtain what would in fact be a multi-disciplinary assessment. At the hearing of the application, anyone upon whom it had been served would be entitled to appear and make representations. The court would also have a discretion to allow anyone else to appear and make representations.

The court would not be able to make a guardianship order unless guardianship would be in the best interests of the disabled person and would be of substantial benefit to the disabled person. The court would be able to appoint a guardian if satisfied that the disabled person is an adult who is often or always unable to care for himself (or herself), who is often or always unable to make reasonable judgements in personal matters, and who needs a guardian.

The court would be able to appoint as guardian any adult willing to act, if the court were satisfied that he (or she) would act in the best interests of the disabled person, would be suitable and able to act, and would not be in a position of conflict of interest. As in Alberta, it would not be a conflict of interest to be a potential beneficiary or a relative. The court would be able to call the proposed guardian before the court for questioning to establish whether the proposed guardian complied with these requirements. When making or reviewing a guardianship order, the English court would also be able to appoint an alternate guardian to take over in the event of the death of the guardian. Under the English proposals the guardian would also be able to authorise the alternate guardian to act during temporary absence of the guardian. The qualifications for an alternate guardian would be the same as for a guardian. It would be necessary to give adequate notice of both the proposal to appoint an alternate guardian, and of any such appointment, to all those entitled to have the original guardianship application served upon them.

The powers of a full guardian would include power to make all decisions that in England can be made by the father of a child under the age of 14. The full guardian would also have all the powers in a list similar to the list from which powers would be selected for partial guardians. The list from which powers would be selected for partial guardians contains exactly the same nine items as the Alberta statute (see page 38). An additional item at the end is: "any other matters specified by the Court and required by the guardian to protect the best interests of the dependent adult". The English court would also be able to impose conditions or restrictions, and to restrict, modify, change or add to anything in the list.

All guardians under the English proposals would have the same duties as guardians in Alberta. They would have to exercise their powers in the best interests of the disabled person. They would have to encourage the disabled person to become able to care for himself and to make reasonable judgements in personal matters. They would have to exercise their powers in the least restrictive manner possible.

Where an Alberta guardianship order has to be reviewed after a maximum of three years, the English court would be able to specify a review date up to six years later. The English court would specify who should apply for the review, and any other requirements in relation to the review. An application for review could be made at any time by the disabled person, or by anyone in the list of those on whom applications would normally require to be served.

At a review hearing the court would consider whether the criteria for appointing a guardian still applied, and also whether the guardian had acted in accordance with the guardianship order and statutory requirements. Procedure would be similar to the original appointment as regards obtaining reports and hearing representations. The court would be able to amend, cancel, terminate, continue, vary or replace the guardianship order, subject to any conditions or requirements considered necessary.

The English proposals also contain a procedure for discharging a guardian. An application for discharge would be brought by the guardian himself (or herself) or by any interested person. The provisions for serving review applications would also apply to discharge applications. The court would be able to discharge the guardian from office if the guardian were unable or unwilling to continue to act, or refused or failed to act, or failed to act in accordance with the guardianship order, or acted improperly, or endangered (or risked endangering) the disabled person's wellbeing, or were no longer suitable to be guardian. In any of those circumstances the court would be able, as an alternative to discharge, to make any other order considered appropriate in the circumstances.

Before making any discharge or alteration order, the court would have to be satisfied that "suitable arrangements" had been made for the disabled person, or would be made. Any discharge order would be served on the usual list of persons entitled to have applications served on them.

These proposals, prepared in England, appear to be intended to apply throughout the United Kingdom. Some modifications would be necessary if they were to be applied to Scotland. County courts exist only in England: one would probably substitute the Sheriff Court in Scotland. The Court of Protection neither exists nor has any equivalent in Scotland. While the draft relates to dependent adults, in Scots law it would probably be appropriate for statutory guardians to be available for boys over 14 and girls over 12, as well as to adults. In Scotland it might be possible for the Mental Welfare Commission to be given functions similar to those of the Public Guardian in Alberta.

I am aware of no immediate likelihood of a Bill along the lines of the English draft being introduced in Parliament. The need in England is even greater than in Scotland, because of the lack of any stop-gap such as our tutor-dative procedure. However, the work of the English Law Society's Group remains in the meantime something of an academic exercise, at least as far as England is concerned. It is in Scotland that we have been able to make some practical use of their work, and of the Alberta model on which it was based, as we shall see in the next chapter.

42

VI

TUTORS DATIVE AS PERSONAL GUARDIANS
IN MODERN SCOTS LAW

The *Morris* petition of 1986 concerned a young adult who needed a guardian. In the terminology of the Alberta code and the English proposals described in the last chapter, he would have needed a partial guardian, not a plenary or full guardian. Translated into available procedure in Scots law, he required a tutor, but with less than the full powers of a tutor.

The last previous reported case of appointment of a tutor-dative *(Dick -v-Douglas* in 1924) was a precedent for limited powers in the sense that the tutor-dative in that case was given powers of personal guardianship only, and no powers to manage property. In the *Morris* case the further step was taken of asking the court to grant only limited powers of personal guardianship, and to limit the duration of the appointment.

The list of powers in the Alberta code and the English proposals (see pages 38 and 41) was used as a basis for selecting appropriate powers. There was no change in the basic procedure. Two medical certificates were obtained. The certificates listed the particular matters in which the disabled person required supervision, help and guidance. The doctors certified that in their opinion the petitioners were suitable people to provide the necessary supervision, help and guidance. They also stated that there could be some improvement in the disabled person's capability and capacity, and that his needs should be reviewed after three years – though in the course of these particular proceedings the review period was extended from three years to five years.

The court made the appointment as asked. Mr and Mrs Morris were appointed joint tutors-dative for a period of five years. The powers granted in this particular case were powers (a), (d), (e), (f), (g) and (h) of the Alberta list, together with power to provide general care, support and guidance. Mr and Mrs Morris were given the right to apply for variation of the court order in the event of a change of circumstances. In future cases it would probably be appropriate to give "any interested person" a similar right to apply for variation of the appointment.

The *Morris* case did not introduce a full modern personal guardianship code into Scots law. It refined and updated the existing tutor-dative procedure, without fundamentally altering it. Specifically, it established that if, in a petition to appoint a tutor-dative, the court is presented with medical evidence that it is appropriate to limit the appointment as to powers granted and as to duration, and if the court is asked to limit the appointment in these ways, the court will do so.

The Alberta list of powers has no status in Scots law. It simply happens to have been used as a helpful checklist when the *Morris* case was being prepared. Any such list can only be a guide and a starting point. The principle underlying it is that one should evolve an individual list, as specific as possible, of the guardianship needs of each disabled person requiring a guardian.

There has been speculation as to whether the courts would henceforth insist that the powers granted to tutors be tailored to need in each particular case. That issue has not yet been put to the test. One would hope that the courts would accept that it would be inappropriate and unjust to grant greater powers than were needed in any particular case, and would be alert to avoid such injustice. Likewise it is reasonable to suggest that it is now good practice for lawyers preparing such petitions to enquire as to the appropriate powers, and the appropriate duration, and to frame their petitions accordingly.

To ask whether the courts would insist upon powers being tailored to individual need, is perhaps to ask the wrong question. The courts proceed on the basis of the evidence laid before them. A judge will question evidence if it seems to him that relevant factors have not been taken into account in the evidence laid before him. However the crucial items of evidence in this procedure are the two medical certificates. If it is inappropriate and unjust for unnecessary powers to be granted, the best safeguard is the care taken by doctors in the wording of the medical certificates. One recent reported case concerning appointment of a curator bonis – for which purpose two medical certificates are also required – indicated that insufficient care was taken at that stage (see page 99). It is a very serious step for personal decision-making to be taken away from an individual and placed in the hands of another. Doctors are given a heavy responsibility in our procedures for doing this. They should not issue a certificate in terms with which they do not entirely agree. In particular, if supervision, help and guidance is required in some matters, but not all, the certificates should say so. The certificates which doctors issue are the crucial documents from which further procedure and the eventual appointment are likely to follow. A suggested form of medical certificate for tutor-dative petitions is given later (pages 48-49).

The onus on doctors providing medical certificates is heavier in tutor-dative proceedings, and in proceedings to appoint curators bonis, than it is in proceedings to appoint statutory guardians. As explained in

Scots Law and the Mentally Handicapped (page 20), when appointment of a statutory guardian is sought, the two doctors certify that the disabled person is mentally handicapped, and that the degree of handicap warrants guardianship, while the mental health officer is responsible for recommending whether guardianship is necessary in the interests of the welfare of the disabled person. The mental health officer has no role in petitions to appoint tutors or curators bonis, because mental health officers were created by recent legislation and did not exist when those older procedures were established. There is scope here for a possible extension of the role of mental health officers. One possibility would be to follow the precedent of statutory guardianship, and to require reports from mental health officers as well as medical certificates in all petitions to appoint tutors or curators bonis. Another would be a requirement to intimate all such petitions to social work authorities, so that social work comments or reports could be submitted wherever the authorities consider it appropriate. In the meantime, petitioners and their lawyers should perhaps consider whether social work reports should be sought, if necessary from other sources. It is certainly my view that if the only professional evidence before the court is the two doctors' certificates, the doctors should not restrict themselves to medical, as opposed to welfare, matters. If the doctors are unwilling to deal with welfare aspects, a social work report should be sought.

One aspect of the *Morris* precedent is in my view an improvement on models such as the Alberta code. Mr and Mrs Morris were both appointed to be joint tutors-dative. On the analogy of the law of parent and child, it is surely appropriate that when a married couple are the appropriate people to be tutors, both should be appointed. Under models such as the Alberta code and the draft English Act, it would appear that only one of them could be personal guardian.

It is not possible under tutor-dative procedure to appoint an alternate guardian, but appointment of two joint tutors-dative can be used to achieve the same purpose of ensuring continuity, should one tutor die or become unable to act, temporarily or permanently.

Comparison of Powers of Statutory Guardians and Tutors-Dative

The powers of the modern statutory guardian are limited to those set out in section 41(2) of the Mental Health (Scotland) Act 1984, as quoted on page 29. It would be quite possible for a mentally handicapped person to have both a tutor and a statutory guardian. Within the scope of the statutory guardian's powers, the statutory guardian's powers would prevail and those of the tutor would be excluded, because under section 41(2) the statutory guardian's powers are conferred "to the exclusion of any other person". Beyond the scope of the statutory guardian's powers, the tutor would still have authority. Let us consider what this means in relation to the statutory guardian's specific powers.

Under power (a) the statutory guardian can decide where the mentally handicapped person should live. This power can be used to take a mentally handicapped person out of an unsuitable or harmful home environment. Even though tutors had been appointed, the statutory guardian would be able to take the handicapped adult out of the tutor's home. The availability of this power may lend strength to efforts to improve the home regime, without the power actually being exercised or even taken. Power (a) has also been used to place in residential care people who refuse to accept such care voluntarily.

Power (a) is the appropriate method of resolving a "custody dispute". Two examples will illustrate what I mean by this. Firstly, parents who separate may both wish the adult handicapped son or daughter to reside with them. In matrimonial proceedings the courts can award custody of children under 16, but they have no power to award custody of an adult, however handicapped (even though I am aware of one unreported case in which such custody was initially sought). The appropriate solution in such a case would be for a statutory guardian to be appointed, and for the statutory guardian to decide where the handicapped person should live.

A second example would be a case where a mentally handicapped adult has left institutional care for a "foster" home. The "foster" family might feel a degree of insecurity in building a long-term relationship with the handicapped person, because of the fear that relatives who had shown little interest for many years might appear to "claim" him. It could be reassuring for them to know that if such fears were to materialise, a statutory guardian could be appointed with power to confirm that the mentally handicapped person should reside with the "foster" family; or a member of the "foster" family could perhaps be appointed statutory guardian.

There is one practical limitation on power (a) which causes concern. If the handicapped person runs away from the place where the guardian says he should reside, then the handicapped person can be taken into custody, and returned. This can be done by a local authority officer, a policeman, or anyone who has written authorisation from the guardian or the local authority. This power is contained in section 44(1) of the 1984 Act, but the Act contains no power for the handicapped person to be locked or otherwise detained in the place where the guardian has said he should reside. So if the handicapped person runs away twenty times, he can be brought back twenty times, but he cannot be confined so as to stop him running away again. A tutor has power not only to bring him back, but also to restrain him from running away in the first place.

Section 44(2) of the 1984 Act provides that if the mentally handicapped person runs away and stays away without leave for twenty-eight days, then guardianship ceases and he can no longer be brought back. The appointment of a tutor does not terminate in any similar way.

Powers (b) and (c) also have limitations. As regards medical treatment, under power (b) the guardian can specify times and places at which the handicapped person is to attend for medical treatment, and under power (c) the guardian can require that a doctor should be able to see the handicapped person at home. These powers probably envisage a situation where those having care of a handicapped person are preventing medical examination or treatment. However there are no powers of compulsion in relation to a handicapped person who himself refuses to co-operate. Moreover, the statutory guardian does not have power to consent to medical (or dental) treatment on behalf of the handicapped person. A tutor does have power to consent to treatment. The question of medical consent is an important one, and is dealt with in more detail in Chapter VIII.

There are similar problems of lack of power of compulsion where the handicapped person refuses to co-operate in relation to the other matters under power (b) – regarding attendance for occupation, education or training, and under power (c) – regarding access by mental health officers and others.

Guardianship orders tend to be sought only in cases where persuasion has failed. It is in those very cases that the lack of back-up compulsory powers is likely to cause difficulty. The view is frequently expressed that guardianship is of little use, because in the very cases where guardianship powers are required, they often cannot be enforced. The problem seems to arise because of lack of clarity about the role of new statutory guardianship. It still carries a legacy of statutory provisions dating back to the old statutory guardianship introduced in the 1913 Act and 1914 regulations. The person to whom a guardian is appointed is still termed a "patient" – with the connotation that guardianship is similar in kind to compulsory detention in hospital, though lesser in degree. The exclusion of property management, the prohibition of corporal punishment, and the power to bring back runaways are all similar to provisions in previous legislation. It might perhaps have been better to have wiped the slate clean, recognised that the new statutory guardianship was not personal guardianship in the sense of regularisation of a normal relationship between carer and mentally disabled adult, but an interventionist tool to be used occasionally and as a last resort in unsatisfactory cases; and then to have created a package of powers limited to that purpose, but designed to achieve it effectively.

None of these difficulties affect a tutor. A tutor can have all of the powers of a statutory guardian, and can exercise such reasonable restraint and control as may be necessary to make those powers effective. The powers of a tutor are in this respect similar to those of the parent of a young child – except, of course, to the extent that in any particular case the tutor's powers are limited by the court, following the *Morris* precedent.

Legal Aid

Initially, interest in appointment of tutors-dative was tempered by concern about cost. The Scottish Legal Aid Board have however made a helpful ruling that entitlement to Legal Aid will be determined in relation to the means of the handicapped person, not those of the guardians or other petitioners. In response to a specific enquiry about Legal Aid for petitions for appointment of tutors-dative, the Secretary to the Scottish Legal Aid Board wrote as follows (letter to the author, dated 5th June 1987):

> Where an application is made by a person for appointment in a representative or fiduciary capacity, the means assessment is based on that of the proposed ward or incapax.
>
> Neither the previous legislation nor the present legislation (I think) were clear on this point but that is the practice which we are adopting.

Procedure

Petitions for appointment of tutors-dative require to be submitted to the Court of Session in Edinburgh. They are usually presented to a single judge sitting in the Outer House of the court, though the *Morris* case was heard by the Inner House – a bench in this case of three judges, sometimes of more. Petitions are often presented by the proposed appointee or appointees, but that is not essential. If the appointee is not one of the petitioners, the court would require to know that the proposed appointee was willing to act.

Two medical certificates require to be submitted with the petition. There is no prescribed form for the certificates, but in a partial guardianship case a certificate along the following lines would be appropriate:

> I, AB, a Bachelor of Medicine and a Bachelor of Surgery of the University of __ and a member of the Royal College of Psychiatrists hereby certify:

1. that I have for ＿ years known CD, date of birth ＿ who resides at ＿, and that I have this day at ＿ further seen and examined him;
2. that he is mentally handicapped, that he requires supervision in many but not all aspects of everyday life, that he requires help and guidance in making reasonable judgements in many but not all of the ordinary things involved in the process of daily life, and that he is unable continuously to care for himself;
3. that the particular matters in which he requires supervision, help and guidance are as follows, namely:

   (list particular matters – see page 38);
4. that I also know ED and FD, spouses, residing at ＿ aforesaid, parents of the said CD, that I am familiar with the care and assistance which they have hitherto provided to him, and that I consider them to be suitable persons to be empowered to provide such supervision, help and guidance as is above specified;
5. that in my opinion the said CD is likely to continue to require supervision, help and guidance in at least some of the foregoing matters for the remainder of his life, but that there could be some improvement in his capability and capacity and that it would be appropriate to review his needs in ＿ years time; and
6. that service of the petition for appointment of tutors upon said CD will not be harmful to him, though he is unlikely to understand the petition.

The petition narrates who are the nearest relatives, and is served on them. It is also served on the disabled person, unless the medical certificates indicate good reasons for not doing so. Even though only personal guardianship is sought, the nearest relatives for the purpose of serving the petition would normally be those who would succeed to the disabled person's estate, if any, if the disabled person were to die (without leaving a Will). There might however be other people on whom the petition should be served. For example, if the disabled person lived with carers other than the petitioners or proposed tutors-dative, the petition should be served on those carers. Likewise, if the disabled person had a curator bonis, the petition should be served on the curator bonis.

The petition should briefly describe the disabled person's handicap and medical condition, and also the history of accommodation, care and training, up to and including present and any proposed future arrangements.

The petition should state whether the disabled person has any assets. If so, they should be specified, and the present and any proposed future arrangements for administration should be described.

The petition concludes by setting out the precise duration and terms of the appointment sought.

The petition could be opposed by anyone on whom it was served, including the disabled person, or by anyone else concerned about the welfare or interests of the disabled person. An opposed petition would normally be decided following a hearing in court.

So far as I am aware, no such petition has yet been opposed since the procedure was revived in 1986. Petitions are normally granted without a hearing in court if the judge is satisfied with all of the information presented in the petition and the evidence provided by the medical certificates.

Further developments

Revival of tutors-dative was initially seen as being relevant mainly to the situation of a family unit of parents and adult son or daughter who has a mental handicap. The next step in development, which has already been taken, is for a parent to seek appointment of himself (or herself) along with a younger person such as a non-handicapped son or daughter. In a recent petition an elderly widow whose only child was mentally handicapped had a trusted and eminently suitable friend of the same generation as her son appointed joint tutor-dative with herself. This goes some way towards achieving the same result as the provision in some countries' guardianship codes for a substitute guardian to take over automatically upon the death or incapacity of the guardian (see last chapter).

Another variation, considered in at least one recent case, though apparently not yet carried through to a formal petition, is for older parents to petition for appointment of persons younger than themselves as tutors-dative, in the expectation that these tutors-dative will be able to continue to provide personal guardianship after the deaths of the parents. There was a direct precedent for this in the old case, mentioned on page 24, in which the nearest agnate felt that he was too old and too infirm to act as tutor, and petitioned for someone else to be appointed tutor-dative.

Two trends are now focusing interest on further extensions of the use of tutor-dative procedure. The first is the well known trend towards deinstitutionalisation. The second is the recognition that if handicapped people should be allowed to live as near "normal" a life as the handicap permits, then this should include the "normal" life-pattern of moving away from the family home. Where a suitable home, with necessary support, can be arranged, that is healthier for both parents and handicapped son or daughter. The alternative is that parents take on a lifelong burden, with the risk that the handicapped person will suffer the double trauma of bereavement or serious illness of parents, and at the same time a complete and abrupt change of lifestyle. Increasingly, parents see it as better that the move away from home should take place in a way and at a time which has been planned and chosen, when they are fully able to help with preparation beforehand and support afterwards.

Both trends – deinstitutionalisation and promotion of "normal" life-patterns – result in mentally handicapped people moving into hostels, group homes and the like, and sometimes "foster" homes, where professionals or volunteers will be largely responsible for providing such day-to-day care, help and support as may be necessary. Carers who are not relatives are often in practice more concerned about what rights, if any, they have to make decisions for handicapped people, and to exercise guidance and control. Strictly speaking, parents or other relatives of adult handicapped people are in the same position as unrelated carers, as their relationship does not of itself confer any greater rights upon them. However, it is understandable that carers who are not relatives should be particularly concerned about these questions. Tutor-dative procedure can be used to meet those concerns.

One way in which that can be achieved is for tutors-dative to be appointed, and for them to give the necessary authority to the carers by delegating some or all of the tutors' specific powers. This can take the form of a written agreement, if so desired. It is not essential that tutors should themselves provide care in their own homes. Just as parents can entrust the care of their children to schools or hospitals for longer or shorter periods, so can tutors authorise others to care for, and supervise, mentally handicapped adults.

Another solution is for the carer to be appointed tutor-dative. That would be particularly appropriate where there is a long-term "fostering" arrangement. It might also be possible to appoint as tutor a carer in a hospital or group home, or an official of the body providing the facility. There would have to be a reasonable probability of the carer establishing a long-term relationship with the handicapped person. The problem here is that, at least in the area of care of people with profound mental handicaps, experience indicates that the work is so demanding that a carer does well to last two years in the same post.

The worry that sometimes arises when handicapped people come out of institutions into other forms of accommodation, particularly "foster" homes, is whether relatives who have shown no interest for years may appear upon the scene to "claim" the handicapped person. Of course, in some cases it may be a positive and beneficial thing for family contacts to be re-established. There are other cases where it would not be beneficial, and these include cases where the handicapped person is able

51

to communicate a strong preference. This is a situation in which appointment of a statutory guardian could be helpful, as mentioned on page 46. But what would happen if the "foster parents" sought appointment as tutors-dative, and if relatives competed for appointment as tutors-dative, or the nearest agnate sought appointment as tutor-at-law?

The answer, I think, is to go back to the historical development of the two kinds of tutor. As we have seen, under the older Scots law suitability was more significant than kinship. The tutor-at-law, with his prior claim based on kinship, arrived in the sixteenth century masquerading as an import from Roman law, when in fact Roman law was in this respect closer to the older Scots law in emphasising suitability rather than kinship. This was due either to a misconception – which would be surprising – or to a deliberate response to social conditions and perceptions of the time which placed greater emphasis on the claims of kinship. Either way, it seems reasonable that when considering such issues in a modern context, the courts should look to modern social conditions and perceptions, rather than to those of four centuries ago. If modern society gives relatively more weight to suitability, rather than kinship alone, then the courts should be able to reverse the shift in emphasis which occurred four centuries ago. The tutor-at-law is still part of our law, and the question would still be "Is the nearest agnate a fit person?" rather than "Would an existing or proposed tutor-dative be better?" The courts should however be reluctant to appoint a tutor-at-law in the face of opposition based on any significant indications of unsuitability. In dealing with competing candidates for appointment as tutors-dative, it is probably reasonable that kinship (or closeness of kinship) should prevail if other considerations are equally balanced; but otherwise suitability should be the determining criterion.

One possible modern use of tutors-at-law is identified in Chapter XI. Apart from that, it seems to me that tutor-at-law procedure would only be used in preference to the less cumbersome tutor-dative procedure in an attempt to press claims of kinship above considerations of suitability.

There would be a further, and major, objection to revival of the tutor-at-law in a modern context. Appointment is limited to the nearest male relative. Women are excluded from appointment. That problem does not exist in relation to tutors-dative. For example, in the Morris case both parents were appointed joint tutors-dative, and in another more recent case two women have been appointed joint tutors-dative.

Finally, tutor-at-law procedure does not lend itself so well to the modern refinements which are now being applied to tutor-dative procedure.

Local Authority as Tutor-Dative?

A recent legal article which referred to the *Morris* case suggested that a local authority could be appointed tutor-dative (Thomson, 1988 – see Appendix I). There is no precedent for a tutor-dative being anything other than an individual, or two individuals acting jointly. The courts have held that only an individual may be appointed curator bonis, and if it is important that management of property and affairs should only be placed by a court in the hands of an individual, then that must be even more important in the case of personal guardianship. As we have seen, modern guardianship codes in other countries require guardians to be individuals. A local authority can be appointed statutory guardian under the Mental Health (Scotland) Act 1984 (and could be appointed under the 1960 Act, though not the 1913 Act), but it would be quite unsatisfactory and contrary to principle for a tutor or other true personal guardian to be an impersonal corporate entity such as a local authority.

Criticisms of tutor-dative procedure

Revival of tutor-dative procedure has caused some disquiet. The most cogent criticism is along the following lines. It is suggested that in practice the procedure will tend to reinforce the parental role in a rather indiscriminate way. As well as strengthening the position of parents who are making an entirely positive and beneficial contribution to the wellbeing and development of handicapped sons and daughters, it will also tend to strengthen home regimes in which the role of parents is unduly dominant, or over-protective, or in other ways considered to be less than ideal. It is felt that the idea that appointment limited by time will result in effective review is over-optimistic and illusory, and that the procedure both upon appointment and upon subsequent re-appointment affords little or no scope for consideration of views other than those of the petitioners themselves.

It is certainly the case that many parents who consider appointment as tutor-dative are motivated partly by a feeling, or a fear, that professionals ignore them and make unsuitable decisions over their heads. They will tend to see some professionals as domineering, and in need of restraint.

Where there is such divergence between parents and professionals, what is needed, of course, is a careful balance between the two. Tutor-dative procedure tends to take matters from one extreme to the other, and to that extent the criticism may well be valid. One way of introducing a degree of balance might be a requirement that such petitions be intimated to the social work authority, and a report invited from the mental health officer.

Underlying this criticism, however, is a very worrying trend. The gap between many parents and many professionals seems to be widening, rather than narrowing. The problem is certainly not limited to cases where parents could fairly be described as unduly dominant or over-protective. It extends to many concerned, responsible and caring parents, who feel that their role and views are largely ignored by professionals who appear on the scene for a year or two, then flit off to pastures new, while the parents bear the lifelong load of care and responsibility, and have to live with the consequences of decisions which are made. Professionals who criticise parents, and criticise parents' use of tutor-dative procedure, should perhaps ask themselves why they have failed to secure the confidence and co-operation of parents.

That having been said, it cannot be stressed too strongly that modern use of tutor-dative procedure is no more than a useful stop-gap. Employed appropriately and responsibly, the procedure meets needs for which there is no other provision at all in our law. However it is neither an ideal nor a comprehensive solution. It lacks sufficient checks and balances. We require an integrated statutory code designed to meet the various needs of adults who lack (or lose) full legal capacity, including needs in the area of personal guardianship. This is discussed further in Chapter XVII.

VII

PERSONAL GUARDIANSHIP OF MENTALLY DISABLED MINORS

So far, we have considered tutor-dative procedure only in relation to mentally disabled adults. There is clearly no need for any special procedure to appoint personal guardians to mentally disabled children who are "pupils" (girls under 12, boys under 14) because the tutors of all such children, whether the children are mentally disabled or not, have full powers of personal guardianship (see *Scots Law and the Mentally Handicapped,* Chapter IV).

The law is not clear in relation to mentally disabled children who are minors (girls 12-18, boys 14-18). Some older legal texts indicate that the father of a mentally disabled child remained tutor until the child reached majority, and only required to petition for appointment as tutor once his son or daughter became an adult. If that is correct, then translated into modern law it means that the parents retain the role of tutors in relation to their mentally disabled children until they reach 18. However, this proposition is not well supported either by authority or in practice. It creates difficulties as to the degree of mental disability which causes the role of parents as tutors to extend automatically up to 18, and how the degree of disability is ascertained. The difficulties arise because the texts in question date from times when mental disability was seen simplistically (in terms of "idiocy", "furiosity", and so on) and when management of property and affairs was viewed as more important than personal guardianship. It is probably unsafe for parents of mentally disabled minors, and those dealing with them, to assume that parents retain all the powers of tutors up to majority. The less severe the disability, the less safe would such an assumption be.

Parents of all minor children, handicapped or not, do retain some powers of personal guardianship into minority. As I explained in *Scots Law and the Mentally Handicapped* (pages 11-12) they have limited power to control place of residence, conduct and upbringing. Their powers may be diminished or lost before the child reaches majority. In the case of mental handicap, the greater the degree of handicap, the more likely are parents to retain these powers, undiminished, until 18. In relation to some mentally disabled minors, these normal parental powers may provide adequate powers of personal guardianship. However these powers probably do not extend to all the personal guardianship powers of a tutor with unlimited powers.

Unfortunately - and surprisingly - there is some doubt and debate about the precise scope of parental powers in relation to all minors, handicapped or not. For example, on the question of consent to medical treatment, which is the subject of the next chapter, the Scottish Law Commission wrote in a consultative memorandum published in June 1985 (*Legal Capacity and Responsibility of Minors and Pupils*) that: "The law is by no means clear". They took the view that girls over 12 and boys over 14 can give legally effective consent to medical treatment; that "logically, the consent of a parent . . . would be ineffective"; but that "possibly" this particular power is within those of a parent of a minor; and accordingly that "it may be" that either the minor or the parent may consent. The tentative wording demonstrates that not even the Scottish Law Commission can state with clarity and certainty what are the powers of parents in relation to their minor children.

A line of academic argument which has been developed recently approaches the problem from a different angle. It concentrates on the question of what are the attributes of "custody". It has been suggested that rights in relation to the care and upbringing of children are conferred by reason of having custody, rather than as a consequence of being tutor, or parent. This is only of academic interest where the parents or tutors both have custody. It has practical importance where a court has awarded custody to one parent and not to the other, or has awarded custody to someone other than the parents. It is then important to know what rights have been conferred on the person who has custody, and what rights have been taken away from the parent or tutor deprived of custody. The "custody theory" would define custody as including all of the parental rights of personal guardianship of children. Even if that is correct, I doubt the suggestion (which has been made) that because parental rights in relation to minors derive from having custody, rather than from being parents, those rights are greater than they would otherwise have been. It seems to me that debate about the source of such rights - whether they derive from custody or parenthood - is relevant to allocation of existing common law rights, but cannot increase them. If I am correct, then the "custody theory" does not throw any more light on what, precisely, are the rights of parents in relation to their minor children.

There has been much recent statutory law concerning custody and custody orders. Most of these provisions concern children up to the age of 16, though some categories of court orders (including custody orders) can be made in respect of minors up to the age of 18. There is nothing in this legislation to suggest that a parent, or other person, awarded custody of a child in judicial proceedings, should have greater rights in the area of personal guardianship than the parents of that same child would have had if there had been no such proceedings and the child had remained in their custody. Nowhere does this legislation attempt to list the attributes of custody, nor does it imply that "custody" means the same thing in relation to children of all ages. Custody is not defined in such a way as to grant to parents, or others having custody, rights greater than existing common law rights of parents (whatever those rights may be!)

As an example, let us take what is perhaps the closest to a definition of custody in recent legislation. (It appears in the *Convention on the Civil Aspects of International Child Abduction*, included as a schedule to the Child Abduction and Custody Act 1985.) For the purposes of the Convention "rights of custody" are defined as including "rights relating to the care of the person of the child and, in particular, the right to determine the child's place of residence". The most important aspect of custody is the right to determine abode. There are also "rights relating to the care" of the child, but these rights are neither specified nor defined. The definition simply covers such rights as already exist in our law in relation to the care of the child in question. Again, we are taken no further towards clarification of what those rights are.

Until these issues have been clarified, the safest advice is this. If decisions in personal matters need to be made, and the mentally handicapped minor is not capable of making them, and if those decisions are in areas (such as giving medical consent) where it is doubtful whether anyone else has automatic right to make them, then application should be made to a court. One possibility would be to apply for appointment of a tutor-dative. If the court were to refuse the petition as being unnecessary, on the grounds that the parents already had the necessary powers, that would authoritatively solve the problem.

An alternative course of action has been created by the Law Reform (Parent and Child) (Scotland) Act 1986. Under that Act the court has power to "make such orders relating to parental rights as it thinks fit". The parents or anyone else claiming interest can apply for such an order. At least one legal writer (Professor J.M. Thomson – see Appendix I) holds the view that this power is wide enough to cover applications for the court's approval of a proposed exercise of parental rights. If the court held that the matter in question lay outwith parental rights, then it would be clear that it would be necessary to apply for appointment of a tutor-dative. The advantage of the procedure under the 1986 Act is that it can be brought in the local Sheriff Court, whereas petitions for appointment of tutors-dative require to be presented to the Court of Session in Edinburgh. On the other hand, under tutor-dative procedure only one court application would be required: the court would either appoint a tutor, or declare such appointment to be unnecessary because parents already had the necessary rights. Under the alternative of applying to the Sheriff, if the Sheriff held that the matters to which the application related lay outside parental rights, the parents would have to start again with an application to the Court of Session to appoint a tutor.

VIII

MEDICAL CONSENT

In 1987 an English court authorised sterilisation of a mentally handicapped girl of 17. The case, and subsequent debate, hit the headlines. The case is generally called the *"Jeanette* case", though lawyers know it as *"In re B".* Not all of the comment seemed to be based on an understanding of what actually took place. Even less were the significant differences in the Scottish position explained, or the relevance which the decision did have in Scotland identified.

In 1989 the House of Lords, in another English case, approved a decision authorising sterilisation of an adult woman with a mental handicap. The 1989 case is known as *F -v- West Berkshire Health Authority.* I shall call it simply the *"F* case". The *F* case was probably more significant than the *Jeanette* case, but seems to have attracted less popular comment, though it has caused some unease among legal commentators.

Over recent years increasing interest has been focused on the question of medical consent in relation to people with mental handicaps. The *Jeanette* case brought the debate into the wider public arena. Here we are concerned with the general issue of medical consent, not just the particular and rather dramatic question of consent to sterilisation. And what I have to say is in general equally applicable to related matters, such as consent to dental examination and treatment.

We can encapsulate the issues in a few simple questions. When – and why – is medical consent needed? Who can give that consent? Should they give that consent?

Subject to the points which I shall make shortly, it is wrongful for medical examination to be carried out or medical treatment to be administered without the patient's consent. By wrongful, I mean potentially an assault, and also a civil wrong giving rise to possible liability in damages. To touch someone, without his consent or other justification, is an assault. To carry out intimate examination, or to render him unconscious (albeit by anaesthetic), or to cut him with a knife (albeit surgically), are all potentially assaults if done without consent.

This does not mean that surgeons can do nothing if a patient is carried unconscious into hospital, in urgent need of surgery. Lawyers are agreed that in such cases the surgeons may carry out the necessary operation. As to the legal basis, there were until recently two theories.

While there is often little practical difference between the two theories as they affect patients who are not mentally handicapped, there is – as we shall see later – a considerable practical difference in relation to mentally disabled patients.

One theory is that of implied consent. The patient would certainly have consented if he had been conscious and able to be consulted. Implied consent also operates more mundanely: when we go to a doctor with a complaint, he will often proceed to investigate it without specifically asking for consent, for by seeking his help we have impliedly consented to necessary investigation.

The other theory is based on the principle of necessity. Acts otherwise wrongful can in some circumstances be justified by necessity. Applying this theory to the unconscious patient, the otherwise wrongful act of giving treatment without consent is justified because the treatment is necessary to avert greater harm to the patient.

Under either theory, it is clear that giving essential treatment to an unconscious patient is not wrongful, but neither theory justifies anything other than essential treatment. This issue sometimes arises in relation to cases where, during an operation for one purpose, a surgeon has discovered and dealt with something else. Such action is only justified if it is essential that it be done there and then to avert risk to health or life. If there is no such urgency, if the action taken is convenient rather than essential, then the action is wrongful. This demonstrates how limited are the circumstances in which examination or treatment without consent is permissible.

The House of Lords decision in the *F* case was based upon the necessity principle, and it would appear that the "implied consent" principle was not even considered.

We shall come back to the two theories of implied consent and necessity when we look at the topic of treatment without consent of people with mental handicaps. We shall then also look at the question of the extent to which the English case of *F* can be seen as clarifying Scots law.

Who Can Consent - Children

Pupil children (girls up to 12, boys up to 14) cannot themselves give valid consent to medical examination or treatment. The parents, or other tutors, can consent for them. The parents can delegate the power to consent, and often do so when someone is temporarily put in charge of their children. If the custody theory (mentioned on page 56) is correct, any person having legal custody of a pupil child can consent to medical treatment.

Minor children (girls 12-18, boys 14-18) can give medical consent for themselves, unless prevented from being able to do so by mental disability (or, perhaps, by lack of sufficient understanding without mental disability). As explained on page 56, it is possible that parents (or perhaps others having custody) may also be able to consent, but the law as to such parental consent in relation to minors is not clear.

In England the age of medical consent is 16. In Scottish medical circles there is a widespread, but erroneous, belief that 16 is the relevant age here as well. As the Scottish Law Commission have put it: "Medical practice does not make law".

Who Can Consent - Mentally Handicapped People

Adults and minors with mental handicaps may be unable to give valid medical consent if their disability is such as to incapacitate them from doing so. Legal capacity to give medical consent is tested by criteria similar to those applied to establish legal capacity for other actions and transactions (see *Scots Law and the Mentally Handicapped*, pages 36-37). It is not valid consent for a mentally handicapped person to give apparent consent – verbally or in writing – if he lacks adequate understanding of what he is doing. The consent is only valid if the mentally handicapped person has reasonable understanding of the significance of the consent which he is giving. Where a doctor would normally explain to a patient the risks of alternative courses of action, or the relative advantages and disadvantages, then the mentally handicapped person must be able to understand those risks, advantages, and disadvantages to a sufficient degree to be able to make a reasonably informed choice and decision, if his consent is to be valid.

If the mentally handicapped person is an adult, and if he is unable to give valid consent, then only a tutor can consent for him. If the tutor's powers are limited, then the tutor can only give medical consent if he has specific power to do so (see power (h) of the list on page 38). Statutory guardians can require the patient to attend for medical treatment, and can ensure that a doctor has access to the patient, but cannot consent on behalf of the patient to medical treatment.

In the case of a minor who cannot consent for himself, if a tutor is appointed the tutor can certainly give valid medical consent for the minor, provided that the tutor has unlimited powers or limited powers which include specific power to consent to health care. But if the minor does not have a tutor, then we run into the uncertainties already described. The parents (or perhaps anyone having custody) may be able to consent, but until the law is clarified or changed, it is not safe for anyone to assume this. The safe course is to seek either an "order

61

relating to parental rights", or appointment of a tutor-dative, as suggested on pages 57-58.

Treatment Without Consent - Mentally Handicapped People

In relation to people with full legal capacity, the differences between the theories of "implied consent" and "necessity" are largely academic, because both generally have the same practical consequences. When we consider people who lack capacity to consent, the consequences of the two theories are more important.

In relation to people who lack legal capacity, the "implied consent" theory runs into an obstacle. Can one be assumed to have given implied consent when one lacks legal capacity to give valid explicit consent? Can one be held to have done impliedly when unconscious something which one is legally incapable of doing when conscious? The implied consent theory proceeds on the basis that "although the [unconscious] patient was clearly unable to consent to treatment, his consent could be implied or presumed on the grounds that if he were conscious he would probably consent". That is a fiction, and in the case of the mentally disabled patient we would have to add the further fiction that "if he were conscious and if he had adequate legal capacity he would probably consent". It is doubtful whether the theory can be stretched so far. The "implied consent" theory runs into difficulties even in relation to essential treatment to an unconscious patient, and is unlikely to take us further than that.

There is no equivalent difficulty with the "necessity" theory. Necessity justifies the giving of essential treatment to the unconscious patient, whether mentally disabled or not. The necessity theory takes us further. If essential treatment is justified on grounds of necessity when the patient is unable to give consent, then logically that justification is equally valid whether the inability to consent results from the temporary disability of unconsciousness or the permanent disability of mental handicap.

The Scottish courts have made no clear decisions on such matters. In the English case of *F*, mentioned earlier, the House of Lords proceeded on the basis of the necessity principle, apparently without even considering the implied consent theory. Shortly, we shall look further at questions of the extent of "necessity", and how it should be determined. For the meantime, it is, in my view, clear that in the *F* case the court was right to look to the "necessity" principle rather than the "implied consent" theory, and equally clear that on this point we can regard the *F* case as being authoritative also in Scotland.

If I were wrong in this, the result would be absurd. It is certainly the law that essential treatment may be given without express consent to an unconscious patient, whether mentally disabled or not. If the justification were to be "implied consent" rather than "necessity", we would have a situation in which mentally disabled patients incapable of valid consent while conscious could nevertheless be held to have given implied consent when unconscious. Doctors would perhaps have to wait for the mentally disabled patient to lapse into unconsciousness before being able to give essential treatment!

How is necessity defined and determined?

Criticism of the *F* case centres on questions about the extent of "necessity", and how it should be determined. In my view, moreover, there are in relation to these issues differences between the Scottish and English position which may limit the extent to which this English decision, albeit a decision of the House of Lords, is authoritative in Scotland.

The decision in the case of *F* frequently uses the phrase "in the best interests of the patient", rather than the word "necessity". It might be thought that what is in the best interests of the patient goes much further than the relatively restricted area of necessity. However, in the leading judgement, Lord Brandon stated that treatment was in the best interests of patients "if, *but only if*, it was carried out in order to save their lives, or to ensure improvement or prevent deterioration in their physical or mental health" [my italics]. A dozen lines later in his judgement he appears to use "on ground of necessity" as being synonymous with "in the best interests of the patient". Nevertheless, this case has given rise to concern as to the extent of "best interests", and how they should be determined.

In the *F* case the House of Lords stated that the test laid down in a 1957 case should be applied in deciding whether a proposed operation was or was not in the best interests of the patient. The 1957 case is called *Bolam -v- Friern Hospital Management Committee*. It was a case about alleged medical negligence. In it, the court stated that "a doctor is not negligent if he acts in accordance with a practice accepted at the time as proper by a responsible body of medical opinion".

The House of Lords has been criticised for applying to the question of defining what is in a patient's best interests a test designed to be applied to the very different question of what is medical negligence. It is one thing to consider whether proposed treatment is so clearly in a patient's best interests that it may be given without the patient's consent. It is quite another thing to decide whether giving particular treatment, or the way in which it was given, fell short of accepted medical standards to the extent of being negligent, and giving rise to liability in damages.

The nub of the criticism is that the decision as to what is in a patient's

63

best interests should involve objective enquiry into wider considerations than simply whether a body of doctors – not necessarily a majority – would consider particular treatment to be appropriate. It has been suggested that the decision in the *F* case "reinforces medical paternalism". It is certainly true that there has been unease about the *Bolam* principle even in relation to negligence cases. It has been questioned whether the courts should permit doctors to define the extent to which they themselves can impinge upon the fundamental legal right of a competent adult to give informed consent (e.g. see dissenting opinion of Lord Scarman in *Sidaway* [1985] 1 All E.R. 643).

In the *F* case the House of Lords themselves seemed to feel that more was required than just a doctor's opinion (albeit in accordance with "a responsible body of medical opinion"). In a rather strange part of their judgement they appeared to be trying to defend their decision from criticisms along the lines which I have described, by saying that in practice those involved in the care of the mentally disabled person would be involved in the medical decision. In his leading opinion, Lord Brandon said that adults suffering from mental disability would normally be either in the care of guardians and referred to doctors for treatment, or reside or be detained in mental hospitals. He said that if they were detained in mental hospitals, it would then again be the duty of the doctors concerned to use their best endeavours to do, by way of operation or other treatment, that which was in the best interests of such patients.

Particularly in relation to people other than mental hospital patients, this is a strange and quite inaccurate assertion. The only form of guardianship of adults in England is statutory guardianship similar to Scottish statutory guardianship. As in Scotland, only a very small proportion of mentally disabled adults have statutory guardians. To this extent, the *F* decision proceeds upon an assumption which is simply factually wrong.

This passage does however point to a fundamental problem of English law, underlying the decision. Whereas in Scotland a tutor-dative can give consent to medical treatment on behalf of a mentally disabled adult, English law has no-one at all who can give such consent. While in Scotland we have revived the tutor-dative as a stopgap to make good the lack of any other provision for true personal guardianship, English law has no such provision at all. This had already been recognised as a serious gap in English law. As we shall see, it had for example resulted in the *Jeanette* case being rushed through before she reached the age of 18, in the belief that there was no mechanism for authorising her operation after she reached adulthood.

Put simply, in England either a proposed operation is justified by the necessity principle, or it cannot be carried out. In Scotland, either it is justified by the necessity principle, or else the consent of a tutor-dative will be required, and then the operation may still be carried out. To avoid unacceptable consequences, English law needed a wider definition of necessity than is required in Scotland. It was right that, in the case of *F,* the House of Lords should seek to put in place in England a regime for treatment without consent which would not result in a mentally disabled patient failing, for want of consent, to receive treatment which was in the patient's "best interests".

Because of the difference between the Scottish and English positions, it is in my view unsafe to assume that the Scottish courts would adopt an equally broad definition of the area in which consent is not required. The Scottish courts may do so, but in my view it would be unwise to make that assumption unless and until a suitable case arises in Scotland, and is decided.

In the case of *F,* the House of Lords also considered the role of the court in such cases. One might have thought that, if any proposed treatment were covered by the necessity principle, then there would be no need to obtain any form of authorisation from a court. Lord Brandon, in his leading judgement, said that in his opinion, while involvement of the court in such cases was not strictly necessary as a matter of law, it was nevertheless highly desirable as a matter of good practice to involve the court in cases of proposed sterilisation. He felt that there might be other special operations to which this same principle would apply, though he did not give examples. The appropriate procedure, in sterilisation or other similar cases, was for the court to decide whether the proposed operation was in the best interests of the patient and therefore lawful, or not in the patient's best interests and therefore unlawful.

One of the other judges, Lord Griffiths, went further. He said that he could not agree that it was satisfactory to leave the grave decision to sterilise, with all its social implications, in the hands of those having the care of the patient with only the expectation that they would have the wisdom to obtain a declaration of lawfulness before the operation was performed. He felt that, in the public interest, sterilisation of a mentally disabled woman with healthy reproductive organs should be declared unlawful unless the operation had been enquired into and sanctioned by the High Court. However, Lord Griffiths was in a minority on this point, and his view did not prevail. His view is however one which should commend itself to Parliament in any new legislation dealing with the question of medical consent in respect of mentally disabled adults.

In my view, the broad principles of the case of *F* regarding the role of the court do apply in Scotland. I consider that the Scottish courts would be likely to hold that they could not make lawful a proposed procedure which was unlawful, but that they do have jurisdiction to declare whether, in any particular case, a proposed operation is covered by the principle of necessity and may therefore be carried out without consent. I think it likely, also, that the Scottish courts would take the view that for certain types of operation (including sterilisation) an application to the court was at least "highly desirable as a matter of good practice". If I am correct in my view that the scope of the necessity principle may be narrower in Scotland than in England, the Scottish courts may even take up the view expressed by Lord Griffiths that in at least some circumstances the court's approval is not only highly desirable, but essential.

In Scotland, similar principles about the role of the court require to be considered in relation to a situation which does not exist in England. That is the situation where there is a tutor who is empowered to give consent, but a question arises as to whether or not the tutor should give consent. This decision takes us to the next topic.

When consent should be given

Wherever there is a degree of doubt as to whether an available medical procedure is in the best interests of a mentally handicapped person or not, the tutor (or other person empowered to consent, in the case of a child) faces a dilemma. The tutor has the legal authority to give, or to withhold, consent. How should that power be exercised? Some such decisions require careful thought and sensitive guidance when we make them for ourselves. It is even more difficult to make them for someone else, who cannot be meaningfully consulted. This is one of the fundamental dilemmas considered in Chapter II.

The tutor should not give consent to treatment which is not in fact in the best interests of the handicapped person. It has been suggested that in such circumstances the consent might be invalid. Even if it were valid, it would still be wrongful, so that the tutor might be held liable to compensate the handicapped person – and might also be removed from appointment as tutor. Except perhaps in the case of minor procedures where risks and potential consequences are insignificant, the proper course for a tutor to take, in any case where there is doubt as to whether a proposed procedure is in the best interests of the handicapped person, is to seek authorisation from a court. The court may find it equally difficult to decide what is in the best interests of the handicapped person, but the court's decision is authoritative, and is a protection for the tutor and for those administering the treatment, as well as for the handicapped person.

The court can be asked to approve consent to a proposed medical procedure at the same time as making the appointment of the tutor. A tutor who has already been appointed can go back to the court to apply for approval. The Legal Aid position would be the same as for petitions for appointment – eligibility for Legal Aid would be determined on the basis of the means of the mentally handicapped person, not those of the tutor (see page 48).

In the case of a child, the parent or other person proposing to consent should likewise apply to a court to approve the proposed procedure. The application should be made to the local Sheriff Court for an "order relating to parental rights" as described on page 57.

Sterilisation - The *Jeanette* Case

In some cases sterilisation may be an unavoidable consequence of essential treatment. Where sterilisation is an objective, rather than a consequence, the operation comes into the category to which the above criteria apply. Except where sterilisation is an unavoidable consequence of an essential procedure, a mentally disabled person should never be sterilised unless the person who has power to consent is authorised to do so by a court. This applies whatever the age of the person to be sterilised.

The *Jeanette* case was an application to the English Courts to authorise the sterilisation of a 17 year old mentally disabled English girl. The case was appealed, and ultimately decided by the House of Lords. Some important features of the case were peculiar to England, and would not apply in Scotland. Other points which arose in the *Jeanette* case have now been superseded by the case of *F*. Nevertheless, the *Jeanette* case provoked considerable debate, not all of it well informed, and caused worry – some of it needless – to parents and others, including many in Scotland.

One major consideration in the *Jeanette* case never applied in Scotland, and since the case of *F* that consideration is now known to have been a misconception in England. This was the doubt as to whether, in the absence of any procedure in English law for personal guardianship of mentally disabled adults (apart from a form of statutory guardianship similar to Scottish statutory guardianship), anyone would have had the power to consent to sterilisation once Jeanette reached 18. An unfortunate and unsatisfactory aspect of the case, accordingly, was that it was thought that if she was to be sterilised at all, the operation had to be authorised and performed before she reached the age of 18. The courts were therefore under pressure to make a speedy decision, and had to decide "yes" or "no". "Wait and see" was not considered to be an available option. These pressures have never existed in Scotland, where the tutor of an adult can seek authorisation to consent to sterilisation.

Another difference from the Scottish position is that Jeanette was made a "ward of court". That is an English speciality with no direct equivalent in Scotland. When a person under 18 becomes a ward of court in England, the court itself becomes guardian. So the court itself as guardian had to decide whether to authorise sterilisation, rather than authorising some person having guardianship powers to consent to the sterilisation.

The *Jeanette* case provides two lessons which are relevant in Scotland. Firstly, it emphasised that only with the authority of a court should a procedure such as sterilisation be carried out upon anyone unable to give valid consent. The local authority, which had parental rights, was willing to consent to sterilisation. The girl's mother agreed that she should be sterilised. Yet the local authority still had her made a ward of court so that the matter could be decided by the court. This feature of the *Jeanette* case has been confirmed by the case of *F*, though on the basis of "good practice" rather than outright legal requirement.

The second lesson for us in Scotland is the basis on which the court determined the matter. It must be stressed that the court did not make any decision in general terms that mentally handicapped women should or should not be sterilised. The court refused to proceed on the basis that "therapeutic" sterilisation could be permitted, but "non-therapeutic" sterilisation could not. The court also rejected the argument that sterilisation of a mentally disabled person would contravene her fundamental human right to reproduce. What the court did do was to focus on this particular girl and her circumstances. The court stressed that the decision had to be made on the basis of what was in her own particular and individual best interests. One of the judges summarised the evidence which would normally be required to enable a court to decide any such case. The court would require to be told about the girl's medical history and foreseeable future. Evidence would be required as to the risks of pregnancy occurring, and the consequences if there were a pregnancy. The court would also need to hear what were the various alternative ways in which pregnancy could be avoided. While the court was considering the case of an under-18 English girl, a Scottish court would be likely to have similar requirements if asked to authorise the sterilisation of a Scots girl or woman.

All of the above points were covered by the evidence, and considered by the court, in the *Jeanette* case. She had a "moderate" degree of mental handicap, with limited intellectual development. She was "unlikely to develop beyond a mental age of 6". She suffered from epilepsy and was obese. She had in the past shown extremes of mood, and had been violent and aggressive. She had a high tolerance to pain, and would open wounds.

She was showing signs of becoming sexually aware. She was said to be capable neither of forming an adult relationship, nor of maternal feelings, nor of bringing up a child. She did not understand the link between sexual intercourse and pregnancy. She was not capable of making an informed choice about contraception. Her obesity could well hide any pregnancy until it was too late to terminate. Any birth would require to be by Caesarean section. She would probably prevent the operation wound from healing.

Of the various ways in which pregnancy could be avoided, supervision sufficient to prevent the possibility of intercourse was ruled out as incompatible with humane management. Contraception by mechanical methods was ruled out because of her limited intellectual capacity. The possibility of using a contraceptive pill was carefully considered, but was also rejected. She would have had to take the pill without interruption for some 30 years, and the side effects of this were unknown. A daily dose was necessary, but might be prevented by her periodic spells of aggression and violence. Finally, because she was almost 18, there was no time to experiment with the pill, because it was feared that if such an experiment were unsuccessful, by then it would (in England) be too late to sterilise.

On this question of the principles to apply in deciding whether sterilisation should be approved, the *Jeanette* case contains sensible guidance which could well be looked to by a Scottish court considering whether to approve a proposed sterilisation as being in the best interests of a mentally disabled woman. In this regard, I do not think that the helpfulness of the *Jeanette* case has been displaced by the more recent case of *F*, which appears to have proceeded on the basis that there was "complete agreement" that sterilisation of *F* was in her best interests, without the same degree of anxious consideration of the point as occurred in the *Jeanette* case.

The usefulness of the *Jeanette* case in this regard is however subject to one important qualification. One should not underrate the pressures and limitations caused by the belief that a decision had to be made before Jeanette reached the age of 18. This appeared to preclude some options which would have been available in Scotland, and which since the case of *F* are now known to be available in England. It might otherwise have been thought appropriate to wait and see how far sexual awareness developed; to use the pill for a trial period; to see whether these could be combined with practical management which was not in fact unacceptably restrictive. A later application to a court would still have been available. The court's task would perhaps have been easier, and its decision less controversial, if experience of such courses had still indicated that sterilisation was in the woman's best interests.

This is not the place to consider or even summarise the many arguments and viewpoints expressed in the wake of the decisions in the *Jeanette* case and the case of *F*. I will limit myself to two footnotes.

Firstly, I would suggest that it is not necessarily illiberal to question the assumption that supervision to prevent such a woman having intercourse would be bound to be impractical or unacceptably restrictive. For such a woman to engage in intercourse is almost certainly tantamount to a crime being committed against her – see Chapter IX. If this cannot be prevented, or at least not prevented without unacceptable restrictions, is she being adequately safeguarded in other ways? Is this at the end of the day a question of resources – an unwillingness to make available sufficient resources to enable such women to be adequately safeguarded without being subjected to unacceptable restrictions? Perhaps also an unwillingness to make available sufficient resources to enable them to experience and cope with sexual awareness without undesirable consequences? I am not sure of the answers to such questions. I suggest that they have not been adequately answered. In my view the answers to such questions should be sought and scrutinised before sterilisation is sanctioned. In the *F* case, Lord Jauncey's judgement is brief, but includes the following: "In the case of a long-term incompetent, convenience to those charged with his care should never be a justification for the decision to treat". There is no reason to suppose that this is other than a statement of the law. To my mind, it has significant implications, particularly if we assume – as seems reasonable – that "convenience" includes matters of the making available of sufficient human and other resources.

Secondly, I would question whether attention should always be focused exclusively upon the best interests of the woman in question. It may sometimes be necessary to consider questions relating to the health, circumstances and welfare of any child who might result from any pregnancy (which considerations can by statute be relevant considerations in relation to proposed abortion, and are clearly no less relevant to sterilisation). My particular concern here, however, is the need to focus greater attention upon the parents, and sometimes other relatives, of such women. The point can be made most clearly in relation to parents. In many cases, if such a woman were to have a child, the parental role in relation to that child would in practice fall upon the mother's parents. It is those grandparents who would in practice be forced to choose between the burdens of parenthood and the trauma of distancing themselves from their "own flesh and blood". The mentally handicapped woman may be at risk of a pregnancy in relation to which she is incapable of making choices and decisions for herself; but in a very real sense it is the woman's parents who will often be at risk of having thrust upon them parenthood which is in no way of their choice. If it is right to consider the best interests of the woman who might fall pregnant, it must surely be wrong to take no account of the position of those at risk of having the role and responsibilities of parenthood thrust upon them. Not far away, of course, there again lurks the question of the resources which our society chooses to devote towards those in need of help. To the extent that questions of resources do arise, it cannot be right to allow decisions as to the best interests of the mentally handicapped woman to be circumscribed by limitations on provision for her supervision and care, but at the same time to disregard the practical consequences for her parents or other relatives of similar lack of provision.

Abortion

Abortion is subject to special controls. It is lawful only if certain statutory criteria are met. Those criteria were recently reviewed by Parliament: they were not changed on that occasion, but may be reviewed again. The statutory criteria apply to all women, including mentally handicapped women. Even where the current criteria are met, there is still a requirement for consent, except in cases of necessity. The principle of necessity could well justify termination of a dangerous pregnancy. Otherwise the consent of a tutor, authorised by a court, is likely to be required, on the same basis as for sterilisation, in the case of a woman lacking the legal capacity to give valid consent for herself.

Examination

The principles of law which apply to treatment are relevant also to medical and dental examination. It is probably reasonable to suggest that medical and dental examinations are justified if they are the only practicable way of checking whether essential treatment of any kind is required, and where reasonable care and concern for the wellbeing of the mentally disabled person indicates that such examinations be carried out. If the principles of the case of F apply fully in Scotland, then any examination considered by a responsible body of medical opinion to be in the patient's best interest may be carried out without consent, in the case of a person incapable of giving valid consent.

Partial Capacity

Our law has not yet even begun to address the issues which arise if a person with some degree of mental disability is able to express a view about proposed treatment, but there is doubt about his or her ability to give fully informed and rational consent. Such problems would arise where the patient's strongly expressed views are contrary to professional opinion as to what is truly in the patient's best interests.

Summary

1. It is certainly the law that essential treatment may be given without consent to an unconscious patient, mentally disabled or not.
2. It is very probably the law that essential treatment may be given without consent to a conscious patient with a mental disability which prevents him from being able to give valid consent.
3. In England treatment may be given without consent if the treatment is considered by a responsible body of medical opinion to be in the patient's best interests (as defined in the case of *F*). However, that principle has evolved in the absence of any English provision for obtaining consent, such as the Scottish tutor-dative procedure. Unless and until a Scottish court decides otherwise, it is not safe to rely on this English principle in Scotland, and it is better to assume that non-essential treatment may not be given without valid consent.
4. If there is a degree of doubt as to whether treatment is essential or not, it is to the same degree unsafe to give treatment without valid consent.
5. It is probably the law that examination may be carried out without consent where the examination is indicated by reasonable care and concern for the wellbeing of the mentally handicapped person, and is the only way of establishing whether any kind of essential treatment is required.
6. Except when justified by the above principles, examination or treatment without consent is a criminal assault and a civil wrong.
7. Where consent is required for a mentally disabled adult who is not able to give valid consent, such consent can be given only by a tutor, who should be appointed with power to give health care consent.
8. Approval of a court should be sought in any of the following situations:
   (a) Where there is doubt whether proposed treatment may lawfully be given without consent.
   (b) Where a tutor is in doubt whether to consent or not (except, perhaps, in relation to simple and minor procedures).
   (c) In any case where sterilisation, or a similarly serious procedure, is proposed (except in cases of urgent medical necessity, for example where reproductive organs are seriously diseased and sterilisation is a consequence of necessary treatment, rather than the objective).

Part X of the Mental Health (Scotland) Act 1984

Under Part X of the 1984 Act medical treatment may in certain circumstances be given without the consent of the patient. These provisions apply only to patients detained under certain provisions of the Act. They apply to patients detained under 28-day short term detention, and patients detained under the normal procedure. They do not apply to patients detained under the procedure for two-hour detention, or 72-hour emergency detention. (These procedures are summarised on pages 29-31 of *Scots Law and the Mentally Handicapped*.)

In the case of a patient to whom the provisions do apply, the general rule is that consent is not required for any medical treatment for the patient's mental disorder, if the responsible medical officer is in charge of the treatment.

There are two groups of qualifications to this general rule. Special procedures apply to both. Firstly, the patient's consent is required for certain categories of treatment including any involving destruction of brain tissue, or destruction of the functioning of brain tissue. In addition, certain statutory requirements and procedures must be complied with. The requirements include three certificates by persons appointed by the Mental Welfare Commission to issue such certificates. All three certificates must confirm that the patient has consented, and that the patient is capable of understanding the nature of the proposed treatment, and its purpose and likely effect. One of the certificates must be a medical certificate confirming that the treatment should be given, having regard to the likelihood of the treatment alleviating the patient's condition, or preventing deterioration. The doctor who issues that certificate must first consult those primarily concerned with the patient's medical treatment.

Secondly, there are special provisions for a group of cases which include any case where medication is administered over a period of three months or longer. If the patient consents, a medical certificate is required confirming that the patient has consented, and is capable of understanding the nature of the treatment, and its purpose and likely effects. The certificate may be issued by the responsible medical officer, or by a doctor appointed by the Mental Welfare Commission to issue such certificates. If the patient does not consent, or is not capable of giving valid consent, a medical certificate is required that the treatment should be given, having regard to the likelihood of the treatment alleviating the patient's condition, or preventing deterioration. Such a certificate can be issued only by a doctor appointed by the Mental Welfare Commission to sign such certificates.

Copies of certificates issued under the above procedures must be sent to the Mental Welfare Commission within seven days.

Finally, there are some defined situations which fall generally within the "necessity" principle where the above procedures do not require to be followed. These are situations where the treatment is immediately necessary (a) to save the patient's life; (b) to prevent serious deterioration in the patient's condition, provided that the treatment is not irreversible; (c) to alleviate serious suffering by the patient, provided that the treatment is not irreversible and not physically hazardous; (d) to stop violent behaviour, or to stop the patient being a danger to himself or others, provided that the treatment represents the minimum interference necessary to achieve this, and provided that the treatment is not irreversible and not physically hazardous.

In these four categories of situation the special procedures do not require to be followed, and the general rule applies that treatment can be given without consent to patients detained under the 28-day and normal detention procedures.

Statutory Provision for Medical Consent

In some jurisdictions, but not in Britain, there is specific statutory provision which attempts to overcome the problem of medical consent for examination and treatment of mentally disabled people.

As in the case of guardianship, the Dependent Adults Acts of Alberta contain provisions which were adopted for the proposed English *Dependent Adults Act* (see pages 36-42). The provisions apply when an adult is not capable of understanding proposed examination or treatment, and is incapable of consenting because of "mental or physical disability". They only apply when the adult does not have a guardian empowered to consent to health care (power (h) of the list on page 38).

In such circumstances, the Alberta Act (and the English proposals) simply require the written opinion of two doctors that the adult is "in need of" the proposed examination or treatment. In the case of dental treatment, the written opinion of two dentists is required. A doctor or dentist may then carry out the proposed examination or treatment "in the manner and to the extent that is reasonably necessary and in the best interests of the person examined or treated", just as if the patient had been an adult with full legal capacity who had consented. However, the proposed examination or treatment may not be carried out if either of the certifying doctors (or dentists) is aware that the patient had previously withheld consent to the proposed examination or treatment.

I would not recommend the uncritical importation of similar provisions into Scots law. The provisions quoted, if brought into our law, would be likely to create difficulties of interpretation, and would still leave some problems unsolved. The procedure only applies when doctors can certify that the patient is "in need of" examination or treatment. Only examination or treatment which is "reasonably necessary" and in the patient's "best interests" can be given. This could be interpreted as equivalent to enshrining the necessity theory in statute, and going no further than that. There would still be problems when there was room for doubt as to whether treatment was necessary or not, or as to what would be in the patient's "best interests". It could well be necessary to refer doubtful cases to a court for decision, and indeed it may well be better that the courts should continue to have a role, at least in doubtful cases of significant importance, such as the example, discussed above, of sterilisation.

I would suggest that statutory provision for Scotland, coupled with a statutory code for personal guardianship, should contain the following elements:

(a) There would be statutory confirmation of the "necessity" approach to treatment without consent.

(b) In the case of adults without a guardian, there would be an authorisation procedure in "necessity" cases, perhaps similar to the Albertan provisions described above.

(c) A guardian with power to consent to medical treatment would nevertheless be able to apply to a court for guidance or authorisation in cases where the guardian was in doubt as to how to exercise his powers. This could perhaps be a general provision applying to any of the guardian's powers. There might be a specific requirement to follow such procedure in defined circumstances, covering cases such as proposed sterilisation.

(d) There would be a specific procedure for obtaining authorisation of the court in any case not covered by the "necessity" provisions or by a guardian's consent.

(e) Such provisions would require to be co-ordinated with the provisions of the Mental Health (Scotland) Act 1984 described in the previous section of this chapter.

Drug Testing in Sport

Sport and recreation is increasingly seen as an important area in which people with mental handicaps can develop a sense of self-worth and achievement. The trend towards normalisation has meant that sportsmen and sportswomen with mental handicaps have increasingly come under the jurisdiction and rules of governing bodies of mainstream sport. Nowadays such rules include provisions regarding drug testing.

The position of mentally handicapped people in relation to such drug-testing requirements should be approached by applying the principles outlined above in relation to medical consent. In medical terms, such drug-testing procedures are non-essential. Valid consent must therefore be obtained, and cannot be implied.

In the case of an athlete who has the capacity to give valid consent, there is no reason why rules which apply to non-handicapped people should not be complied with. If a mentally handicapped athlete lacks sufficient capacity and understanding to be able to give valid consent, but has a tutor with powers to give such consent, then the tutor can consent. On the assumption that the testing procedures carry no risk of harm, there is no reason why the tutor should not consent. If however the mentally handicapped athlete is not capable of giving valid consent and does not have a tutor, then such testing simply cannot be carried out, because no-one can validly give the necessary consent. There is no question of the athlete either giving consent or refusing to give consent. The athlete is legally incapable of doing either, and it is not legally possible for testing to take place. To carry out such a test in such circumstances would be to commit an assault. Any rule of any sporting (or other) organisation which cannot be complied with without commission of an offence is to that extent of no effect.

There is of course the further point that if an athlete is not capable of giving medical consent, then the athlete cannot be legally capable of consenting to the administration of performance-boosting drugs. Even if such substances were by some means to be detected, that would be evidence only of wrongful conduct towards the handicapped athlete. The athlete could not be "guilty" of "taking" such drugs.

IX

SECTION 106 OF THE MENTAL HEALTH
(SCOTLAND) ACT 1984

Sexual feelings and their expression are for most people very personal and private matters. For people with mental handicaps, these areas of their lives do not escape the problems of giving necessary protection without unjust restriction. Indeed, such problems intrude with a particular sharpness, with the result that this subject has become one of the focal points of concern and discussion about the rights and status of people with mental handicaps, and about the role of those who seek to help them to live fuller and more normal lives.

In relation to Scots law, these concerns have centred upon a statutory provision designed for the "protection of mentally handicapped females". The provision is now contained in section 106 of the Mental Health (Scotland) Act 1984. Substantially the same protective provisions were previously contained in section 96 of the Mental Health (Scotland) Act 1960, and it is under that heading that I described those provisions in *Scots Law and the Mentally Handicapped*, on pages 51 and 52. I briefly pointed out the importance of these provisions to carers and others. I did not anticipate the huge amount of debate and concern which would ensue, particularly among professionals and voluntary workers involved in the provision of counselling and accommodation.

This is not an area in which the law itself has changed or developed. However the social environment in which the law operates has changed, with consequent changes in the way in which the law is perceived and is likely to be interpreted. Section 106 imposes criminal sanctions. A great deal of concern developed about the possible imposition of criminal sanctions on providers of counselling and accommodation. In 1985 I was asked to take up these concerns with the then Lord Advocate. His response was considerate and helpful, and the guidance which he gave is summarised later.

Before going further, it is necessary to put matters in perspective, for some of the comment on the issues raised by section 106 has been unbalanced. On the one hand, the statutory provisions are archaic and unsatisfactory in that they seek to provide protection without acknowledging the sexuality of those who are to be protected. However, it would on the other hand be quite wrong to suggest that such protection is unnecessary. There are cases of sexual exploitation of women with impaired ability to safeguard themselves from sexual abuse. Prosecutions do from time to time take place. It is right that guilty offenders be prosecuted and punished. Indeed, in 1985 the European Court of Human Rights ruled that the Netherlands was in breach of the European Convention on Human Rights in failing to provide such protection in its criminal law (see Appendix I). A man had forced a young mentally handicapped woman to undress and have sexual intercourse with him. It was not possible for him to be prosecuted under Dutch law. The court held that there was a breach of the right of the young woman and her father to private and family life under Article 8 of the Convention.

Section 106 is not to be criticised because it seeks to prevent exploitation. It is to be criticised to the extent that it might be perceived as hindering those seeking to serve the best interests of people with mental handicaps in a genuine and responsible way. It is to be criticised for treating mentally handicapped women as if they themselves have no sexuality, when they are in fact likely to develop physical maturity despite their intellectual handicaps.

The Provisions of Section 106

Section 106 seeks to protect certain women with handicaps by creating three offences. All of the provisions of this section apply also to girls, but there is no equivalent protection for men and boys (though a male with mental deficiency cannot give the necessary consent to prevent a homosexual act from being a crime). The offences concern intercourse outside marriage with women who come within the definition of those protected. A woman is protected

> . . . if she is suffering from a state of arrested or incomplete development of mind which includes significant impairment of intelligence and social functioning.

We will look more closely at that definition shortly.

The three offences are as follows. Firstly, it is an offence for a man to have intercourse outside marriage with a woman protected by the section. Secondly, it is an offence for anyone to "procure or encourage" any such woman to have intercourse outside marriage. Thirdly, an offence is committed by anyone who owns, occupies, manages or controls premises, or assists in their management or control, if they induce such a woman to be on the premises (or to resort to the premises) for the purpose of intercourse outside marriage.

The offences are prosecuted on indictment, and are punishable by up to two years imprisonment, or a fine. It is a defence to any of the offences that one did not know that the woman came within the

78

definition of those protected, and had no reason to suspect that she came within the definition.

The Problems

These provisions worried many people and organisations involved in activities such as giving education and counselling in sexual matters to people with mental handicaps, and in the provision of accommodation. Were they likely to be accused of "encouraging" protected women to have intercourse? Or be accused of "inducing" them to "resort to or be upon" premises for the purposes of having intercourse?

These worries led to over-reaction. In some quarters it was suggested, with apparent authority but quite incorrectly, that any provision of sexual education and counselling to mentally handicapped people was unlawful. This produced two opposite but equally undesirable reactions. One was to conclude that the law was an ass, and to proceed to give education and counselling without any regard to the need of some women for protection, and to the provisions of section 106. The other was to stop giving such education and counselling.

The latter reaction was particularly unfortunate. Those who give sexual education and counselling in a caring and responsible way are trying, among other things, to achieve the same objective as section 106. They seek to help mentally handicapped people to cope with and express their own sexuality, and to make genuine decisions and choices for themselves, and thus to safeguard themselves from exploitation.

In practice, one encounters individual situations in which it would be hardly feasible, and certainly harmful, to refuse help and support, or to disrupt accommodation arrangements. The following two examples will be recognised as typical by most readers involved in the management of residential accommodation for people with mental handicaps.

(1) After many years in hospital, Miss A moved to a residential development. Initially she occupied a shared flat with two other women. Then she moved into a smaller flat as sole tenant. It was discovered that she had formed a steady and loving relationship with Mr B. Mr B was awaiting a divorce. Miss A became pregnant to Mr B. The pregnancy was troublesome, and at one stage she almost lost the baby. She asked if Mr B could move into her flat with her. Her doctor strongly advised that he should do so, because the doctor felt it important that she should have the support and help of his presence with her during the remainder of her pregnancy.

(2) Miss C and Mr D resided in the same complex, she in hostel-type acommodation, and he in a training flat. They formed a regular sexual

relationship which had lasted for some four months before staff became aware of it. So far as could be ascertained, both were willing partners, and there was no question of Mr D having forced Miss C or having taken unfair advantage of her. Staff felt that both were well placed in their present accommodation, and were reluctant to move them. Miss C was found to be pregnant, and after discussion and counselling decided to have a termination. Both she and Mr D required further help and counselling in a difficult and confusing time for them, and staff did not think it right to disrupt their accommodation arrangements at such a stage.

In both examples the woman had become pregnant. The second pregnancy was unwanted and could perhaps have been prevented by counselling and advice, including advice and help with contraception. Alternatively, both pregnancies could have been avoided by denying the women the opportunity to form and develop relationships which resulted in the risk of pregnancy. That would probably entail an unacceptably restrictive regime. Most people with mental handicaps mature physically at the same age as other people. They have the same range of sexual needs and drives, and they behave sexually in the same way as non-handicapped people. Many mentally handicapped people live quiet lives and develop satisfying friendships, social activities and stable marriages, apparently with no more problems than non-handicapped people. People with more severe mental handicaps are less likely to have the capacity to perform the complex social or physical skills required in intimate and sexual relationships; but many of them do express sexual and friendship needs, and problems can arise if they are not enabled to have those needs met. The ability of many mentally handicapped people to give informed consent in relation to intimate and sexual relationships is enhanced if they are provided with normal life experiences, sex education, counselling and support.

If we accept that people with mental handicaps should be allowed as normal a lifestyle as possible, then they should be protected from exploitation, but those able to form loving relationships of their choice should be given necessary help and support, not prevented from doing so. In the words of Article 1 of the *Declaration on the Rights of Mentally Retarded Persons* by the General Assembly of the United Nations, dated 20th December 1971, to which this country subscribed: "The mentally retarded person has, to the maximum degree of feasibility, the same rights as other human beings".

The fears and worries of professionals working with mentally handicapped people were nevertheless very real. On the one hand, a prosecution would be very damaging, even if it were unsuccessful. On the other, there was the unfortunate tendency to restrict unduly the provision of education and counselling, and decisions about the provision of accommodation, because of fears about the way in which section 106 might be interpreted by the prosecuting authorities. It was felt that it would be helpful to ascertain whether the prosecuting authorities, in deciding whether to bring a prosecution under section 106, would take the view that the whole purpose of the section is to protect women from those seeking to take unfair advantage of their handicaps, and whether prosecution would be considered appropriate when it could be shown that those concerned were endeavouring, responsibly and in good faith, to act in the best interests of mentally handicapped women.

It is not difficult to envisage the way in which, sooner or later, circumstances might arise in which there might be a complaint of breach of section 106 by a professional. When a mentally handicapped adolescent remains immature and dependent in many respects, it can sometimes be difficult for parents and others to accept that she is nevertheless becoming sexually mature. If she were to become pregnant, they might well be very angry and very upset. Their reaction may well be entirely justified, particularly if the pregnancy is unwanted, inappropriate, or potentially harmful. The professionals who have tried to educate and counsel her to cope with her sexuality may themselves feel that they have been unsuccessful, but that does not mean that they were wrong to try. The risk of not trying may have been greater. One can understand, nevertheless, how the anger of distressed parents may be turned upon those professionals, out of a feeling that the professionals had somehow created sexuality where none would otherwise have existed, and that the woman's sexuality had been abused. Such feelings could lead to a demand for prosecution. This could in turn result in the circumstances being reported to the prosecuting authorities, who would have to decide whether to proceed with a prosecution. Because offences under section 106 require to be prosecuted on indictment, the case would be reported to the Crown Office in Edinburgh and a decision whether to prosecute would be made by Crown Counsel.

The person ultimately responsible for prosecutions in Scotland is the Lord Advocate. These concerns were taken to him on behalf of certain organisations concerned with the provision of education, counselling and accommodation. It is important to understand that the Lord Advocate is not in a position to change the law, or to say that he would never enforce an offence created by Parliament. Moreover, if there is doubt whether or not an offence has been committed in particular circumstances, it is the function of the courts to decide the law. The prosecuting authorities, of which the Lord Advocate is head, do however have a duty in every case to consider whether facts reported to them, if proved, would be sufficient in law to warrant conviction of an offence. The prosecuting authorities also have a fairly broad discretion to decide in any particular case whether it is in the public interest and in the interests of justice that a prosecution should proceed. Normally, such decisions are made case by case, on an individual basis. It was however reasonable to approach the then Lord Advocate in general terms regarding section 106 because services to the mentally handicapped were being inhibited by fears as to whether, even though given in good faith, they could result in prosecution. It was not in the public interest that services intended to help and benefit mentally handicapped people should be impaired by fears which might in fact prove to be groundless.

Good Practice - The Definition of Women Protected

A crucial question is: what is good professional practice in these matters? That question is linked to the statutory definition of women protected by section 106 (see page 78). The guidance given by the Lord Advocate was based upon what he was told about modern professional practice in these matters.

A similar test must be satisfied whether a professional proposes to give advice and counselling which is supportive of an intimate relationship or likely to result in an intimate relationship being formed or continued, or whether a decision is being made about accommodation arrangements which is likely to result in the formation or continuation of an intimate relationship. The test is: does the woman have sufficient intelligence and general understanding of relationships to make a genuine and informed choice to enter or continue a particular relationship? There should be a deliberate and careful assessment, using all available information and expert opinion, and the assessment should be recorded. If there is doubt, psychological or medical advice should be sought, and recorded. After making the initial assessment, one must remain alert to the possible need to reconsider in the light of further experience or changed circumstances.

This test should be applied having regard to the statutory definition of women protected by section 106. In giving guidance, the Lord Advocate pointed out that if an offence were alleged, the Crown would require to prove not only that the woman was suffering from "a state of arrested or incomplete development of mind", but also that that state included "significant impairment of intelligence" and "significant impairment of social functioning". In the Lord Advocate's view, "significant impairment of . . . social functioning" would have to be interpreted taking account of recent developments and advances in relation to assisting mentally handicapped people to live in the community and in as normal a way as possible.

In relation to any decision to prosecute, the Crown would be likely to take account of steps taken to obtain expert advice as to whether the woman came within the definition of those protected by section 106. The Lord Advocate took the view that in the type of situation under discussion a fairly narrow interpretation might appropriately be placed on that definition.

The interpretation of the phrase "significant impairment of intelligence and social functioning" is of considerable importance. The approach to interpretation outlined above gives considerable weight to the context in which the phrase is used in section 106. In my view, that is the correct approach. I think it appropriate to interpret the phrase rather as if the definition contained a rider something along the following lines: ". . . in relation to coping with and expressing her own sexuality, and guarding herself from sexual exploitation".

There is however the problem that draftsmen of legislation have latched on to the phrase "significant impairment of intelligence and social functioning" as if it had a clearcut area of meaning with a precise borderline. Thus, for example, the same phrase appears in the definition of "mental impairment" in the 1984 Act. With "severe" in place of "significant" it appears in the definition of those exempted from payment of the Personal Community Charge ("poll tax") under the Abolition of Domestic Rates Etc. (Scotland) Act 1987. Definitions such as "significant impairment of intelligence and social functioning" trip off the tongue easily enough if one knows little about mental handicap, and do in a generalised way indicate the main characteristics of mental handicap. However they are virtually meaningless if one tries to apply them with legal precision from the viewpoint of some understanding of mental handicap and some experience of people with mental handicaps. It seems to me that the most that one can hope to do is to interpret the phrase in relation to a particular mentally handicapped person in particular circumstances and in relation to specific areas of functioning. Even that can be very difficult.

It is nevertheless possible that an attempt might be made to argue that if a person is categorised as "suffering from significant impairment of intelligence and social functioning" for one purpose, then that person comes within that definition for all purposes. For example, it could be argued that a woman registered for exemption from Community Charge must be within the protection of section 106 (particularly on the basis that "severe" includes the lesser concept of "significant"); or that a woman compulsorily detained in hospital under the detention provisions of the 1984 Act is likewise automatically within the protection of section 106. My view is that such an argument could only be advanced from a standpoint of ignorance of mental handicap.

Unfortunately, in one English case the court did rather give the impression of opting to approach such questions of interpretation from a basis of uninformed ignorance. The case was called *Regina -v- Hall*, reported in the Times of 15th July 1987 under the heading "Medical Evidence on Mental Defective Irrelevant". The principal of a residential college for the education of profoundly mentally handicapped young people was unsuccessful in an appeal against conviction of indecent assault on a young woman at the college, for which he was sentenced to six months imprisonment. He had been prosecuted under English provisions which deem a woman unable to give consent if she suffers from "severe impairment of intelligence and social functioning", the same phrase as appears in section 106, except with "severe" in place of "significant". The report gives no indication of the nature or circumstances of the offence, or of the motives for the activities which gave rise to the charge. The report declared that the court had decided that "any 'severe impairment of intelligence and social functioning' was to be measured against the standard of normal persons, and although medical expert evidence was admissible to establish the extent of a victim's intelligence, the opinion of a medical expert as to whether there was severe impairment had no real weight, if indeed it was admissible at all". The court's actual decision does not seem to have been quite as sweeping as that. It was apparently argued that the woman suffered from severe impairment of intelligence and social functioning in comparison to non-handicapped people, but only moderate impairment when compared with other mentally handicapped people. The court rejected that argument on the grounds that the words of the definition were "ordinary English words and not terms of art".

It was also argued in *Regina -v- Hall* that the degree of impairment could only be proved by expert evidence, or, if that was not the case, then expert evidence was certainly the most cogent evidence. The court held that medical evidence was admissible to establish the extent of the woman's intelligence, but that "their Lordships were unable to accept that an expert's opinion that a woman of, say, 30 with the intelligence of a girl of five was not severely impaired was of any real weight, if indeed admissible at all".

One is left with the very clear impression that the English court came just close enough to grappling with this definition to glimpse how meaningless it is –"not a term of art" – and then retreated into the platitude that it should be interpreted "as ordinary English words". One trusts that a Scottish court would face up to the difficulties of

84

interpretation and utilise all available assistance, including appropriate expert evidence, in attempting to interpret such statutory definitions in individual cases. In particular, one trusts that the court would accept that the most which it could hope to achieve is to place a mentally handicapped person within or outwith the scope of the definition for the purposes of the particular question before the court, and not in any general sense.

Encourage

Those involved in the provision of advice and counselling are mainly concerned about possible allegations of contravention of the second offence, that of procuring or encouraging a woman protected by section 106 to have intercourse outside marriage. That offence could also be of concern to those involved in the provision of accommodation. In considering a prosecution for that offence, the Crown would require to have regard to the appropriate interpretation of "encourage". The Lord Advocate in his guidance pointed out that the Crown would, for example, require to take account of the House of Lords decision in the *Gillick* case.

The *Gillick* case concerned the provision by doctors of contraceptive advice and treatment to girls under 16. The courts were asked to consider whether such doctors would be guilty of aiding and abetting unlawful sexual intercourse by the girls. Lord Fraser pointed out that the case was concerned with doctors who honestly intended to act in the best interest of such girls. He said: "I think it unlikely that a doctor who gives contraceptive advice or treatment with that intention would commit an offence" [under the relevant statute]. Lord Scarman was more definite than that: "The *bona fide* exercise by a doctor of his clinical judgement must be a complete negation of the guilty mind which is an essential ingredient of the criminal offence of aiding and abetting the commission of unlawful sexual intercourse".

Lord Scarman also had this to say on the general subject of applying old law in modern social conditions. He described the court's task as "to search the overfull and cluttered shelves of the Law Reports for a principle, or set of principles recognised by the judges over the years but stripped of the details which, however appropriate in their day, would, if applied today, lay the judge open to a justified criticism for failing to keep the law abreast of the society in which they live and work".

Purpose of Section 106

The side heading to section 106, as printed in the 1984 Act, is "Protection of mentally handicapped females". Technically, such side headings are not part of the Act. However, in his guidance the Lord

Advocate confirmed that he was in no doubt that the purpose of the provisions of section 106 is indeed to protect mentally handicapped women from exploitation. One of the factors which a prosecutor will consider, when deciding whether to prosecute a statutory offence, is the purpose of the statutory provisions, and whether a prosecution would be likely to achieve that purpose. In relation to the purpose of section 106, it would be counterproductive to prosecute professionals who try, responsibly and in good faith, to help mentally handicapped women, among other things, to learn to safeguard themselves from exploitative relationships. A letter from the Crown Office following the discussion with the Lord Advocate put it this way: "It may be doubtful whether prosecution would generally be necessary or appropriate to achieve that purpose in the types of situation which were described and discussed at our meeting" (letter to the author, 16th December 1985). The same letter concluded:

> You will appreciate that, while he recognises [SSMH's] concerns and is sympathetic to the work which is currently being undertaken in the area of enabling the mentally handicapped to lead as normal lives as possible, the Lord Advocate could not properly undertake that an offence provided by Parliament will never be enforced. The decision in each case of an alleged contravention of Section 106 of the Mental Health (Scotland) Act 1984 will depend on the particular circumstances of the individual case. From our discussion and what I have said above, it will be apparent, though, that we do not think it likely that prosecution of a person responsibly concerned with the provision of sexual education and counselling, or of accommodation to mentally handicapped adults would normally be considered appropriate.

It cannot be stressed too strongly that nothing in this chapter should be read as indicating that a complaint such as that which I have described above will always be unfounded. Professionals must exercise great care in these matters. They would be open to the severest criticism if they failed to exercise proper professional standards in assessing whether it was appropriate to provide sexual guidance and counselling to a woman, and in particular whether to provide such guidance and counselling in such a way as might encourage an intimate relationship. On the one hand, on the basis of the guidance given by the Lord Advocate, a professional carefully and conscientiously following proper professional practice, as described above, is not likely to face prosecution, even though in a particular case things may have gone awry. The converse, however, is that a professional who cannot show that he (or she) has followed proper professional practice could be at risk of prosecution in such circumstances.

Men

There is no provision providing protection for men directly equivalent to section 106. If a country which failed to provide such protection to women was held to be in breach of the European Convention on Human Rights, then it is presumably a breach of the Convention not to protect men in the same way. (In relation to homosexual activity, if one participant lacks capacity to consent to the activity then the other is guilty of a crime.)

However, in the provision of education and counselling, and in decisions about accommodation, the position of men under section 106 must be borne in mind. It is an offence for a man to have intercourse outside marriage with a woman protected by section 106. The interpretation and application of the statutory definition of women who are protected is equally important here, and responsible professionals will require to give careful thought to the position of the male partner in any relationship, particularly if he is also receiving guidance from them.

If Prosecution is Threatened

So far as I am aware, the fear that someone involved in sex education and counselling or provision of accommodation might be prosecuted under section 106, has not yet materialised. If however such a prosecution were to be threatened, then it would be perfectly proper to provide relevant detailed background information to the Procurator Fiscal or to the Crown Office. If for example the recommendations on page 82 have been followed, full details should certainly be submitted. The Lord Advocate confirmed in his guidance that account would be taken of such information.

The Gap between Professionals and Non-Professionals

Discussion of section 106 with professionals sometimes leads on to criticism of parents, or non-professional management committees, and the like. It is suggested that mentally handicapped people have a "right" to sex education, and indeed a "right" to sexual fulfilment. The complaint is that non-professionals refuse to acknowledge the sexuality of mentally handicapped people and deny them these "rights".

If we listen to the non-professionals, their attitude is often not as extreme as that. They may be suspicious about the degree of interest shown by some professionals in the sexuality of the mentally handicapped people with whom they deal. Resistance is likely to be stiffened by any suspicion that those professionals seek to apply in these matters a personal view of sexual morality seen as deviating from acceptable norms.

Without doubt the responsibility here rests with the professionals. It is for them to communicate effectively what they seek to do, why, and how, and to respond to any concerns. It is for them to explain that what they seek to do is necessary, in order to enable some mentally handicapped people to cope with their own sexuality, to express their sexuality, to fulfil their human need to form close and loving relationships, and so forth. It is for them to demonstrate sufficient professionalism, responsibility and integrity to dispel any worries or suspicions. If they cannot do that, the failure is theirs.

And if any readers who have reached this point feel that this subject has been given disproportionate space, and that there are not real and significant issues to be faced and considered, then that failure is mine!

The Case for Law Reform

Some of the more extreme fears about section 106 can be dispelled. The need remains for the type of protection which section 106 was designed to provide. There is however a case for reform of the law.

When the predecessor of section 106 was drafted, there is little doubt that Parliament was directing the three offences at clear sexual exploitation, either directly or in the form of activities akin to those of the pimp and the brothel-keeper.

That protection should be retained, but it should be embodied in a code in which the starting point for this and other offences should be the rights and needs of mentally handicapped men and women. Such reform must follow a discussion and assessment of those needs which is beyond the scope of this book. Issues will include questions about what help in coping with sexuality should be given to very handicapped people who, without doubt, in this context do suffer from "significant impairment of intelligence and social functioning" (by any reasonable interpretation of the phrase); whether existing criminal law requires amendment to avoid depriving them of such help; and how necessary protection – including protection from misguided professionals – can nevertheless be provided.

X

MANAGEMENT OF AFFAIRS – THE CURATOR BONIS

We come now to an area of law which has remained fossilised in archaic form, leaving an ever-widening gap between legal provision and the needs of modern society. For many people with mental handicaps that gap is unhelpful. For some it is disastrous. Law reform by Parliament is needed. In the meantime, however, the inherent flexibility of our common law should provide scope for at least some improvement, possibly significant improvement. As a matter of urgency, these possibilities should be explored and tested to the full.

This area of law is called "management of affairs" in *Scots Law and the Mentally Handicapped*. There I explained how, by and large, the law deals separately with matters of personal guardianship on the one hand, and matters of management of money and property, transaction of business, and so forth, on the other. Up to this point, most of the topics discussed in this book can be grouped under the general heading of personal guardianship and personal decision-making. In those areas there has been much ongoing development to consider. But when we turn to the management of affairs, I cannot report any such significant development since I wrote *Scots Law and the Mentally Handicapped*. However, I doubt whether there is any other area of law more urgently in need of development and reform.

The Curator Bonis

If a mentally disabled adult has affairs which he is unable to manage himself, no-one – neither parents nor anyone else – has any automatic authority to manage them for him. Someone has to be appointed to manage them. For some specific types of asset, there are relatively simple procedures for making such an appointment. Examples are appointees who receive social security benefits, and special arrangements for vaccine damage payments and National Savings Certificates. In the case of hospital patients, there is a simple procedure under which the hospital management can be authorised to look after money and valuables, up to specified limits. For everyone else – and for hospital patients above the limits – it is necessary to petition a court for appointment of a "curator bonis". Under present law and practice, only a curator bonis has general authority to manage the assets and affairs of a mentally disabled person. The law covering curators bonis is described in Chapter VIII of *Scots Law and the Mentally Handicapped*. There I also mentioned some more specific arrangements, such as appointment of a curator to look after the interests of a mentally disabled person in a court action; and the procedure for administration by hospital management. In addition I mentioned what I described as "informal voluntary arrangements", under which the problems of lack of legal capacity are solved either by agreeing to ignore the lack of capacity, and the resultant lack of legal validity, or by allowing someone to act for the mentally disabled person without having, strictly speaking, any authority to do so.

Mental handicap, however severe, does not disqualify anyone from owning property or assets. The problem is how to manage property and assets, and how to carry through necessary legal actions and transactions, how to make legally effective decisions, and so on. The problem does not arise in relation to trusts, because when a trust is established for the benefit of a mentally disabled person, the trustees are legal owners of the trust fund, and they administer it. Trusts are discussed at some length in *Scots Law and the Mentally Handicapped*. They can be used to avoid the disadvantages of having a curator bonis, provided that funds are put in trust at the outset. However, if funds or assets become the property of a mentally disabled person, then under Scots law they cannot thereafter be retrieved and put into trust.

So if we set aside trusts, informal voluntary arrangements, and a few specialities, we come back to the general proposition that under present law and practice, if a mentally disabled adult has affairs which he cannot manage himself, the only available solution is to appoint a curator bonis. Bearing that in mind, let us look briefly at the history of the curator bonis, and more closely at the problems.

Curator Bonis - History

As we have seen (pages 22-23), curator bonis procedure had its origins at the beginning of the eighteenth century as a response to the delays and difficulties of cognition. Cognition was the procedure by which tutors-at-law were appointed. Tutors-at-law, once appointed, were managers of affairs as well as personal guardians. However the procedure to appoint them was slow, cumbersome and expensive, and in any event only available in the case of people who came within the extreme definitions of "furious" or "fatuous".

Curators bonis met two needs. They could be appointed relatively quickly, to act as managers of affairs pending appointment of a tutor-at-law. They could also be appointed to people incapable of managing their own affairs, yet not so severely ill or handicapped as to be classified as "furious" or "fatuous".

Regulations made by the Court of Session (termed an "Act of Sederunt") in 1730 narrated that the judges of the court "have often been applied to" for appointment of curators bonis. The regulations laid down rules for the conduct of curators bonis (and certain other persons given similar powers). A fresh code of rules was established by the Judicial Factors Act of 1849, which narrated that such applications had become "very numerous". In 1868 appointment of tutors-at-law was extended to anyone incapable of managing his affairs because of unsoundness of mind, but appointments of tutors-at-law dwindled. In 1880 the Sheriff Courts were empowered to appoint curators bonis to small estates, and they can now appoint curators bonis in estates of any size. In this century the curator bonis has become the sole manager of affairs of mentally disabled people.

The two codes of rules, of 1730 and 1849, give us the key to many of the problems encountered today. Both are codes of rules for the conduct of curatories. The 1849 code set out what is still the basis of the regime under which curators operate.

The 1730 rules envisaged that the typical curatory involved the management of a landed estate. Under the first rule, the curator bonis was responsible for "all rents and profits whatsoever which he shall recover, or by diligence might have recovered". Under the second, his first duty after appointment was to "make a distinct and special rental of the estate committed to his management". And so forth.

The 1849 rules still envisage a substantial landed estate. After appointment and finding security for the proper performance of his duties, the curator bonis was required to prepare and lodge

> a distinct rental of all lands committed to his management, specifying the rents, revenues and profits of such lands, the existing leases, and other rights affecting the lands, and the public burdens and other burdens thereon, and a list of all monies and funds belonging and debts due to the estate, specifying the particulars of each item, and the interest or revenue arising from the same, the document by which the same is vouched, and the nature and value of any security held for the same, and also an inventory of any household furniture, farm stocking, goods, or moveables, including rights moveable, forming part of the estate.

The 1849 Act narrated that "it has been found that the existing regulations and the present means of enforcing them are imperfect and insufficient for preventing in many instances the occurrence of great irregularity in the conduct of curators bonis and others, and in consequence thereof great loss has resulted to the funds and estates under their charge and to the parties interested therein". The narrative concluded that it was "expedient to make provision for the more regular accounting and official management of persons who shall hereafter be served as curator to any insane person or idiot". So the problem was that irregularities on the part of curators were resulting in losses to funds and estates, and the solution was the provision of more regular accounting and official administration. Thus was established the present-day regime – expensive to administer, cumbersome and rigid, insensitive and remote, heedless of the rights and status of the mentally disabled person, dominated by the requirements of "regular accounting and official administration".

Not surprisingly, curatories nowadays function best in cases which approximate most closely to those perceived as the norm in the era when the procedure evolved. These are cases where the mentally disabled person is wealthy, quite clearly has no legal capacity whatsoever, is institutionalised, and is considered to have very simple financial needs which can be met by regular payments at a fixed rate, or occasional isolated items of expenditure which are clearly defined and not urgent; and where all concerned accept that the main objective of administration is to maximise the amount of estate which will pass to those entitled to succeed to it on the death of the mentally disabled person. That description applies only to a tiny fraction of the people who have assets and affairs which they are unable to administer themselves. Let us look at various categories of problems which afflict the majority.

Expense

Curatories are expensive. The funds of the mentally disabled person have to pay for the court petition to appoint the curator, for the curator's ongoing remuneration, for annual audit costs, and for other expenses such as the costs of further court applications to authorise various steps or decisions which the curator proposes to take. For very large estates these costs may not be an undue burden. For medium estates they are a significant burden. For small ones, they are absurdly high. In July 1989, the Mental Welfare Commission, after consultation with the Accountant of Court, raised from £10,000 to £50,000 the minimum level of estate at which the Commission would normally consider appointment of a curator to be appropriate, in the absence of circumstances justifying the setting up of a curatory at a lower level. It is now accepted that curatories are uneconomic for estates less than about £50,000, yet there is no alternative procedure for smaller estates. Of those mentally handicapped people who have significant funds or assets at all, the majority have relatively modest means. If anything, the less capital someone has, then the more important it is to safeguard that capital. What happens in practice is that if a curator is appointed, then the costs of the curatory eat up the funds until nothing is left. In other words, the mentally handicapped person is deprived of his funds and assets by the system designed to protect them.

Cases where this has happened are coming to light with depressing regularity. They often occur as a result of deinstitutionalisation. They also tend to raise questions as to whether the handicap was sufficient to justify appointment of a curator at all, but that is a separate issue dealt with later. These are the salient facts of one case:

> A left hospital and went to supported accommodation in the community. She had about £2,000 held by a curator bonis. Assessment in connection with her placing in the community suggested that her degree of disability did not justify curatorship. This was eventually established, and some three years after she had left hospital the curatory was terminated. During those three years she had received less than £400 of her money. The rest disappeared in costs, and she was told that she owed a balance to the former curator.

It is the system which produces such results, not ill-will on the part of curators. Indeed, case-histories reported to me include those where curators have waived charges, and must have expended significant amounts of professional time and effort without remuneration. Even in such cases, costs have depleted meagre funds by a wholly disproportionate amount.

So long as we have a system designed for the administration of very large estates, and dominated by the requirement to meet meticulous standards of "regular accounting and official administration" the problem will remain of disproportionate costs in relation to less wealthy people with mental handicaps.

It is difficult to find comparable situations where administrative costs are so high. The most common tool for avoiding the need of a curatory is to establish a trust. Smaller trusts can be run at a fraction of the cost of equivalent curatories, yet there is no evidence of widespread abuses or losses – indeed, trusts are generally much more successful in meeting satisfactorily the needs of those whom they are designed to serve.

Cumbersomeness and Rigidity

"We cannot buy him an ice cream cone without getting a receipt" was the complaint of the parents of a young adult who was mentally handicapped, and who had a curator. The curatory system is dominated by meticulous accounting for accounting's sake. The curator has to be able to vouch and justify his own intromissions down to the last penny. Yet when the Accountant of Court approves payment by a curator to parents of a weekly allowance from the funds held in the curatory, the requirement on the curator is to show that the payments are made. Thereafter, the controls in practice disappear, and unless obvious abuses are drawn to the curator's attention, there is no control on whether the parents spend money wisely or unwisely.

In practice, curators tend to see it as their priority to meet the auditing requirements of the Accountant of Court. Otherwise, their role is passive, not active. If particular needs are drawn to their attention, they may react. But there is no incentive or requirement to assess the needs of the mentally disabled person, or to seek to identify any unmet needs. Indeed, the qualification for the job of curator is to be a competent and careful accountant: there is no requirement that the curator should have any skills in understanding the disability or social circumstances of the person whose funds he administers, nor even a requirement that he should ever meet the person.

Even when needs are drawn to the attention of a curator, the curator may have to seek agreement from the Accountant of Court, or the authority of the court itself, before acting. And he may find himself unable to do what is suggested. An example of the problems which can arise appeared in a court case reported in 1988. A curator had been appointed to a Mrs Paterson, who had a substantial shareholding in a private family company. All concerned wished the curator to retain the shares. The only person who disagreed was the Accountant of Court. He took the view that the shares were not "authorised investments" and could not be retained. The matter went to court, where the judge over-ruled the Accountant of Court. In our present context, however, the important point is that the family had to contend with the opposition of the Accountant of Court, and the matter had to go to court to avert the disruption of a family company which would otherwise have occurred, contrary to everyone's wishes, due to the restrictive view adopted by the Accountant of Court.

In many cases the Accountant of Court is blamed unfairly. His interpretations of curators' powers under our present system are usually correct. Moreover, I hear many complaints of reasonable requests for expenditure from curatory funds being turned down by curators because "the Accountant of Court would not approve", when in fact the Accountant of Court way well have been prepared to approve the proposal had it been carefully thought out and explained to him. In such situations, the truth of the matter is often that the problems can be traced back to the question of expense, in the sense that the curator is a professional person whose time is costly, and he may feel that the expenditure of his time which would be demanded would not be cost-effective.

Lack of effective supervision in cases of serious mismanagement

Paradoxically, supervision by the Accountant of Court does not always guarantee that there will not be serious mismanagement. On the one hand, a curator who can produce only a paid cheque, rather than a receipt, for some obvious and reasonable disbursement of a few pounds, is likely to receive an unending stream of letters until he is eventually able to produce a receipt. On the other hand, cases have arisen where it has been claimed that serious neglect giving rise to substantial losses has gone undetected and uncorrected, sometimes for years. There have been well publicised criticisms of the Accountant of Court's office, which have not necessarily been fair criticism, yet the fact remains that the existing system does not prevent such complaints from arising.

If one looks at the realities of the quality of management, rather than petty auditing and accounting requirements, then there seems to be no evidence that supervision by the Accountant of Court achieves a higher standard than equivalent situations, such as trusts, where there is no such supervision. This makes it even harder to justify the cumbersomeness, rigidity, expense and other disadvantages of the present system.

Insensitivity and Remoteness

One can only assume that curators, and the Accountant of Court's office, simply do not realise how cruelly distressing for relatives and other carers can be the insensitivity sometimes shown to them. Let us go straight to an example:

As a little girl, B sustained brain damage when struck by a hit-and-run driver. By the time she reached adulthood, the damages award had built up almost to a six-figure sum, administered by a curator bonis. Despite the stresses of doing so, her parents continued to provide a home for her and to care for her. She had a typewriter, and could copy-type. She liked to socialise with friends – to have suitable clothes, to visit a hairdresser on occasions. She told her parents' solicitor how she once went to a christening, and bought little presents. She liked swimming.

A welfare rights officer discovered that the income which B received from the curatory to live on was less than she would have received if she had been on supplementary benefit. In other words, in terms of current income she was poorer than she would have been if she had never received the substantial damages payment, and had been dependent on state benefits. The welfare rights officer wrote to the curator, who passed the letter on to the Accountant of Court. The response from the Accountant of Court's office included the following: "With regard to the social worker's letter, this really has no bearing on this case. The DHSS have their own policies and guidelines and act accordingly, whereas the Factor has been entrusted by Court with the Ward's estate to maintain and preserve the estate as far as possible so that, in case of recovery by the Ward, the Factor would be in a position to hand over the estate virtually intact". In an earlier letter, about monthly allowance and payment for clothing, the Accountant of Court's office had written: "When considering these matters, however, the Factor should bear in mind that it is his duty to preserve the estate as far as possible". The Accountant of Court's office did not disclose the basis on which they regarded the possibility of B's "recovery" from brain damage sustained sixteen years earlier as being sufficiently significant to form a major factor (or form any factor at all) in the administration of her funds. And whoever wrote that letter did not see the expression on the parents' faces produced by the glib reference to "recovery".

The parents claimed that when they tried to explain to the curator their concerns that the curatory was not being administered in their daughter's best interests, they were made to feel that "he queries our integrity". At their first meeting with the curator, he had told them: "This is not a meal-ticket for life". When a solicitor consulted by the parents first met the curator, the curator's first words were: "B has money. Mother is working, father is not. Father would like to get his hands on a bit more of the money. That's the way I see it". Prior to the meeting he had written to the parents that he was "prepared to meet with [the solicitors] to explain the situation which they do not seem to appreciate".

He appeared to have little or no understanding of B, or of her abilities and disabilities.

He had never met her.

This particular case had a happier ending. A reasonable working relationship was establised between curator and family. This was achieved after the curator had been told rather more about B and her family, and their situation and concerns; and after the parents had been told rather more about the workings of a curatory and the constraints upon a curator.

Often the underlying cause of problems with curatories appears to be a huge gap in understanding between curators and families. The Accountant of Court's office are well aware of the problem, and have recently prepared a helpful booklet entitled *Information for Families of Persons Subject to Curatory*. Any families who do not have this booklet should obtain a copy through the curator, or from the Accountant of Court's office.

This initiative by the Accountant of Court is to be applauded. Unfortunately, it is not balanced by any requirement for curators, or even the Accountant of Court's staff, to have any particular degree of knowledge or expertise about mental disabilities. I do not know how many curators of mentally handicapped people have never even met those whose affairs they administer: it would not surprise me if they were in the majority. The Accountant of Court is aware of both sides of the problem, but has explained that he simply does not have the resources to apply an effective "quality control" to the performance of individual curators.

There is no obligation on curators to consult with families or other carers, on a regular or indeed any basis. There is no obligation to consult with the mentally disabled people themselves, or to try to involve them in decision-making, in the many cases where at least some limited involvement along these lines would be possible and beneficial. There is no requirement to prepare and regularly update an account of the mentally disabled person's capabilities and requirements, present and anticipated, and a plan for the management of the curatory, geared to that assessment. Even if professional curators volunteered to do any of these things, it is doubtful whether they would be remunerated (and if they were remunerated, the costs would deplete unacceptably the funds of smaller curatories).

We come back yet again to the basic ethos of the curatory regime, which is that of a sterile and impersonal accounting exercise, rather than a skilled and sensitive service made available to meet the needs of mentally disabled people and their families and carers.

Loss of Capacity

Curatory procedure is based upon the simplistic and inaccurate assumption that everyone falls neatly into one of two categories: that they either have complete capacity to manage all of their affairs, however complex, or alternatively have no capacity whatsoever to play any part in the management of any of their affairs, however simple. Of course, most mental disabilities, and certainly most mental handicaps, place people somewhere between these two extremes. However, a curator bonis has never been appointed with a limited remit. If a mentally disabled person has some assets or affairs which he cannot handle, the only available solution is to appoint a curator bonis, who completely takes over administration of all of the affairs of the mentally disabled person. The mentally disabled person is deprived of the legal capacity even to manage simple matters which he may in fact be quite capable of managing. As I pointed out in *Scots Law and the Mentally Handicapped,* our law imposes upon those who already have to cope with a mental handicap, a further unnecessary and artificial legal handicap. It is a scandal that in this area our law remains out of touch with reality, and far behind the accepted standards of modern legal systems.

Inadequate Certification Procedures; Lack of Review

Curators are generally appointed on the flimsiest of evidence. Two doctors provide certificates saying no more than that the person is "of unsound mind and incapable of managing his/her own affairs or of giving directions for their management". On the basis of no greater assessment or information than that, a fundamental change is made in the status of a mentally disabled person, with far-reaching consequences for that person and for family and carers. Moreover, the change is likely to be lifelong: there is no requirement for review. There is no requirement for any other professional assessment (such as the assessment by a mental health officer in statutory guardianship procedure).

The remarkably brief and uninformative certificates usually accepted by the courts when appointing curators bonis should be contrasted with the forms of certificate for tutor-dative procedure described in Chapter VI (pages 48-49). Obvious queries arise. Do doctors obtain full information as to the person's affairs before issuing a certificate? If not, how can they certify that the person is unable to manage them? If they do obtain information as to affairs, why do they not spell out the person's disabilities and relevant degrees of capability and incapability, relating them to that person's affairs, and explaining why the person is completely incapable of managing any of them?

It seems that doctors give too much deference to lawyers, and lawyers give too much deference to doctors. Doctors either sign, or decline to sign, the certificate submitted by the lawyers, without challenging form and content. Lawyers accept whatever the doctor's certificate contains, without further enquiry, provided that it will enable them to obtain the outcome which they have been instructed to achieve.

Increasingly, evidence is emerging of inappropriate curatories. As most of the examples relate to mental handicaps which are unlikely to have varied greatly in degree, it is probable that in most cases curators have been appointed when they should not. Even if there has been some change in capacity, inappropriate curatories have remained in force, and this must be attributed to the lack of any requirement for regular review of appointments. One example has been given in another context on page 93. These are two further examples:

(1)   C lived in hospital for many years until 1986. A curator administered his relatively modest funds. Administration costs depleted his funds substantially. On discharge from hospital he was assessed as being "able to live independently within the community with minimal support and supervision". He took up the tenancy of a flat. His curatory was eventually terminated. His "affairs" had never amounted to more than relatively modest

savings, and on the evidence of assessment and actual capability following discharge from hospital, it is unlikely that he was ever "unable to manage his affairs".

(2)   D had very substantial funds and assets. He was mentally handicapped. He wished to make a Will. He appeared to have a clear understanding of his assets and affairs, to be aware of the various choices before him when considering the terms of his Will, and to be capable of making sensible decisions and giving adequate instructions. However, there was concern as to whether the Will would be valid. D was seen by a doctor most eminent and skilled in this field, who produced an admirable report showing that all relevant medico-legal factors had been considered, and expressing the firm conclusion that D had the necessary capacity to make a valid Will. On D's subsequent death the Will was accepted by all concerned as being valid. Yet for many years prior to making the Will, D's affairs had been administered by a curator, and the curatory remained in force until his death. There appears to have been no review of the appropriateness of the curatory. It is possible that he may have been able to make a Will, yet still unable to manage all of his affairs, but what is significant is that even in this situation there was no review of whether D still needed a curator.

Concern about the quality of certification in a curatory was expressed in a judgement which appeared in the law reports in 1987, concerning the same Mrs Paterson who featured in the 1988 case mentioned on page 94. Mrs Paterson had suffered a stroke. Relatives disagreed as to whether she required a curator bonis. A petition for appointment was opposed. The petitioners had lodged the usual medical certificates by two consultant psychiatrists who had certified on soul and conscience that Mrs Paterson was "of unsound mind and incapable of managing her own affairs or giving instructions for their management". As the case progressed, much evidence was tendered to the court regarding Mrs Paterson's condition, abilities, and disabilities. After summarising this evidence in his judgement, Lord Jauncey had this to say about the original certificates:

It is absolutely clear from the foregoing detailed material that it contains nothing to support the description of Mrs Paterson as 'of unsound mind', as was thought appropriate in the two soul and conscience certificates accompanying the petition. Indeed the material all points in the same general direction, namely that while Mrs. Paterson has very severe difficulties of communication she is very far from being of unsound mind in the sense in which that term is normally accepted by doctors and lawyers. It would not be profitable to speculate upon the circumstances in which the two learned psychiatrists came to express their brief opinion.

Mrs Paterson was not mentally handicapped, and had not been a long-term hospital patient. The majority of cases which come to light of apparently inappropriate appointment, or at least of failure to review and terminate curatories, concern people who have been institutionalised. A common pattern seems to emerge. In most, if not all, cases the affairs of the mentally handicapped person have first been administered under the much less formal procedure now governed by section 94 of the Mental Health (Scotland) Act 1984. This procedure is considered in a little more detail later (pages 111-113). Briefly, hospital management requires only one doctor's certificate, and no other procedure, to hold and administer money and valuables up to a limit, currently, of £3,000 (which can be increased by the Mental Welfare Commission in individual cases). When funds have built up further, a curator has often been appointed. Many inappropriate small curatories seem to have originated in this way.

The availability of the section 94 procedure is no doubt a considerable administrative convenience for hospital management. There is no equivalent procedure available for mentally handicapped people in the community. Those concerned with the care of mentally handicapped people in the community expend considerable effort helping them to manage their money and affairs themselves. If the provision under section 94 were removed altogether, similar efforts would have to be made for hospital patients. That would probably be a good thing in many cases, if the resources were available to give such help. In practice, the easy option provided by section 94 is taken, and thereafter a curator is appointed apparently without any great consideration as to whether such a step could be avoided.

A professional engaged in projects to accommodate mentally handicapped people in the community, who reported several such cases to me, wrote that in his view "it would help enormously if curatories were reviewed at the point of the individual leaving hospital and, where appropriate, dissolved". However, the criteria for appointing curators are the same for hospital patients as for people in the community. If – as seems to be the case – many curatories for mentally handicapped people require to be discharged as unnecessary once the patient leaves hospital, it is likely that the initial appointment was inappropriate. It is necessary for doctors to take more care in issuing certificates, and for the courts to scrutinise applications more carefully. The mentally handicapped person normally has no-one to represent his (or her) own interests in the curatory procedure.

A requirement for regular re-assessment would also help in identifying and terminating appointments which were either inappropriate, or had become inappropriate. The procedures for detention in hospital and for statutory guardianship both require regular review, and it is now good practice in tutor-dative cases for appointments to be of limited duration, to ensure periodic review.

A Possible Way Forward

Curator bonis procedure is a tool which works best when applied in the situation for which it was designed. I have already described that as being the situation of the wealthy person who clearly lacks any legal capacity, is institutionalised, and is considered to have simple and modest financial needs. Many curatories which do not meet all of those criteria nevertheless work satisfactorily. Indeed, in recent years a thoughtful and more flexible approach on the part of some curators, and the Accountant of Court's office, has achieved much in cases in many ways ill-suited to curatory procedure. However, even in skilled hands, the only available tool is simply not suited to many of the jobs for which it is used. We require a new and more adaptable tool, or perhaps a selection of tools, custom-designed to meet modern needs. Only legislation can provide us with a new toolkit. I can think of no other area of law of similar importance where the gap between need and provision has become so wide, without reforming legislation.

In the meantime, can we make better use of the existing tool, and perhaps refurbish it?

Curator bonis procedure was not devised by the legislature. The procedure was invented by the courts, and thereafter regulated, in some respects, by rules and by statute. We have seen that the courts have been willing to update tutor-dative procedure to meet modern needs, perceptions and conditions. I see no fundamental reason why the courts should not also update curator bonis procedure. Tutor-dative procedure had fallen into disuse, whereas curator bonis procedure has remained in full use; but that, I would suggest, is no reason in principle for updating one and not the other, if the need for such updating is equally great in both cases.

In the early eighteenth century the courts created curator bonis procedure to meet needs not met by a procedure which – as I have already mentioned – came to be regarded as "very absurd, very cumbrous, and very expensive". Curator bonis procedure, through failure to develop and adapt, is itself open to those same criticisms, in some of the situations in which it is the only available remedy. If the courts can create a remedy to meet need, then surely they still have at least some scope to update and adapt that remedy to meet modern needs, perceptions and conditions.

In many areas of law the courts have been able to develop the law in response to changing social conditions, changing needs, and changing perceptions. Parties to cases before the courts have argued for such development, drawing the attention of the courts to the fundamental

101

principles of law and justice underlying the existing law, and suggesting how those principles should be applied to new circumstances.

Perhaps one reason why curator bonis procedure remains ossified and undeveloped is that the mentally disabled people to whom curators are appointed have not been able to draw the attention of the courts to the injustices described in this chapter. In curator bonis procedure no-one represents before the court the interests of the mentally disabled person himself (or herself). In such a situation justice will only be achieved if the judges take a more active role than is customary in the more usual situation in litigation, in which the judge's role is to listen to the evidence and arguments presented by opposing parties, and make his decision on the basis of what he has heard.

In relation to tutor-dative procedure, I suggested on page 44 that the starting point is the medical certificate, and that care in the preparation of medical certificates is the main safeguard against the granting of unnecessarily extensive powers to a tutor. A similar degree of care is necessary in curatory cases. There is nothing sacrosanct about the formula: "of unsound mind and incapable of managing his/her own affairs or of giving directions for their management". I have quoted Lord Jauncey's criticism of the inappropriate use of this formula in the circumstances of Mrs. Paterson's case, the only recent reported case in which the formula has been considered by the courts.

Mrs Paterson's case is perhaps the key to the updating which I advocate. The case came originally before Lord Mackay of Clashfern, then a Court of Session Judge, now Lord Chancellor. Already, back in 1984, Lord Mackay followed the course which I suggest above. Having been presented with two certificates in traditional form, he remitted to another doctor to report as to Mrs Paterson's capacity. When Lord Jauncey took the case over, he sought further medical evidence.

My own view is that there are many cases in which the "traditional formula" is woefully inadequate, and also misleading. No doctor should use it unless he is satisfied that it provides the court with accurate and fully adequate evidence upon which to make a major decision which will have a fundamental effect upon the status of the person to whom it relates.

Where would this more careful approach to certification take us? Let us hypothesise. Let us suppose that the medical certificates in a curatory petition were something along the following lines:

I AB [state qualifications], hereby certify:

1. that I have for __ years known CD, date of birth __ , who resides at __, and that I have this day further seen and examined her;

102

2. that she is mentally handicapped, that she can manage some of her affairs herself, that she requires help and guidance in managing others of her affairs, and that there are yet further matters which she is unable to manage either herself or by instructing others;

3. that in relation to those of her affairs which she is unable to manage unaided and unable to manage at all, she is vulnerable to exploitation and may require protection;

4. that it is important to her development and wellbeing that she be encouraged, so far as she is capable, (a) to take responsibility for her own affairs, (b) to deal herself with those matter which she is able to manage unaided, (c) to receive only the minimum necessary assistance in those matters in which she requires assistance, and (d) to be consulted, and to be encouraged to participate, in decisions regarding the management of those of her affairs which require to be managed for her;

5. that for the last __ years she has been, and still is, resident in hostel-type accommodation at __ ; that throughout her period there hostel staff have assisted her in dealing with her state benefits, in budgeting, and in managing a deposit account with __ Bank, in which she has kept her savings, and that with appropriate assistance and guidance she is able to achieve a reasonable level of understanding of such matters and to make reasonable decisions; that such budgeting assistance has included budgeting for food, which she now purchases herself, though she at times requires guidance in selecting a suitable diet; and that with such assistance, she also budgets for an amount of weekly spending money, which spending money she is able to manage unaided, her purchases including toiletries and tapes for her cassette player, and on occasions such as birthdays small presents for her friends in the hostel;

6. that I am informed that she is one of several nephews and nieces of the late ED, who recently died a bachelor, leaving the residue of his estate equally among his nieces and nephews; that his estate includes shop premises at __ let to a tenant, and that it is proposed that at least for the remaining duration of the lease the shop should be retained and held jointly by the nephews and nieces, including CD; and that the other estate to be divided equally among the nephews and nieces, including CD, comprises mainly stock exchange securities;

7. that I am of the opinion that CD will not be able to manage the estate which she has inherited from her uncle, or unaided to give instructions for its management; that she is unlikely to be able to understand the arrangements regarding the shop, or to understand aspects of the management of other items inherited, that her ability to participate in decision-making in such matters is likely to be limited, but that it would nevertheless be important for her to be encouraged to participate to such extent as she is able, and for efforts to be made to explain to her matters such as the effect of this inheritance upon her social security benefits;

8. that FG is also a mentally handicapped resident at __ hostel; that CD and FG have formed a stable friendship, regularly assisting each other in matters such as cooking and shopping; that I am aware that it is proposed that __ Housing Association should offer joint tenancy of a flat to CD and FG; that I am aware that appropriate practical support and supervision is available; that in the circumstances I consider that it will enhance CD's quality of life and her development towards the maximum degree of independence of which she is capable for her and FG to take up such a tenancy; but that CD will require assistance in many matters at the outset of such tenancy, including understanding and executing a lease, in furnishing and equipping the flat, in making appropriate joint arrangements with FG, in arranging necessary services, in budgeting for household costs, and so forth;

9. that I know HJ, the proposed curator bonis, and have been present on occasions when he has been discussing CD's affairs with her and helping her regarding them; that he is skilled and patient in explaining matters to CD in ways which she can understand; that he is able to encourage her interest and participation in the management of her affairs; that she appears to like and trust him; that he has a reasonable understanding of her capabilities, the likely scope for future development of her capabilities, and her handicap; and

10. that HJ appears to me to have an understanding of CD's affairs and that I am aware of no reason why he should not be a fit and proper person to provide CD with such assistance as is necessary in the management of her affairs, and to manage for her such of her affairs as she is unable to manage herself.

This hypothetical certificate is entirely fictitious, but in general terms it encompasses elements applicable to many people with mental handicaps. If certificates such as the above were produced in a petition for appointment of a curator bonis, then I consider it unlikely that the court would insist upon simply appointing a curator bonis with blanket powers in what has up to now been the usual way. Given the precedent established in the Morris case for refining tutor-dative procedure, it should be possible to persuade the court to apply equivalent refinements to curator bonis procedure.

On the basis of certificates along the lines of the above example, it would in my view be reasonable to ask the courts to include in orders appointing curators bonis some or all of the following elements:

(a) The curator's exclusive powers of management to be limited to certain specified items. The handicapped person to be kept informed, and to be consulted and involved in decision-making, as far as is practicable. The accounting obligations of the curator to be limited to the estate under the curator's exclusive management.

(b) A declaration that the handicapped person suffers no loss of legal capacity by reason of the appointment of the curator bonis, except only as regards the management of items placed under the curator's exclusive management.

(c) Authority to the curator bonis to guide and assist the handicapped person where necessary in all matters of management of affairs outside the curator's exclusive control, and a direction that the curator shall provide such guidance and assistance.

(d) Also as regards affairs outside the curator's exclusive control, authority to add the curator's signature to the signature or mark of the handicapped person on any document, as an indication of the curator's agreement and approval; coupled with a declaration that no document signed by both the handicapped person and the curator bonis in this way shall be open to challenge on grounds of the mental disability of the handicapped person (or on grounds of "facility and circumvention" – see *Scots Law and the Mentally Handicapped* page 38).

(e) Similar validation of transactions by the handicapped person alone, if they come within general arrangements sanctioned by the curator bonis. Examples would be operations by the handicapped person on a bank account, within general arrangements agreed by the curator bonis, and cash transactions using money budgeted for personal spending under a budget agreed with the curator bonis.

(f) The curator bonis would be required to consult with tutors, close relatives, carers, and the handicapped person; and to have reasonable regard to their views and wishes.

(g) At an early stage of the curatory the curator would be required to prepare and submit a plan for the management of the curatory, having regard to the capabilities and whole circumstances of the handicapped person. In preparing the plan the curator would be required to pay particular regard to the information provided in the medical certificates, to the views of parents, carers and the like, and to the views of the handicapped person (so far as ascertainable). As regards management of affairs within the scope of the plan, accounting and auditing requirements would be simplified to a more common-sense basis.

(h) There would be a direction that at specified intervals fresh medical certificates be obtained, and any changes in the handicapped person's capabilities be reported to the court so that the court can consider whether the terms of appointment of the curator should be varied, or the appointment terminated.

Finally, there should be a fundamental shift in emphasis in the criteria for suitability for appointment as a curator. The main qualification for appointment should be understanding of the handicapped person's capabilities, disabilities and potential, and of the handicapped person's personal circumstances. There should be less emphasis on professional accountancy or similar qualifications, though the curator should still be a person of competence and integrity in financial management.

A person with professional qualifications should only be appointed where the estate is sufficiently large that costs will not be disproportionate, bearing in mind the additional work for curators which the above requirements would be likely to entail. This could, however, be offset at least partly by a simpler and more down-to-earth approach to accounting and auditing requirements.

A parallel shift in emphasis within the Accountant of Court's office would be beneficial. Auditing skills will always be required, but they should be exercised in a supportive and helpful way, based on a sound understanding of the various disabilities giving rise to the appointment of curators. The Accountant of Court's office should be orientated towards enhancing the "customer satisfaction" provided by the curatory service.

All of these suggestions point to ways in which the operation of the existing curatory system could be improved, without reform of the law by Parliament. Reform of the law is still required. Lawyers and others should continue to press for such reform. But they should not content themselves with doing that, and nothing more. Lawyers in particular have a primary obligation to explore every possibility for achieving better and more appropriate provision for the needs of those whom they serve, within the framework of the law as it stands. The Scottish lawyer has the advantage of working within a system which is based upon principle, rather than detailed rules, and which accordingly has an inherent flexibility. His obligation is to use that flexibility creatively, and where necessary to the utmost. If this is done, and our ossified curatory system updated and developed as far as the existing framework permits, then when law reform eventually takes place we shall have practical experience of the application here in Scotland of at least some of the features which one would wish to see embodied in a modern code. Without doubt, the experience which is currently being gained from the development of tutor-dative procedure will be valuable whenever Parliament updates our law of personal guardianship. As we shall see in Chapter XII, the best results will probably be achieved by a single Act of Parliament covering both personal guardianship and management of affairs. It will be helpful to have equal experience in both areas of trying to develop existing common law principles to meet modern needs.

Management of Affairs in Other Legal Systems

Other legal systems provide comparative material relevant to management of affairs similar to that discussed in Chapter V in relation to personal guardianship. Here also, this material from other legal systems provides pointers both for suitable updating and refinement of existing common law procedures in Scotland, and also for future law reform.

As mentioned on page 34, the United States model statute envisages that needs in relation both to personal guardianship and to management of affairs would be dealt with in the same procedure. Conservators and limited conservators are available in relation to management of affairs, just as guardians and limited guardians are available to meet needs for personal guardianship. There is a third option in relation to management of affairs, and that is to create a trust. It was recognised in the United States that a trust is a "less restrictive and more normal device" than other forms of intervention in the management of affairs. The same could be said in Scotland. In Scotland however, as already mentioned, once property has passed outright to a mentally disabled person, it is too late to retrieve it and put it into trust. The model statute recognises this problem and empowers the court to create a trust over property of the mentally disabled person. This is seen as a lesser form of intervention than conservatorship or limited conservatorship.

A limited conservator may be appointed to a "partially disabled person", to provide assistance in the management of financial resources, and to act in place of the partially disabled person only in relation to those financial resources specifically placed under the control of the limited conservator. A conservator may be appointed to a disabled

107

person, and takes on complete management of all financial resources. However, both limited conservators and conservators have a duty to encourage disabled people to participate in decisions "to the maximum extent of their abilities", to act for themselves as far as they can, and to develop "to the maximum extent possible" their capacity to manage their financial resources. Limited conservators and conservators are both required to prepare an "individual conservatorship plan".

Other steps available to the court under the United States model statute include to direct that various services be provided; and to authorise or ratify particular contracts or transactions. This latter power obviates the need for appointment of a conservator to carry out a single transaction.

Under the Dependent Adults Acts of Alberta (see pages 36-39) there are separate procedures for guardianship and for orders regarding management of affairs. The procedure leading to the making of an order regarding management of affairs is however very similar to the guardianship procedure described on page 37. An order for the management of affairs is called a "trusteeship order", and the manager appointed is a "trustee". The trustee may be an individual, a trust company, or the Public Trustee. A trustee may be appointed for a specified period, not exceeding three years, to an adult who is "unable to make reasonable judgements in respect of matters relating to all or any part of his estate", and who is deemed to need a trustee. The Public Trustee makes a trusteeship application if a trustee is needed but no-one else is able or willing to apply. An alternative trustee may be appointed, to take over automatically in the event of the death of the original trustee.

The trustee may be appointed to the whole or to a specified part of the dependent adult's estate, of which the trustee takes possession and control, and which the trustee thereafter manages. The court may select from two lists of specific powers. Such specific powers may be exercised without further sanction from the court. The first list contains powers which may be made subject to restrictions or conditions imposed by the court, and is as follows:

(a) grant or accept leases of real or personal property for a term not exceeding 3 years;
(b) invest any money in investments in which trustees are authorised to invest trust money under the Trustee Act;
(c) deposit any money in the manner in which trust money can be deposited under the Trustee Act;
(d) transfer property held in trust by the dependent adult, either solely or jointly with another, to the person beneficially entitled to it;

108

(e) give a consent to the transfer or assignment of a lease if the consent is required;

(f) perform a contract entered into by the dependent adult or by his guardian;

(g) draw, accept and endorse bills of exchange and promissory notes, endorse bonds, debentures, coupons and other negotiable instruments and securities, and assign choses in action;

(h) give or receive a notice on behalf of the dependent adult that relates to his estate.

The second list contains powers which may be granted on any terms and conditions which the court considers appropriate, and is as follows:

(a) purchase, sell, mortgage, grant or accept leases for more than 3 years or otherwise dispose of real or personal property;

(b) exchange or partition property and give or receive money for equality of exchange or partition;

(c) carry on the trade or business of the dependent adult;

(d) surrender a lease, with or without accepting a new lease, or accept a surrender of a lease;

(e) exercise a power or give a consent required for the exercise of a power vested in the dependent adult;

(f) exercise a right or obligation to elect, belonging to or imposed on the dependent adult;

(g) compromise or settle a debt;

(h) compromise or settle a court action;

(i) notwithstanding the Trustee Act, invest funds in any securities and assets that the Court approves;

(j) do any other thing approved by the Court.

Within six months of appointment the trustee must file with the Clerk of Court an inventory of the assets and liabilities of the estate placed under the trustee's care. Accounts must be filed at least every two years.

The appointment of a trustee (or of a guardian) does not automatically take away the capacity of a dependent adult to make a valid Will.

The English draft *Dependent Adults Act* described on pages 39-42 deals only with personal guardianship, and not with management of affairs (at least in the version of the draft which I have seen).

The new regime in New Zealand is described in Chapter XII.

Curator Bonis Must be an Individual

It has long been understood that only a single individual can be appointed curator bonis. A case reported as long ago as 1835 decided that a partnership of solicitors could not be appointed curator bonis: an individual partner can be appointed, but not the partnership. In a case decided in 1983 and reported in 1986 the court confirmed that a limited company could not be appointed as curator. Lord Allanbridge said

. . . a factor or curator is an officer of the court and must always be an individual who is fully subject to the control of the court. It would be quite impractical to appoint a company or partnership to the office of curator or factor. Such a person may have to give advice or take decisions, always subject to the overall authority of the court. To appoint a company would only cause confusion in such a situation and make it more difficult for the accountant of court and the court to supervise and control the administration of the ward's estate in the case of an incapax.

Responsibility to Avoid Need for Curator Bonis

While curator bonis procedure can be improved, the problems are still such that it will normally be wise to avoid such appointment if possible. Indeed, I would suggest that it is normally the responsibility of professional advisers to avoid the need for a curatory by using alternative techniques, of which the most common is the trust. Most trusts will avoid almost all of the disadvantages of curatories.

Various alternative techniques are considered in the next chapter.

Note: The Law Reform (Miscellaneous Provisions) (Scotland) Bill published December 1989 proposes to permit a simplified procedure for discharging curators bonis and proposes a modest widening of curators' powers of investment.

XI

MANAGEMENT OF AFFAIRS - TECHNIQUES OTHER THAN CURATOR BONIS

Management of Property of Hospital Patients

Money and valuables belonging to hospital patients may be looked after for them by the hospital management. This procedure is described on pages 41-42 of *Scots Law and the Mentally Handicapped*. The procedure is now contained in section 94 of the Mental Health (Scotland) Act 1984. The procedure applies to patients who are liable to be detained, or who are receiving treatment for mental disorder. The only procedure required is a certificate by the doctor in charge of treating the patient. In it, the doctor certifies that in his opinion the patient's handicap is such that he is incapable of managing and administering his property and affairs. The certificate permits the hospital management to "receive and hold money and valuables". They can expend the money for the patient's benefit. They can also dispose of valuables for the patient's benefit, but must have regard to their actual or likely sentimental value.

Money and valuables may be held up to a limit set from time to time by the Secretary of State. In August 1989 the limit was raised from £1,000 to £3,000. The hospital management must seek the permission of the Mental Welfare Commission to go above the limit in any case. In the past, hospital managements often arranged for a curator to be appointed once the limit was reached. As mentioned on page 92, the Mental Welfare Commission have now increased from £10,000 to £50,000 the level at which they would normally consider it appropriate to appoint a curator, except in cases where circumstances require the setting up of a curatory at a lower level.

This procedure appears to give rise to problems in three areas.

1. A certificate under section 94 can be given if a person "is incapable, by reason of his mental disorder, of managing and administering his property and affairs". In practice, this question seems to be addressed in the context of the level of encouragement and support currently available, or not available, to the patient. When the same person leaves hospital, and greater encouragement and support become available, it is frequently found that the person can manage his own affairs. While this procedure does not itself result in any general loss of legal capacity, it seems that in practice, if funds build up, there is a risk of an inappropriate curatory ensuing (as we have seen in Chapter X - see page 98).

2. In practice, procedure under section 94 seems to give rise to problems of insensitivity and remoteness similar to those encountered in relation to curator bonis procedure. Relatives find it particularly hurtful when hospital authorities take over the patient's affairs, and exclude them from involvement and consultation. Here is an example:

> Mr A was seriously mentally disabled. For many years his wife cared for him at home. As she became older, her physical health deteriorated, and he was admitted to hospital. The hospital followed the procedure under section 94. Without consulting the wife, they arranged that they should receive a substantial pension to which Mr A was entitled. These funds were simply accumulated, without being used in any way to benefit either husband or wife. Her only income was state benefits. The journey from home to hospital was not an easy one, but she was not even assisted with the costs of travelling to visit her husband. She was excluded from all consultation and even information regarding her husband's affairs. She described her feelings as being "as if the hospital stepped in and divorced us from each other". (An application was submitted to the European Commission on Human Rights claiming that the hospital had interfered in the private and family life of the couple in breach of Article 8 of the European Convention on Human Rights, and had deprived them of the peaceable enjoyment of funds which they were entitled to possess, in contravention of Article 1 of the First Protocol to the Convention. The Commission refused to entertain the application.)

3. The scope for management is limited. Money held by hospital management may be expended "for the benefit of" the patient. Valuables may be disposed of for the patient's benefit, but management must have regard to sentimental value, including sentimental value which an article would have had but for the patient's mental disorder. Insurance policy proceeds received by the hospital may be used to reimburse some other person who may have paid the premiums, if that person is legally entitled to such reimbursement. These are not wide and general powers of administration, though they may be adequate in many individual cases.

Apart from these problem areas, section 94 procedure is an improvement on curator bonis procedure. It provides a quick and inexpensive method of administering funds and possessions of modest value. It avoids the cumbersomeness of accounting to, and supervision by, the Accountant of Court. It does not impair any existing legal capacity. The problems are not so much inherent in the procedure, as a result of the way in which it is operated in an institutionalised context. A similar simplified procedure would probably work better in a non-institutionalised context. If such a system of management is acceptable in the case of hospital patients,

112

there is no reason in principle why a similar procedure should not be available for mentally disabled people who are not in hospital. Indeed, it is strange that the only context in which this simplified procedure should be available is one in which the first two areas of disadvantage identified above are more likely to occur. It is also rather strange that, apparently without any review of the procedure as a whole, the substantial step should recently have been taken of increasing from £1,000 to £3,000 the limit up to which notification to the Mental Welfare Commission is not required, and that the level up to which the procedure is likely to be operated should have been increased from £10,000 to £50,000.

One point of interest is that section 94 procedure is not available when there is a curator bonis, tutor or judicial factor; and hospital management must account to any curator bonis, tutor or judicial factor who is appointed. The reference to tutors appears to cover all tutors, even although modern tutors-dative have so far been appointed only as personal guardians, and not as managers of property.

The Dependent Adults Acts of Alberta contain special procedure for "trusteeship without court order" for dependent adults resident for any period of time in a "facility" (defined in regulations). However, the safeguards are much greater than in Scotland. Two doctors sign the "certificate of incapacity". One of the doctors must immediately notify the Public Trustee, and send copies of the certificate to the Public Trustee, to the Public Guardian, and to the person's guardian (or nearest relative, if there is no guardian). The Public Trustee gives further notification, including a notice to the dependent adult. The estate is administered by the Public Trustee, not the management of the "facility". There is a system of Appeal Panels to hear appeals regarding certificates of incapacity. The Public Trustee must have every certificate of incapacity renewed by an Appeal Panel at least once every two years.

Judicial Factor

A judicial factor is a person appointed by a court to hold, administer or protect another person's funds or property. A curator bonis is accordingly one type of judicial factor. Judicial factors are appointed for a variety of other purposes.

In cases of damages awards, a judicial factor is nowadays sometimes appointed. Most commonly, the damages payment is compensation for injuries which have included some form of mental impairment. A judicial factor can be appointed to receive the damages payment, and thereafter to administer it. With one important difference, administration by a judicial factor is subject to substantially the same regime as administration by a curator bonis. Strictly speaking, this should be put the other way round: the regime described in the last chapter applies to all judicial factors, including curators bonis.

The difference is that a judicial factor appointed in this way administers, and is responsible for, only the fund entrusted to him. Nothing changes as regards any arrangements for administering any other affairs of the mentally disabled person. There is no automatic loss of legal capacity.

Tutors

Tutors-at-law and tutors-dative, as well as being personal guardians, are also managers of affairs, unless the court specifically limits the appointment to exclude management of affairs. So far, in the modern use of tutor-dative procedure, interest has concentrated on the role of tutors as personal guardians, and I am aware of no recent instance of appointment of a tutor with power to manage affairs. There is, however, no reason why tutors should not be appointed to manage affairs, as well as acting as personal guardians. Let us consider whether there might be circumstances in which such appointment might be sought.

Tutors-dative come under the same general regime in the management of affairs as curators bonis and other judicial factors. One would not, therefore, appoint a tutor-dative in order to escape that regime. Some of the individual disadvantages of administration by a curator bonis could however be overcome. I can envisage only one situation in which tutor-at-law procedure might be revived, and I mention it under the next heading. Appointment of a tutor-dative to administer affairs could achieve some or all of the following:

(a) Most tutors would be relatives, or other persons prepared to act without remuneration, thus reducing costs of administration.

(b) By combining personal guardianship and management of affairs in the same person, problems of remoteness and insensitivity would not arise. There should be no communication gap between administrator and family and other carers.

(c) When both a personal guardian and a manager of affairs are required, use of tutor-dative procedure would mean a single court petition instead of two. The quality of medical evidence placed before the court would be likely to be enhanced if doctors were to consider in conjunction capacity in personal matters and capacity in the management of affairs.

(d) Only one person may be appointed curator bonis, but precedents already exist for appointing joint tutors-dative. The possible advantages of having joint tutors have already been discussed in Chapter VI (page 45). (On the other hand, a joint appointment could be regarded as contrary to the judgement of Lord Allanbridge quoted on page 110. If so, a possible solution might be to make one of the joint tutors responsible to the court in matters of management of affairs with responsibility transferring automatically to the second tutor in the event of the death of the first.)

The refinements to curator bonis procedure proposed in the last chapter (pages 101-107) would of course be equally applicable to tutor-dative procedure, and could fit in well with modern procedure for appointment of a tutor-dative as personal guardian, as described in Chapter VI. Indeed, I would suggest that when preparing petitions to appoint tutors-dative to act as personal guardians, it would in all cases be good practice to investigate whether the handicapped person has affairs which he is unable to manage, or unable to manage unaided, and if so to consider whether the tutor should also seek powers in relation to the management of affairs.

Moreover, in any case where a person already has a tutor as personal guardian, if need should subsequently arise for assistance in the management of affairs, consideration should be given to extension of the existing tutor's appointment, rather than appointment of a separate curator bonis.

Any petition to appoint a tutor-dative as both personal guardian and manager of affairs should include both the modern refinements which now exist in the area of personal guardianship (as described in Chapter VI) and the parallel refinements in relation to the management of affairs proposed in Chapter X (pages 101-107). In any one case, the two are likely to inter-relate closely.

Tutor-at-Law Superseding Curator Bonis

The communication gap between families and curators bonis, described in the last chapter, can mean that some families feel that they simply cannot work with the curator bonis who has been appointed. One hopes that efforts would be made to close such gaps, and that they would be successful. When they are not, the families may or may not find it easy to establish grounds to have the curator removed. Even if the curator is removed, or resigns, another person will be appointed curator in his place.

An alternative approach in such circumstances would be for the appropriate relative to have himself appointed tutor-at-law. Such appointment would automatically supersede the appointment of the curator bonis. The curatory would come to an end and the tutor-at-law would take over.

115

The procedure for appointing a tutor-at-law is described in Chapter IV (page 22).

Negotiorum Gestio

Neighbours have just left for a holiday abroad. You notice that one of their windows has been broken. You arrange for it to be repaired. In law you are a "negotiorum gestor" – one who intervenes to act without authorisation, where it is reasonable to expect that authorisation would be given if it could be sought. The position in law is much the same as if you had been authorised to act on behalf of the absent neighbours. The glazier would be entitled to payment from the neighbours. If you paid him, you would be entitled to be reimbursed by them.

This principle applies in any situation where a person is unable to manage his (or her) own affairs, temporarily or permanently. It includes situations arising from any form of mental disability. It has been mentioned in a recent publication by Scottish Action on Dementia in the context of possible means of management of affairs of people affected by ageing conditions.

The main drawback is the difficulty in persuading others (including banks, insurance companies and so forth) to accept the instructions and actings of the "negotiorum gestor", who obviously will be unable to produce any evidence of authority to act. This principle may occasionally help in emergencies, and can provide a legal basis for "informal voluntary arrangements" (see *Scots Law and the Mentally Handicapped,* pp 42-43). However the principle has very limited value as a vehicle for ongoing management of the affairs of mentally disabled people.

Trusts

The trust remains the generally favoured technique for managing funds and property which a mentally handicapped person is not able to manage for himself. The advantages of the trust were discussed in *Scots Law and the Mentally Handicapped.* Briefly, a trust can be structured so as to operate much less expensively than a curatory; the trust deed can be drawn so as to avoid undue cumbersomeness and inflexibility of administration; trustees can be selected so as to avoid problems of insensitivity and remoteness; there is no supervision by the Accountant of Court; and no automatic loss of legal capacity. The trust deed can specify what is to happen to the trust fund on the death of the mentally handicapped person, thus avoiding intestacy. The trust can be structured so that trust capital is not treated as capital of the mentally handicapped person when eligibility for means-tested benefits is assessed.

One is sometimes asked whether a curatory can be converted into a trust, so as to secure these benefits. It cannot. The reason is that a trust can only be created if the funds or property pass at the outset to trustees, rather than to the mentally handicapped person. If any funds or property become the property of a mentally handicapped person unable to manage them, it is too late to create a trust. The mentally handicapped person is now the owner, so only he (or she) could create a trust; but if he lacks the capacity to manage the funds and property, then clearly he lacks the capacity to create a trust.

The time to consider whether to create a trust is before funds or property are made over to a mentally handicapped person. If the mentally handicapped person lacks the capacity to manage them, then once they have been made over to him it is too late to retrieve them and put them into a trust.

In practice, rather than in strict law, there is sometimes an exception in the area of what I termed "informal voluntary arrangements" in *Scots Law and the Mentally Handicapped* and described on pages 42 and 43 of that book. For example, when funds have been put in a bank account in the sole name of a mentally handicapped person, and problems of administration arise, the bank may be prepared to alter the designation of the account to another person in trust for the mentally handicapped person.

The use of appointees or nominees to receive and manage benefits, pensions, and other funds creates a form of simple trust – what lawyers call a "bare trust". Another available technique is to put funds in joint names of the handicapped person and some other person, so that the non-handicapped joint holder can take necessary steps to manage the fund. Such arrangements should be approached with some degree of care. For example, problems can arise if the appointee, nominee or non-handicapped joint holder should die before the handicapped person. It is wise to know whether any mechanism exists to appoint a substitute, should that happen.

Trusts - Change in Social Security Rules

In *Scots Law and the Mentally Handicapped* (page 89) I warned that the capital of discretionary trusts was likely to be taken into account for the purpose of assessing entitlement to means-tested benefits. I explained that a "discretionary trust" is a trust in which the trustees have discretion to advance capital, or (possibly) discretion to decide who should receive how much income.

This has now changed. Supplementary Benefit has been replaced by Income Support. Matters of entitlement and calculation of means are governed by The Income Support (General) Regulations 1987, which came into force on 11th April 1988. Under regulation 52(2) the capital of a discretionary trust is no longer treated as capital of the beneficiary, so long as it remains in the trust, even though it may be possible to apply to the trustees to pay out capital. If however capital is paid out to the beneficiary, the amount paid out then belongs to the beneficiary, and is taken into account.

Previously, capital available on a discretionary basis was treated as capital of the beneficiary, on the grounds that it was available to the beneficiary whether or not it was actually paid over.

Schedule 10 to the 1987 Regulations lists various categories of capital which are disregarded for means-testing purposes. Included in the list are reversionary interests; the capital or surrender value of an annuity received by the claimant; the capital value of a liferent (the life interest to income under a trust); and the surrender value of a life policy.

Trusts set up by a payment of compensation for personal injury are referred to in both regulation 52(2) and Schedule 10. Regulation 52(2) excludes the availability of capital from such a trust, in the same way as it applies to discretionary trusts. Schedule 10 excludes the funds of such a trust, set up with a compensation payment, for "a period of two years or such longer period as is reasonable in the circumstances". The two-year period starts at the date of the compensation payment if the claimant was then receiving an income related benefit. If the claimant does not start receiving income related benefit till later, the two-year period starts when the payment of income related benefit commences.

Regrettably, these new provisions apply only to Income Support. The old problem remains when resources are assessed to calculate charges for local authority accommodation ("Part IV accommodation"). For these purposes, the rule is that "any sum which is held on a Discretionary Trust for the benefit of a person may be treated as included in his resources".To this extent, the warnings about discretionary trusts which I gave in *Scots Law and the Mentally Handicapped* are still relevant. In the White Paper *Caring for People* the government proposes that such assessments be brought into line with Income Support assessments, with effect from April 1991.

Life Assurance

Surprisingly often, the assertion is made that "you cannot insure a mentally handicapped person". This is not correct.

A policy of life assurance is a contract between the policy owner and the life assurance company. The policy owner may insure his own life, or the life of someone else, but he can only insure someone else's life if he has an "insurable interest". Close relationship is likely to provide an insurable interest.

The policy owner can only enter a valid contract of life assurance if he has sufficient legal capacity. If the policy owner has full legal capacity, it does not matter whether the person whose life is insured lacks legal capacity, unless the insurance company require a statement or declaration from the person whose life is insured. Problems will then arise as to whether the mentally handicapped person has sufficient capacity to make the statement or declaration.

The insurance company may charge larger premiums, or decline to insure, if medical evidence or other information obtained in the proposal form indicates an increased risk, or decreased life-expectancy. That applies whether the person whose life is insured is mentally handicapped or not.

It is for each life assurance company to decide which proposals it will accept, and on what terms. There is no reason in law why life assurance should not be available to a mentally handicapped person who nevertheless has sufficient capacity to enter the contract, and to handle the policy proceeds if they are likely to be received prior to death. Also, there is no reason in law why a relative or other person with an insurable interest should not insure the life of a mentally handicapped person who lacks legal capacity. It is the choice of the life assurance company whether to accept the risk. And if the risk is acceptable, it is the choice of the life assurance company whether to discriminate unfairly on grounds of handicap. Such discrimination is not yet illegal in this country (see page 156). It is the choice of the public whether they in any event wish to deal with a life assurance company which discriminates unfairly on grounds of handicap.

Many problems with insurance arise because someone has put the cart before the horse. In every case, one should first define need, then decide how best to meet that need. The answer may be an insurance policy. It may be something else. So often, people have decided that it would be a "good thing" to have an insurance policy: or they have succumbed to a salesman who tells them so. They do not think through what to do with the policy until after they have decided in principle to take it out; and sometimes no-one thinks about the problems which may arise until those problems are encountered – perhaps years later when the policy matures. In the worst cases, families find that a policy which has cost parents a great deal over many years merely produces a capital sum which disappears in the form of lost state benefits, and which gives rise to all the disadvantages of appointment of a curator.

The Financial Services Act 1986

The Financial Services Act 1986 introduced a new regime for the conduct of investment business. Anyone conducting investment business must comply with regulations made under the Act. Among the obligations imposed by the regulations on those providing investment advice are the following. Firstly, they must "know their clients": they must know their clients' personal and financial situations and investment objectives. Secondly, they must know the investment products available. And thirdly, they must match up the first two elements so as to recommend a suitable investment for each individual client. The definition of "investments" is very wide. The above requirements apply, for example, in relation to life assurances and unit trusts, as well as other forms of investment.

To comply with these requirements, any investment adviser dealing with a family with a mentally disabled member now needs to go through a procedure similar to that which is followed by a solicitor making a Will, as I described in Chapter XVII of *Scots Law and the Mentally Handicapped*. In selecting which investment product to recommend, he requires to be aware of all the factors relevant to the making of financial provision for mentally disabled people, including those described in *Scots Law and the Mentally Handicapped* and in this book. It is to be hoped that the requirements of Financial Services legislation and regulations will cause more people providing investment advice to become better informed about all relevant aspects of mental disability, and that this will in turn lead to a reduction in the "selling" of quite unsuitable investments.

Anyone who feels that he has received bad advice or has been "sold" an unsuitable investment may wish to take legal advice as to whether any remedies are available.

XII

THE NEW ZEALAND MODEL

New Zealand has recently been engaged in a major and comprehensive programme of mental disability law reform. The resulting legislation includes the Protection of Personal and Property Rights Act 1988, which came into force on 1st October 1988. As the title indicates, the Act introduces a regime governing matters both of personal guardianship and management of affairs.

Similar reform is imperative in this country. Until recently we had hardly even begun the process of investigation and discussion which must precede such an exercise. We are beginning to gain useful experience from the modern development of tutor-dative procedure, and I believe that curator bonis procedure is ready for parallel development. Law reform must come next.

The New Zealand Act of 1988 is the most recent statutory code dealing with personal guardianship and management of affairs of mentally disabled adults. Of course, it is designed to meet New Zealand's own needs. However, it follows careful consideration of developments and experience in other jurisdictions, including South Australia and Victoria as well as North America. It is the most recent embodiment of the development of principles which have now achieved a wide degree of acceptance. It is a model worth looking at as we develop existing common law principles here in Scotland, and as we move towards law reform by statute. Of course, I would not advocate the adoption of all of its provisions, nor the adoption of any of them without careful consideration and necessary adaptation.

So far as personal guardianship is concerned, New Zealand seems to have started with a fairly clean sheet: "There is no legislation in force in N.Z. which specifically provides for the personal guardianship of adults". As regards management of affairs, the previous provision in New Zealand appears to have been similar to our own curator bonis procedure in that there was an "everything or nothing" approach. As the explanatory note to the original Bill put it: "The present law can be said to reflect a rather simplistic approach: either a person's property is subject to protection or it is not. If it is, all power to the manager's elbow!"

The question of whether "personal rights" and "property rights" should be dealt with separately gave rise to a "one Bill or two" debate. The New Zealand Justice Department originally favoured two separate

Bills, but most groups representing disabled people preferred a single piece of legislation. The Working Party on Guardianship and Advocacy of Mentally Retarded People of the New Zealand Institute of Mental Retardation argued powerfully that personal rights and property rights do not differ essentially in character, and are closely inter-related. The "one Bill" lobby prevailed, and the result is a well-integrated piece of legislation, from which we have much to learn. The following general principles are particularly noteworthy:

(a) There is a clear declaration that people subject to the Act's provisions retain their rights and legal status in full, except only as specifically provided otherwise by the provisions of the Act or the terms of any order made under the Act.

(b) There is a presumption of competence. Everyone is presumed, until the contrary is proved, to have the capacity to understand matters relating to personal care and welfare, to communicate decisions about such matters, and to manage their own affairs.

(c) There is a statement of two primary objectives of the court in exercising jurisdiction under the Act in relation to both personal and property matters. The first is to make in each case the least restrictive intervention which is possible, having regard to the degree of the individual's incapacity or lack of competence. The second is to enable or encourage the individual to exercise and develop such capacity and competence as he or she may have to the greatest extent possible.

(d) Property orders and personal orders may be sought in a single application, and the court may make an order in either or both categories even though only one type has been applied for.

(e) In the event of any conflict between a personal order and a property order, the personal order prevails.

(f) In any application for a personal order or a property order (or both), the person for whom an order is sought is represented by a lawyer. The court must appoint a lawyer to represent the mentally disabled person, if that person does not appoint a lawyer himself (or herself). Costs incurred to such lawyers are met from public funds, unless the court decides that the mentally disabled person has sufficient funds and should pay the costs.

The Act uses the terms "capacity" in relation to personal matters, and "competence" in relation to property matters. "Property" is given a wide definition. A personal guardian, if appointed, is termed a "welfare guardian". A manager of property is simply termed a "manager". "The person in respect of whom an application is made" is a rather cumbersome phrase used repeatedly: I shall generally refer to "mentally disabled person" or simply "person".

Procedure

Applications are brought before New Zealand's Family Courts. Personal orders may be sought for people who lack, wholly or partly, the capacity to understand decisions concerning their personal care and welfare, or to foresee the consequences of such decisions. They may also be sought for people wholly lacking the capacity to communicate such decisions. Property orders may be sought for people who lack, wholly or partly, the competence to manage their own affairs in relation to their property. The fact that a person fails to exercise ordinary prudence does not of itself justify an application for an order.

Applications may be made by the mentally disabled person; a relative or attorney; a social worker or doctor; or a representative of any non-profit-making group providing relevant services. If the mentally disabled person is a patient in a hospital, the person in charge of the hospital may apply. If the person is resident in a home or other institution, the person in charge of the institution may apply. Personal orders may be sought by a manager, if there is one. Property orders may be sought by a welfare guardian, if there is one, or by a trustee corporation. Any other person may seek leave of the court to apply.

Applications are served on the mentally disabled person, unless the court is satisfied that the person is completely unable to understand the proceedings, or in exceptional circumstances which justify dispensing with service. Applications are also served on parents, guardians or other carers; proposed appointees; any existing welfare guardians or managers; and anyone else specified by the court.

So far as practicable, the lawyer appointed to represent the mentally disabled person must do the following things. The lawyer must contact the person and explain the nature and purpose of the application, find out the person's wishes, and give effect to those wishes. The lawyer must evaluate proposed solutions, having regard to the primary objectives set out in paragraph (c) on page 122. The court can also appoint a lawyer to assist the court. One effect of such provisions must be to develop among lawyers much greater awareness and knowledge of mental disabilities.

A pre-hearing conference may be sought, with the objectives of identifying the problems giving rise to the application, and trying to agree a solution. A judge presides. Normally parties may be represented and the conference held in private, though the judge may direct otherwise. An order may be made of consent, if the judge is satisfied that the person can and does give valid consent. The judge in any event records the matters which are agreed and the matters which

123

are not agreed.

The next step is a hearing. The mentally disabled person should be present, unless his or her presence has been excused by a judge. In practice, the mentally disabled person is often excused from attendance. A New Zealand lawyer describes a typical such case as follows: "It would have been a minor cruelty to inflict upon her the necessity to attend the court proceedings surrounded by strange lawyers talking about her and her property in quite unintelligible terms". If present, the mentally disabled person has the right to be heard and to call evidence. The judge may exclude any party or lawyer while the mentally disabled person addresses the court.

At the hearing, the court may call for medical, psychiatric, psychological or other reports. Lawyers acting in the proceedings must be given copies of reports, but may be ordered by the court not to show them to their clients. The normal rules of admissibility of evidence do not apply: the court may receive any evidence it thinks fit. The court may cite witnesses to attend and give evidence. The proceedings are in private, and may not be reported except with leave of the court.

There are provisions for appealing court orders.

Personal Orders

The Act contains a lengthy list of possible personal orders. The court can order that the person be paid appropriately for work done; that a parent make suitable arrangements for care after the parent's death; that such arrangements made by a parent should be observed, or should be varied; that the person should enter, attend or leave any institution (but not a psychiatric hospital or the like). The court can order that the person be provided with specified kinds of living arrangements, medical advice or treatment, education, rehabilitation, therapy or other services. The court can restrict departure from the country; and can appoint someone to act for the disabled person in court proceedings. The court may specify review dates for any of the above categories of order.

Under the category of "personal orders" the court can also appoint someone to administer small sums. As this is truly a form of property order, I shall deal with it under that heading.

Finally, if certain requirements are met, the court may appoint a welfare guardian. The court can issue supplementary orders and directions to give effect, or to give better effect, to a personal order. The court can make interim orders. And the court can make recommendations instead of an order, in which case the parties, including the disabled person, may come back to the court later for directions relating to the implementation of the court's recommendations.

Welfare Guardian

The "minimum necessary intervention" principle is strongly evident in the provisions regarding welfare guardians. The appointment of a welfare guardian is the last of the list of possible personal orders, and is clearly seen as a last resort. The court may not appoint a welfare guardian unless it is satisfied on certain points. Firstly, the court must be satisfied that the person wholly lacks the capacity to make decisions about one or more aspects of personal care and welfare, or wholly lacks the capacity to communicate such decisions. Secondly, the court must be satisfied that only by appointing a welfare guardian can it ensure that appropriate decisions are made in such matters.

If the court is satisfied on these points, then it may appoint a welfare guardian in respect of specified "aspects of the personal care and welfare" of the mentally disabled person. There is no list of powers, as in the Alberta model. The New Zealand provisions simply refer to "any aspect or aspects of personal care and welfare". No doubt, these possible "aspects" include all those contained in the Alberta list.

The welfare guardian has all powers reasonably required to make and implement decisions within the scope of the appointment. The Act directs that the "first and paramount consideration" of the welfare guardian, in exercising his (or her) powers, must be to promote and protect the best interests of the person for whom the guardian is acting, while seeking at all times to encourage the person to develop and exercise such capacity as the person has. In particular, the welfare guardian must do certain things. The guardian must encourage the disabled person to act on his (or her) own behalf to the greatest extent possible. The guardian must try to facilitate the integration of the person into the community to the greatest extent possible. So far as practicable, the guardian must also consult with the disabled person, and with others who in the guardian's opinion are interested in the person's welfare and competent to give advice (including any non-profit-making voluntary organisations). If there is a property manager, the welfare guardian must consult on a regular basis with the property manager, to ensure that the interests of the disabled person are not prejudiced by any breakdown in communication between guardian and manager.

There are certain things which no welfare guardian can do. The welfare guardian can make no decision regarding marriage or dissolution of marriage, or about adoption of any child of the disabled person. The guardian cannot refuse consent to any standard medical treatment or procedure to save the disabled person's life, or prevent serious harm. The guardian cannot consent to electro-convulsive

125

therapy, destruction of brain tissue or brain function, or medical experiment (other than an experiment for the purposes of saving the disabled person's life or preventing serious harm).

The welfare guardian must be an individual. If possible, the court must ascertain the wishes of the disabled person as to who should be appointed. The court must be satisfied that the proposed guardian is willing to act and is capable of carrying out his (or her) duties satisfactorily, having regard to the disabled person's needs and the relationship between the person and the guardian. The court must also be satisfied that the proposed guardian will act in the best interests of the disabled person, and that there will be no conflict of interest. The court can appoint more than one guardian, but only if in "exceptional circumstances" the court is satisfied that it would be in the best interests of the disabled person to appoint more than one. There is no provision for substitute or alternative guardians.

In the guardianship order the court specifies a review date not more than three years ahead. During the period of guardianship, the guardian can apply to the court for directions regarding the exercise of the guardian's powers. All acts and decisions of the welfare guardian, acting within his powers, have the same effect in law as if the disabled person had done or made them, and had had full capacity to do so.

There are special powers to appoint a welfare guardian specifically to ensure compliance with any of the other categories of personal order. This procedure may be used where someone has failed to comply with a personal order requiring him (or her) to do something. A welfare guardian appointed under these provisions may "take all reasonable steps to ensure compliance with the order of the court by the person who has so far failed to comply with it". In these circumstances, the welfare guardian is appointed for a defined period only. This is the only specific enforcement power for personal orders contained in the New Zealand Act. It will be interesting to see whether in course of time these powers are found to be adequate and effective, and whether a power to "take all reasonable steps" is found to be sufficiently clear and well-defined. By way of comparison, see the discussion on pages 46-47 of the problems encountered here in Scotland in enforcing the powers of our statutory guardians.

It must be remembered that New Zealand welfare guardianship is an entirely new statutory creation, prior to which New Zealand had no guardianship provision for adults. Viewed from a Scottish standpoint, one general aspect causes some concern. In Scotland we are developing two distinct types of guardianship, the purely interventionist statutory guardianship, and the true personal guardianship provided by the tutor. It is not clear that the New Zealand provision fully recognises the value and role of each of these two aspects of guardianship. The guardian appointed in the event of non-compliance is clearly an interventionist guardian, but it is doubtful whether the powers of such a guardian are sufficiently strong and clearcut for the only situation in which such an appointment will be made, namely a situation in which someone has refused to comply with a court order.

Even the general provisions concerning normal welfare guardianship seem to be tinged with a degree of suspicion based on a view of guardianship as interventionist. This is implicit in the treatment of guardianship as a "last resort". It is also implicit in the lack of provision for joint guardianship when the guardians are husband and wife, and in the lack of an alternate or substitute guardian. Guardianship should never be imposed when it is not needed, and guardians should not be given unnecessary powers, but on the other hand personal guardianship can be a valuable and helpful arrangement in cases where it is appropriate. It is not simply a last resort when all else fails. However, these comments should not be read as an attempt to tell the New Zealanders how they could have ordered their own affairs better. They simply identify an aspect which should not be imported unaltered into Scots law. It is necessary to make this comment for the very reason that so much of this New Zealand code is eminently worthy of serious consideration in the context of suitable reform of Scots (and English) law.

"Order to Administer Property"

As already mentioned, one of the "personal orders" is in fact concerned with management of property. It is available only for someone not subject to a true "property order", and is designed to cater for those who need assistance with a small item of property, or a modest item of income such as a social security benefit. No such order may be made in respect of an item of property worth more than $NZ1,000, or any income or benefit of more than $NZ10,000 in any one year (when the Act came into force in October 1988, $NZ1 was worth about £0.35). One person is appointed to administer the property, income or benefit. The court specifies a review date not more than three years ahead.

Property Orders - The Manager

The only form of property order is the appointment of a manager (or managers, or a temporary manager). The manager is appointed to manage all of the property, or any specified part of the property, of the mentally disabled person. The court can appoint more than one manager. The only form of corporate body which may be appointed manager is a "trustee corporation". The definition of trustee corporations includes the public trustee and trustee companies. These provisions contrast with the Scottish position under which only an individual may be appointed a curator bonis (see pages 109-110). The person is presumed, until it is proved otherwise, to be competent to manage any property not included in the order.

The court may appoint a manager if the court is satisfied that the person wholly or partly lacks the competence to manage his (or her) own affairs in relation to property. Although this New Zealand Act does not contain a list of guardianship powers, it does contain a very lengthy list of property management powers. The powers are set out in a schedule to the Act, and are specified in some fifty paragraphs and sub-paragraphs.

The court must be satisfied that the proposed manager is willing to act, and is capable of carrying out his (or her) duties satisfactorily, having regard to the disabled person's needs, and the relationship between that person and the manager. The court must also be satisfied that the proposed manager will act in the best interests of the disabled person. A likely conflict of interest is not a bar to appointment, but must be taken into account. If possible, the court must ascertain the wishes of the disabled person as to who should be appointed.

In the order, the court specifies a review date, not more than three years ahead. During the period of the order, the manager can apply to the court for directions.

The Act directs that the first and paramount duty of the manager is to use the property to promote and protect the best interests of the mentally disabled person, while seeking at all times to encourage that person to develop and exercise such competency as he (or she) may have. The manager may allow the person to have control of, and deal with, any part of the property governed by the property order. Apart from such arrangements, a person subject to a property order cannot exercise any of the powers given to the manager, in relation to property covered by the order, unless the court specifically authorises a particular transaction.

A property order does not automatically disqualify a person from making a Will, though the court may direct that a Will may only be made with the court's permission. When a Will has been made, the court can have enquiries made as to whether the Will "expresses the present desire and intention of the person"; if not, the court can authorise the manager to sign a Will which does express the person's present desire and intention. In any case where a person has a manager and lacks capacity to make a Will, the court can draw up a Will for the person and authorise the manager to sign it.

There is no automatic requirement for managers to give security for the due performance of their duties. Trustee corporations cannot be ordered to give security. The court may order other managers to give security if the court thinks fit. The manager has to lodge in court an initial statement of the property of the person for whom the manager is acting. This appears to cover all property, not just that governed by the property order. Annually thereafter the manager must lodge a similar statement of property, and a statement as to the management of the property. The Public Trustee, or a chartered accountant appointed by the Public Trustee, examines these statements and reports to the court on them. Audit costs may be charged to the managed property. The manager's expenses may also be charged against the managed property, but the manager is not entitled to remuneration unless the court specifically directs otherwise.

As already mentioned, if there is a personal order, it prevails over the property order, and the manager's exercise of his powers and duties is subject to the personal order. So far as practicable, the manager must consult with the disabled person, and with others (including any non-profit-making voluntary organisation) who in the manager's opinion are interested in the person's welfare, and competent to give advice. If there is a welfare guardian, the manager must consult on a regular basis with the welfare guardian, to ensure that the interests of the disabled person are not prejudiced by any breakdown in communication.

All the acts and decisions of the manager, acting within his powers, have the same effect in law as if the disabled person had done or made them, and had had full capacity to do so. In particular, contracts, agreements and arrangements entered into by the manager can be enforced by proceedings brought against the manager in his (or her) capacity as manager.

Proceedings Against Mentally Disabled Person

Once a property order has been applied for, court proceedings or enforcement action cannot be taken against the mentally disabled person without the court's permission, and existing court proceedings or enforcement action cannot be continued.

Temporary Manager

A temporary manager may be appointed to provide interim protection, when an application for a property order has been made or is about to be made. Such an appointment may only be made if a temporary manager is urgently needed to protect any property of the mentally disabled person . Anyone entitled to apply for a property order may apply to have a temporary manager appointed. The appointment lasts for a maximum of three months.

Hospital Patients, etc.

Where a mentally disabled person is a hospital patient, or resident in a home or other institution, the person in charge may not be appointed to administer small sums or to act as manager. This contrasts with the Scottish provisions for management of patients' affairs by hospital authorities (see pages 111-113).

Under the New Zealand Act, when the person in charge considers that a property order may be appropriate and desirable, then the person in charge can notify the Registrar of the Family Court. There are provisions designed to trigger an investigation and an application for a property order, if necessary.

Other Provisions

The New Zealand Act also contains powers under which people can themselves apply to a trustee corporation to act as manager, with a modified procedure for small estates.

There is also provision for enduring Powers of Attorney, as regards both property and personal matters. (A Power of Attorney is a document authorising someone else to manage one's affairs. It may only be granted by someone having legal capacity to do so. Many lawyers consider that in Scotland, if the granter loses capacity, then the Power of Attorney comes to an end. The attorney may have difficulty in persuading people to accept his authority once the incapacity becomes known, though many in practice continue to act. An enduring Power of Attorney is a Power of Attorney which remains fully in force, even though the granter subsequently loses capacity. There is statutory provision for such a Power of Attorney in England, but not in Scotland.)

XIII

THE DISABLED PERSONS ACT

In 1985 a Scottish MP, Mr. Tom Clarke, drew first place in the ballot for Private Members' Bills. With great skill, and with cross-party support, he steered his bill through parliamentary procedures and through some compromises to enter the statute book as the Disabled Persons (Services, Consultation and Representation) Act 1986.

That was not the end of the procedural story. In its final form the Act requires orders by the Secretary of State to bring its various provisions into force. Not all of the provisions are yet (August 1989) in force. This applies to the topics dealt with below under the headings "Notification and Assessment on Discharge from Hospital", "Assessment Procedures", and "The Representative". In each case I have made it clear that the provisions are not yet in force, but I have then described them as they will apply once brought into force, provided that they are not affected by any other changes in the law in the meantime. In describing them, I have used the present tense.

Moreover, in the case of the representative, the detailed provisions will be contained in regulations which have not yet been made. The Act says that the regulations "may" contain certain provisions, which are described only in very general terms. I have limited myself to those provisions of the Act, in describing what is envisaged for the regulations.

The Act contains provisions relevant to people with both physical and mental disabilities. Almost all of its provisions have particular relevance for people with mental handicaps, and their families and carers. The provisions of the Act touch many different areas of law. Even within the Act, provisions dealing with similar matters are not always grouped together. Accordingly, while I quote section numbers, I have not dealt with the sections in numerical order. I have omitted sections 5 and 6, which do not apply to Scotland.

The main thrust of the Act is to improve the effectiveness and co-ordination of existing services for disabled people. Existing assessment procedures are strengthened and new assessment requirements are created. "Citizen advocacy" is given legislative status in the form of the representative. There are new requirements for co-operation in planning among different authorities: these provisions are dealt with in this chapter, though they have been transferred into NHS legislation. There are requirements to give more information – both to individuals in respect of local authority services, and generally in the form of reports to Parliament about the development of services. There are various other provisions, including some changes in relation to the law of special educational needs which I have described in Chapter XIV.

The White Paper *Caring for People* proposes that social work authorities will be responsible for arranging assessments of individual's needs for community care, taking account of their problems, needs and circumstances. The White Paper also states that under the community care proposals it will become even more important that Health Boards should work and plan closely with local authorities and the voluntary and private sectors in the provision of facilities in the community. It seems likely that the provisions of the Act regarding assessment and joint planning which are not yet in force, or provisions broadly similar to them, will be embodied in community care legislation.

Assessment

If people are to receive services which they need, two basic things must happen. Firstly, each individual's needs must be ascertained. Secondly, those who provide the relevant services must be told. The Act seeks to improve both of these elements in relation to disabled people.

Hitherto, education law has been ahead of other areas of law in that it provides for assessing and meeting the special needs of individual pupils. In the last chapter of *Scots Law and the Mentally Handicapped* I suggested (page 116) the possible extension of similar assessment procedures to determine the legal capacity and general legal status of mentally handicapped people. The Disabled Persons Act does not go as far as that, but it does take the important first step of strengthening educational assessment procedures, and introducing analogous assessment procedures outwith education law – in both cases geared to the provision of services.

Assessment of Children and Young Persons (Section 13)

Chapter XIII of *Scots Law and the Mentally Handicapped* described the law of special educational needs. It described how some children with special educational needs may be assessed, and how the assessment may result in the preparation of a Record of Needs. Children with Records of Needs are periodically re-assessed. In about the second-last year of compulsory schooling a Future Needs Assessment is carried out.

The Disabled Persons Act links social work departments into these educational Future Needs Assessment procedures. Most people concerned with the mentally handicapped are aware of problems which can be experienced in ensuring provision of necessary facilities and services at the age when people cross over from educational responsibility to social work responsibility. The government originally resisted some of these provisions on the grounds that "it was always the intention that authorities other than the education authority should be involved in the preparation of [Future Needs Assessments]". However, an express legal requirement is more effective than an intention.

Social work legislation contains various provisions concerning disabled persons. The definition of "disabled person" covers chronically sick or disabled persons, and persons suffering from mental disorder, who come within the provisions of social work legislation. Under the Disabled Persons Act, the education authority must in various circumstances seek an opinion from the social work authority as to whether a child or young person is a "disabled person". They must do this before completing a Future Needs Assessment. They must also do this if they decide to open a Record of Needs for a child or young person already beyond the age of Future Needs Assessment. Finally, they must do this if the child or young person was not a disabled person when a Future Needs Assessment was prepared, but there has been a subsequent change which causes the education authority to believe that the young person is now a disabled person.

The social work authority must respond to such a request for an opinion. If the social work opinion is that the child or young person is a disabled person, that places further duties on both the education authority and the social work authority.

The education authority has the following duties. Firstly, the opinion that the child or young person is a disabled person must be entered in the Record of Needs or Future Needs Assessment report. Secondly, the education authority must enter in the Future Needs report the date on which the person is to leave full-time education. If there is no Future Needs report, the education authority must give the social work authority at least six weeks notice of the date on which the person is to leave full-time education. If for any reason these requirements have not been followed at the proper time, the education authority must follow them as soon as is reasonably practicable.

The social work authority has the following duties. When the social work authority has given an opinion that the child is a disabled person, they must carry out their own assessment. They must assess the person's needs for services provided under welfare enactments, and prepare a report. "Welfare enactments" include various provisons of social work, health, chronically sick and disabled, and national assistance legislation. If the opinion that the child is a disabled person is given in conjunction with a Future Needs Assessment, the social work assessment must be carried out not less than nine months before the child reaches school leaving age. Otherwise, the social work assessment must be carried out within six months from when the education authority asked for the opinion. However, the social work authority do not have to carry out any of the assessment procedures described in this paragraph if the parents (or child, if over 16 and able to do so) specifically request that the assessment should not be carried out.

Finally, both education and social work authorities must keep under consideration the cases of all children and young persons who have had reports prepared, following either a Future Needs Assessment or a social work assessment. Both authorities must review the information in the report "at such times as they consider appropriate". Two points should be noted about this provision. Firstly, in the case of reports following Future Needs Assessments, these provisions apply whether or not the young person has been noted as being a disabled person. Secondly, although the reports referred to will have been carried out by one authority or the other, both education and social work authorities must keep cases under consideration and carry out reviews, whichever of them prepared the report.

The effect of these provisions should be to co-ordinate, and indeed create a deliberate overlap, in the areas of education authority and social work responsibility. Moreover, it should be remembered that it has always been the position that education authorities must send Future Needs reports to the health board, when the education authority consider it appropriate to do so. Accordingly, health boards. will receive the additional information as to whether the person has been assessed as being a "disabled person".

Assessment of Need for Provision of Welfare Services (Section 4)

Under the Disabled Persons Act disabled people and their carers may request the local authority to decide whether the disabled person needs any welfare services. The local authority must make a decision about such needs, if so requested. The Act does not use the word "assessment" here, nor does it specify any assessment procedures, but clearly the local authority cannot decide about needs without assessing them.

The "carer" is one of the new concepts introduced by the Act. A carer is someone who provides "a substantial amount of care on a regular basis" to a disabled person living at home. The carer does not have to be living in the same house. A "carer" under the Act could be a good neighbour who provides a substantial amount of care on a regular basis. The definition covers relatives, companions, friends, neighbours, volunteers and others who provide care voluntarily. It covers people employed by voluntary bodies to provide care. However it does not cover anyone employed to provide care by any authority or agency exercising statutory functions (local authorities, heath boards, and the like).

Any disabled person, and also any carer of a disabled person, can have a decision made by the local authority about need for welfare services. When the provisions about representatives (see pages 138-141) come into force, any representative will also be able to have such a decision made by the local authority.

The welfare services referred to are those available under the Chronically Sick and Disabled Persons Act 1970. The local authority must provide any of these services which they decide are needed, in the case of any disabled person coming within the scope of social work responsibilities. The list of services includes services in the following areas: practical assistance in the home; recreational facilities in the home including radio, television, and library facilities; recreational facilities outside the home including lectures, games and outings; help in taking advantage of any available educational facilities; transport; help in adapting the home, and in providing spcial aids; help with holidays; provision of meals; provision of a telephone, and any necessary special telephone equipment.

Notification and Assessment on Discharge from Hospital (Section 7 — not yet in force)

The provisions of this section have not been brought into force. In *Caring for People* the Government proposes to defer implementation of this section for reconsideration "in the light of several years' experience" of the regime envisaged in that White Paper.

The Disabled Persons Act sets out procedures which are triggered when someone is discharged from long-term hospital care, if he (or she) has received medical treatment for any form of mental handicap or mental illness. The provisions apply if someone has been an in-patient for six months or longer. The six-months period can be built up in more than one hospital. However, these provisions do not apply when a patient is discharged from one hospital in order to be admitted as an in-patient to another, even if in the new hospital the patient is not to receive medical treatment for mental handicap or mental illness.

As soon as reasonably practicable after the date for discharge from hospital becomes known, the hospital management must notify the date in writing to various authorities. This includes an obligation to give notification as soon as practicable after discharge of a detained patient has been ordered by the Mental Welfare Commission or a

Sheriff. In the cases of both adults and children, hospital management must notify the health board and social work authority in whose areas the ex-patient is likely to reside, though the same health board does not have to give notice to itself. In the case of patients under 18, the education authority must also be notified (or at least, that would appear to be the intended meaning of some clearly erroneous cross-references in the text of the Act).

Health boards and social work authorities who receive such notification must make arrangements for assessments, and in each individual case must co-operate with each other in making those arrangements. When a health board has not received notification because it is also the manager of the hospital which the patient is leaving, the health board must still carry out the assessment. Normally the assessments must be carried out before the date of discharge from hospital. Where discharge of a detained patient has been ordered by the Mental Welfare Commission or the Sheriff, the assessments must be carried out as soon as reasonably practicable.

The health board assessment must assess the needs of the person for health services. The social work assessment must assess the needs of the person for services under "welfare enactments". As already mentioned, this covers various services under social work, health, chronically sick and disabled, and national assistance legislation. The person can decline to have these assessments carried out, but in the case of people with mental handicaps the decision not to be assessed would only be effective if the person had sufficient capacity to make a valid decision.

The Abilities of the Carer (Section 8)

We looked at the concept of the "carer" on pages 134-135. The carer is someone, not employed by a statutory authority, who provides a substantial amount of care on a regular basis. The Act recognises that one cannot sensibly assess the needs of a disabled person without considering the abilities of the relative, companion, friend, neighbour or other person who acts as carer. Even though the condition of the disabled person remains unchanged, the disabled person's needs may increase if the carer becomes less able. Under the Act, the local authority must have regard to the ability of the carer to continue to provide a substantial amount of care on a regular basis. The local authority must take the carer's abilities into account in this way whenever the local authority have to decide whether the disabled person needs any services under the "welfare enactments" (covering various services under health, social work, chronically sick and disabled, and national assistance legislation).

136

If the carer has difficulty in communicating (or in being communicated with), the local authority must provide such services as the local authority consider necessary to ensure that the local authority are properly informed about the carer's abilities. In this situation, the local authority must have regard to the carer's own views as to whether help in communicating is required by the carer, and, if so, what help.

Assessment Procedures (Section 3 - not yet in force)

The Act contains provisions, not yet in force, governing assessment procedures. The provisions apply to assessments, both under the Act and otherwise, as to whether a disabled person has needs which call for the provision of any statutory services. The procedure is simpler than the procedure under education law for preparing a Record of Needs (see *Scots Law and the Mentally Handicapped*, pages 64-70), but has some similarities. The procedure can be broken down into the following stages:

1. The local authority must allow an opportunity for representations to be made as to any needs of the disabled person calling for the provision of statutory services by the local authority. The representations may be made by the disabled person, or by the disabled person's representative. They are to be made to an officer of the local authority. The local authority must allow a reasonable period for them to be made. They may be made orally, or in writing, or both.
2. If representations have been made by the disabled person or the representative, the local authority take them into account when making their decision. If no representations have been made, the local authority make their decision after the period for representations has expired.
3. Once a decision has been made, the disabled person or the representative is entitled to ask for a written statement about the decision. They may ask for this whether or not they made representations at stage 1. The Act specifies the information which must be provided in the written statement. If the local authority propose to provide statutory services, they must specify the services to be provided, and the needs of the disabled person which require them. If the local authority are of the opinion that the disabled person has no needs requiring any statutory services to be provided, the local authority must say so. In all cases, the local authority must give an explanation of their decision. In particular, if representations were made at stage 1 identifying any particular need, and the local authority do not propose to provide any

services to meet that need, this must be set out in the statement, with the local authority's reasons. All written statements must also explain the right to make representations at stage 4.

4. The local authority must allow a reasonable period for representations to be made by the disabled person or representative about the written statement issued at stage 3. If the disabled person or representative is dissatisfied with anything in the written statement, either of them may make representations to an officer of the local authority. Again, these representations may be made orally, or in writing, or both.

5. If the local authority receive any representations at stage 4, they must again consider the matter. They must do so even if the point has already been considered at stage 2, and even if representations about it have already been made at stage 1. They must at this stage again consider whether statutory services should be provided by them to meet any needs identified in the representations. If so, they must decide what statutory services should be provided.

6. The local authority must then write to the disabled person or the representative, giving their decision and the reasons for it.

There are further provisions which apply when the disabled person or the representative has communication difficulties resulting from any physical or mental incapacity. They apply whenever either or both is unable to communicate, or be communicated with, orally or in writing (or in either one of those ways). In such cases, the local authority must provide such services as they consider necessary to ensure that the communication difficulties do not prevent the local authority from discharging their functions under the assessment provisions, and do not prevent the making of representations at stages 1 and 4. The local authority must have regard to any views expressed by the disabled person or representative as to whether services to overcome communication difficulties are needed. The local authority must also have regard to any views expressed by the disabled person or representative as to the services which should be provided.

The Representative (Sections 1 and 2 - not yet in force)

The "authorised representative" provided for in the Disabled Persons Act embodies, in somewhat restricted form, the concept of advocacy. Put simply, an advocate is someone who speaks on behalf of another. Usually, the advocate will be someone better able or better placed to communicate, persuade and act than the person whom the advocate represents. That is the function of professional advocates in the courts. Under the next heading are some comments on the subject of advocacy generally. Here, I describe the provisions of the Disabled Persons Act concerning the representative. However, this is another of the provisions of the Act which has not yet been brought into force, and there appear to be no immediate plans to bring it into force.

Under the Act, the initial role of the representative is limited to dealing with local authorities in connection with the provision of services under the "welfare enactments" (which, as we have already seen, cover various services under social work, health, chronically sick and disabled, and national assistance legislation). The Act does however empower the Secretary of State to make orders extending the role of the representative to other local authority services, and to health authority services.

The authority must permit the representative to act as the representative of the disabled person in connection with the provision of services. Also, the authority must permit the representative to accompany the disabled person to any meeting or interview regarding the provision of services, if the meeting or interview is held by the authority or on behalf of the authority. The Act says that the representative may accompany the disabled person "otherwise than as his representative". It is not entirely clear whether this means that the representative may attend even though he (or she) does not act as representative, or alternatively that he (or she) may act as either representative or companion, but not both, at any one meeting or interview.

The authority must do certain things to assist the representative. The authority must give the representative any information which the disabled person himself (or herself) would be entitled to receive. The authority must also let the representative inspect any documents which the disabled person would be entitled to see.

These various rights of the representative can however be restricted or even negated by the authority. The authority can exclude the representative from meetings and interviews, or from parts of meetings and interviews, and can refuse to give information or allow documents to be inspected, if the local authority are satisfied that to do so would be likely to be harmful to the interests of the disabled person. In deciding what might be harmful to the disabled person's interests, the local authority must have regard to any wishes expressed by the disabled person.

In the case of disabled persons living in various categories of accommodation, the representative has the right to visit the disabled person there and interview him (or her) in private, at any reasonable time. The categories include most hospitals, local authority accommodation, registered residential care homes, and the like. Also included is any place specified by a statutory guardian to a disabled person as the place at which the disabled person shall reside.

The Act provides that the rules for appointment of representatives shall be laid down in regulations. Such regulations are unlikely to be made unless and until it has been decided to bring the provisions regarding the representative into force. The Act does however give guidance regarding the content of the regulations.

The regulations will govern the manner of making and terminating appointments as representative, and also the notification of appointments to the authority. It is envisaged that persons over 16, who have the capacity to do so, will normally appoint their own representatives. Disabled persons under 16 will not be able to appoint their representatives: the appointment will normally be made by parents or guardians. A parent or guardian may, if he wishes, himself be appointed representative. The regulations may allow local authorities to appoint representatives to children in their care.

The Act also contains provisions as to the regulations to be made for appointment of representatives to disabled persons who are unable, because of physical or mental incapacity, to make the appointment themselves. It is envisaged that it will be for the local authority to decide whether a person is unable to appoint his (or her) own representative. In making the decision, the local authority are likely to be required to obtain a doctor's opinion and to consult with people whom they may appoint to advise, and also with people "falling within any class or description specified in the regulations".

The Act envisages that the regulations will provide two possible methods of appointment in such cases. The first will be for the local authority to appoint the representative themselves. The second will be for the appointment to be made under delegated arrangements established by the local authority. Under the second method, it is envisaged that the local authority will make arrangements with approved voluntary organisations or persons, under which they will have delegated powers to appoint representatives. Under either method of appointment, it is envisaged that the local authority will again be required to consult with people appointed to advise, and also with people "falling within any class or description specified in the regulations".

It is certainly to be hoped that the class or description of people to be consulted under these provisions will include relatives and carers. However, the Act does not stipulate that they must be included. The Act does say that "nearest relatives" under mental health legislation, and statutory guardians, may also act as representatives. It is not clear why they should be specifically mentioned, while others (such as tutors, curators, and named persons) are not. There appears to be no reason why tutors, curators, named persons or any others with existing roles in relation to disabled people should not also be representatives. Indeed, in the case of tutors, it would seem to be essential that the tutor should also be the representative, to avoid conflict or lack of co-ordination.

When a disabled person has appointed his or her own representative, the representative may only act for the disabled person, attend meetings and interviews, receive information or see documents, if the disabled person so requests. Likewise, a representative to a person under 16 appointed by parents or guardians may only do these things if so requested by the parents or guardians. However, where a representative has been appointed to a disabled person over 16 unable to make the appointment himself (or herself), the representative may thereafter do any and all of these things without any request or permission from anyone. Astonishingly, there is no obligation upon the representative to try as far as is possible to ascertain the wishes of the disabled person, or to involve the disabled person in decisions. Nor is there any obligation upon the representative to consult with parents, carers and others.

It is envisaged that the regulations will require local authorities, in appropriate circumstances, to review whether a disabled person is still unable to appoint a representative himself (or herself). It is also envisaged that the regulations will contain procedures for terminating the appointment of representatives, similar to those for appointing them.

The Representative: Background and Comment

The introduction of the representative builds upon experience gained in various "citizen advocacy" schemes. The key to such schemes is to develop knowledge, understanding, and friendship on a one-to-one basis between a disabled person and a volunteer who is able to speak for the disabled person and to try to ensure that the disabled person's needs and wishes are understood and met. Citizen advocates have helped disabled persons find more suitable accommodation, secure provision of needed services, and free themselves from unnecessary restrictions. Such arrangements are not without risk. There is a danger that the advocate's own views and preferences may intrude unduly, and there is a need for monitoring. However, even with these risks, there is a large unmet need for this type of effective befriending, and it is surely better that the effort be made to meet it.

In my experience, parents who visit a solicitor to make Wills, and express their fears for the future "when we are gone", are in fact less concerned about financial management than about the sort of friendship, support and effective help which a representative could provide. Often a wise choice of tutor-dative will achieve the same purpose. If the representative provisions of the Disabled Persons Act are brought into force, many tutors may seek to be appointed representatives also. However, the main value of citizen advocacy schemes, backed up by the representative provisions of the Disabled Persons Act if they are brought into force, is for those who have no-one sufficiently close and concerned to take the initiative in such ways as seeing a solicitor about having tutors-dative appointed.

In the United States the concept of advocacy has been developed into "protection and advocacy" programmes. In order to qualify for federal funding under the Developmental Disabilities and Bill of Rights Act, states must establish a Protection and Advocacy System. Usually advocacy and legal services are contracted out to private, non-governmental advocacy agencies. The state of New York has an impressively effective Bureau of Protection and Advocacy for the Developmentally Disabled.

Ultimately, however, the value of any advocacy system depends upon the quality of rights and entitlements which the law provides, and which advocates can demand for those whom they represent. Mr William Combes, programme co-ordinator of the New York Bureau, stressed this in the following words (letter to the author of 22nd November 1985):

> I think that it is important to note that the Protection and Advocacy System is reliant on other federal statutes to serve as the underpinnings for our negotiations and litigation. Federal laws with regard to a right to a free and appropriate education, freedom from housing and employment discrimination and entitlement programs for medical and financial assistance give us the administrative structure for appeal and redress should we need it. I would think that a similar structure would assist any advocacy program should it be established in Scotland.

Special Educational Needs (Section 14)

The government decided to take the opportunity of the Disabled Persons Act to make certain alterations to provisions in education law covering assessment and recording of children with special educational needs. These changes are described in Chapter XIV (pages 148-150).

Joint Planning (Section 15 — now repealed)

The joint planning provisions of the Disabled Persons Act were taken out of that Act and transferred to the National Health Service (Amendment) Act 1986. It is however convenient to deal with them here.

The Scottish Society for the Mentally Handicapped was consulted about possible topics for the Disabled Persons Bill. They felt that if one item should be given priority in the context of a Private Member's Bill, then the most important for Scotland would be a provision for joint planning. The needs of disabled people often cross the artificial boundaries between areas of responsibility of different authorities, particularly health boards, social work authorities, and education authorities. In England there are mandatory provisions for joint planning.

In Scotland the only existing provision was in very generalised terms. It is contained in section 13 of the National Health Service (Scotland) Act 1978, which reads as follows: "In exercising their respective functions, Health Boards, local authorities and education authorities shall co-operate with one another in order to secure and advance the health of the people of Scotland".

The Disabled Persons Act sought to amplify this by adding certain more specific duties. However, these provisions of the Disabled Persons Act were repealed without coming into force, and were replaced by the National Health Service (Amendment) Act 1986, which inserted a new section 13A into the National Health Service (Scotland) Act of 1978. This new section 13A is now in force, and the wording is substantially the same as in the Disabled Persons Act, though at one point more specific.

A new section 13B has also been inserted into the National Health Service Act of 1978 by the National Health Service (Amendment) Act of 1986. Section 13B is not yet in force. Although its provisions did not appear in the Disabled Persons Act, it probably reflects more accurately what the Scottish Society for the Mentally Handicapped had in mind when they suggested that the topic of joint planning merited priority.

The new section 13A inserted in the 1978 National Health Service Act imposes various specific duties upon health boards, social work authorities and education authorities, within the general ambit of their existing obligation to co-operate with each other. Where services for disabled persons are of common concern to health boards and social work authorities, they must co-operate with each other in the joint planning of those services. They must also co-operate in planning the development of those services. Likewise, where services for disabled persons are of common concern to health boards and education authorities, they are under similar duties to co-operate with each other in the planning and development of those services.

Under section 13A, health boards, social work authorities and education authorities are also now under a duty to consult with voluntary organisations. This applies where voluntary organisations provide services of common concern to health boards and social work authorities, or health boards and education authorities. Such voluntary organisations must be consulted in the process of joint planning, if such consultations might be expected to contribute substantially to the joint planning process.

Finally, under section 13A, joint plans must now be published, "at such times and in such manner" as the boards and authorities making them "consider appropriate".

Section 13B, which has not yet (August 1989) been brought into force, goes further. It will empower the Secretary of State to order that joint liaison committees be set up. The Secretary of State's orders will set out how such committees should be formed, and what should be their functions. Voluntary organisations may be given a role in joint liaison committees. The general purpose of joint liaison committees will be to advise health boards, social work authorities and education authorities regarding the planning and operation of services of common concern.

There appears to be general agreement among organisations representing "consumers" of such services that the provisions of section 13B should be brought into force, with the necessary orders. It is rather surprising that this has not yet been done in an era when increasing attention is being paid to the wishes and needs of consumers.

Other Provisions of the Disabled Persons Act

Section 9 of the Disabled Persons Act extends local authority duties to give information under chronically sick and disabled persons legislation. Social work authorities had an existing duty to tell any person receiving any social work service about any other services available in the area, which are relevant to that person's needs, and which are provided under social work legislation. This is now extended to all services provided by the local authority, not just those provided under the relevant social work legislation. It is also extended to services which the social work authority knows to be available from other authorities or organisations.

Section 10 refers to various situations in which there is a statutory requirement to appoint or co-opt people with special knowledge of the needs of disabled persons to any councils, committees or bodies. Before anyone is appointed or co-opted, any appropriate organisation or organisations of disabled persons must be consulted. The obligation is only one to consult: there is no obligation to accept any views or recommendations of such organisations. The Act refers to "organisations *of* disabled people", not "organisations *for* disabled people". In practice, this tends to discriminate against people with mental disabilities. Those groups in society who have mental disabilities which render them unable to form their own organisations are represented by bodies formed *for* them. This applies to all of the main organisations concerned with mental handicap, mental health, and particular categories of mental handicap and mental illness. They will be excluded from consultation under this provision if "organisations of disabled people" is given a narrow and limited interpretation. It will be interesting to see whether it is interpreted in such a narrow way, or whether it is interpreted more broadly on the presumption that Parliament did not intend to discriminate against mentally disabled people. The Disabled Persons Act does not in any of its other provisions restrict to one category of disabled people provisions valid for both the physically disabled and the mentally disabled.

Section 11 requires the Secretary of State to make an annual report to Parliament. The report must include the number of people receiving in-patient treatment for mental handicap in health service hospitals, and also the number of people receiving in-patient treatment for mental illness in health service hospitals. The report must in addition include "such information as the Secretary of State considers appropriate" regarding the development of services in the community. The services covered are defined as health and social services in the community for people with mental handicaps and people suffering from mental illness, who are not resident in hospitals. The Secretary of State can also include any other information which he considers appropriate. The government have indicated that the first report under this section is likely to be laid before Parliament "before the end of 1989".

Section 12 refers to legislation concerning chronically sick and disabled people. It makes it clear that people with mental handicaps and people suffering from mental illness are included within the definition of those covered by this legislation.

Scotland and the Disabled Persons Act

During the passage of the Act through Parliament, Scottish organisations tended to feel themselves at a disadvantage. They felt that although Mr Clarke himself had consulted some Scottish

145

organisations at the outset, thereafter they were being largely excluded from consultation and preparation. "London-based organisations have access which simply isn't possible for us". As first introduced in Parliament, the major part of the Bill appeared to have been conceived entirely from an English viewpoint. I was probably not the only one who immediately pointed out the inadequacy and ineptitude of the "application to Scotland" provisions, in clause 8 of the original Bill. The response from one of those involved in drafting the Bill was revealing: "If [Mr Clarke] had not been a Scottish MP I would have omitted clause 8 and waited for someone to notice Scotland had been left out". As the Bill was a Private Member's Bill, this was not one of the official parliamentary draftsmen.

During the committee stage of the Bill an undertaking was given to ensure that the substantive provisions of the Bill as finally amended would be fully applied to Scotland. Nevertheless, Scottish organisations apparently tended to feel that the Scottish Office was resistant to the Bill: it is certainly the case that the Scottish Office consistently lagged behind England in bringing the various provisions of the Act into force.

Scots lawyers are unlikely to be surprised by the lessons learned by Scottish voluntary organisations during the passage of the Bill. Scottish organisations learned that there are significant disadvantages in trying to reform Scots law in a United Kingdom Bill. The English position, and in particular English needs and priorities, tend to dominate. As I pointed out in the first chapter of *Scots Law and the Mentally Handicapped* (page 4), many areas of law most relevant to mentally disabled people were well developed before 1707, and are accordingly among those where the differences between Scots and English law are greatest. Even in modern times, there has generally been separate legislation for Scotland and England in areas of particular relevance to mentally disabled people. For example, Scotland has generally had its own separate mental health and education legislation. Scotland would certainly require its own legislation to make proper provision for personal guardianship and management of property and affairs. Any attempt to introduce a common code in England and Scotland would be likely to take inadequate account of the Scottish position, and to be unsatisfactory here.

In the case of a Private Member's Bill, a well-intentioned Bill which does not reach the statute book is unlikely to help anyone. The Disabled Persons Act succeeded in becoming law because it commanded broad support throughout the UK. Scottish organisations may have felt themselves at a disadvange in the early stages, when the agenda for the Bill was set, but the practicalities of the situation made that virtually inevitable. What matters is the end result. Within the agenda which was

146

set, the Act achieved every bit as much in Scotland as in England. Even if viewed solely in Scottish terms, it has made significant and valuable improvements in our law. It represents a remarkable achievement for a Private Member's Bill.

The Disabled Persons Act also has value beyond its content. At a conference of the British Institute of Mental Handicap in April 1987 Mr Clarke described it as a "framework for future legislation". The Act focused attention on the need for improved legal provision for disabled people, particularly mentally disabled people, and it has set a precedent for innovative law reform.

It is disappointing that there are as yet no indications that all of the remaining provisions of the Act will be brought into force. One can well understand Mr Clarke's argument that the will of Parliament, as expressed in the Act, should be implemented, and the remainder of the Act brought into force.

XIV

SPECIAL EDUCATIONAL NEEDS

The law of special educational needs was described in Chapter XIII of *Scots Law and the Mentally Handicapped*. Since then, there have been some changes and developments. Further changes are proposed in the Self-Governing Schools etc. (Scotland) Bill. These provisions seem likely to be approved by Parliament, and to become law some time in 1989.

Firstly, up till now education authorities have been able to follow assessment and recording procedures in relation to children under school age, but have not been obliged to do so. The Self-Governing Schools etc. (Scotland) Bill proposes in clause 67 to apply to children from the age of 2 onwards the same duties to assess and record as at present apply to school-age children.

The Disabled Persons Act provided an opportunity to make some changes in the statutory framework. Changes have been made to the recording procedure. I described that procedure in numbered stages on pages 64-70 of *Scots Law and the Mentally Handicapped*. Stages 1, 2 and 3 were concerned with a process of assessment. The assessment included a medical examination and a psychological examination, and a report from any teacher employed by the education authority who was (or had been) involved in the child's education. This has now been changed to a process of "observation and assessment". The process includes educational, psychological and medical assessments.

The notice sent at stage 1 now invites parents to allow an assessment of the child (rather than medical and psychological examinations). Examinations are still possible, but not essential. If examinations are proposed, the notice must still say when and where they are to be held. The parents still have the right to be present at any medical examination.

The follow-up notice at stage 2 also now refers simply to "assessment", rather than to medical and psychological examinations. The procedure at stage 3 is now one of observation and assessment, including educational, psychological and medical assessments, without the specific requirement in every case for medical and psychological examinations, and a teacher's report. These changes should give greater flexibility, and allow assessments to be attuned more effectively and sensitively to the circumstances of individual children. The emphasis shifts from specific "one-off" examinations to a process of observation and assessment, allowing the child to be watched and assessed over a period of time, and in various different situations.

Stage 6 is the stage at which the education authority decide whether the child should have a Record of Needs, and draft the Record of Needs if one is needed. At this stage the advice which they must now take into account is that given as a result of the process of observation and assessment.

Parents may now opt not to have a Named Person. If they request the education authority not to appoint a Named Person, then details of the Named Person are omitted from the Record of Needs finalised at stage 9. Some parents objected to having a Named Person. They felt that there was an implication that if a child had special needs, then the parents were automatically less able than other parents to understand and exercise their role. They felt that if a Named Person was needed to assist some parents, that should depend upon the capabilities of the parents, not the special needs of the child. At least one education authority anticipated this change in the law by omitting Named Persons from Records of Needs where parents expressed such objections.

At stage 10 the parents have various rights of appeal, following the education authority's decision at stage 9. I pointed out in *Scots Law and the Mentally Handicapped* that the parents could appeal against a decision that their child should have a Record of Needs, but they had no right to appeal against a decision that the child should not have a Record of Needs. That has now been rectified. At stage 10 parents can appeal against a decision not to record. The procedure for such appeals is the same as described at stage 10(a) for appeals against a decision to record, or against certain details in the Record of Needs.

Unfortunately, there is an apparent defect in the legislation introducing this new right of appeal. It has been added to the list of rights of appeal open to "the parent of a recorded child". If the education authority has decided not to open a Record of Needs, then the child has not become a recorded child. This appears to be an example of careless draftsmanship in the Disabled Persons Act (another was mentioned on page 136). One trusts that the courts will take a broad view and accept that the only possible interpretation is that Parliament intended to introduce this right of appeal.

Stage 10(b) deals with appeals concerning choice of school to be attended, and stage 11 describes the right of further appeal to the Sheriff as to choice of school. These statutory provisions have not been changed, but shortly I shall describe some important developments in relation to placing requests for recorded children, and attendance at establishments abroad.

All of the changes described above also apply to review procedure at stage 12. So the review process is now one of "observation and assessment"; and if at a review the education authority decide to discontinue the Record of Needs, the parents can appeal against that.

Records of Needs can be opened for "young persons" from school leaving age up to 18 (see *Scots Law and the Mentally Handicapped*, page 71). Here assessment is voluntary, and it was already open to the education authority to devise appropriate assessment procedures, with no specific requirement for medical and psychological examinations and teachers' reports. Here also, however, the process is now one of "observation and assessment". Young persons (or their parents) can also now opt to have no Named Person. They can also appeal against a decision not to open a Record of Needs.

Finally, the Disabled Persons Act made a change in terminology. The phrase "child guidance" is dropped from the legislation, so that the child guidance service becomes the regional psychological service (or island authority psychological service).

Placing Requests — Recorded Children

Some special provisions apply to placing requests for children with special needs. Such placing requests may specify a private (fee-paying) special school which is prepared to take the child. The education authority can refuse the request if they can cater adequately for the child's special educational needs in a school of their own, if they can do so at less cost to themselves, and if they have offered to place the child in that school. If the placing request is successful, the education authority must meet the costs of educating the child in the private special school.

Clause 66 of the Self-Governing Schools etc. (Scotland) Bill proposes an alteration to the grounds on which an education authority can refuse a request to place a child in a private special school. It is proposed to drop the requirement that the education authority should be able to cater adequately for the child's special educational needs in a school of their own at less cost to themselves. Instead, the education authority would have to show that they are able to provide for the child's special educational needs in a school of their own, and that it is not reasonable to place the child in the private special school, having regard to comparison of both cost and suitability of the education authority's own school and the private special school. The new element is the comparison of the suitability of provision for the child's special educational needs. If this new provision comes into force, then it is possible for placing requests to succeed on a basis of comparison of suitability of the two schools, even though they would have failed under the existing law. In other words, even though an education authority have offered a place in a school of their own which could cater for the child's special educational needs at less cost to the education authority than the proposed special school, under the new proposals the education authority might still have to meet the cost of educating the child in the special school if the special school was more suitable, and if the advantages as regards suitability outweighed the cost disadvantages.

Placing Requests — Schools outside Scotland

A case decided in 1986 and reported in 1988 concerned a placing request by a Mrs Lamont, mother of a dyslexic child. She requested to have her child placed in a school in England. She did so on the basis that the only schools in the United Kingdom catering for her child's particular needs were in England. The education authority turned down her application, and she was unsuccessful before the appeal committee. She took her appeal to the Sheriff, who found in her favour, turning down an argument by the education authority that the Sheriff had no power to order a placement in a school in England. However, the education authority took this point on appeal from the Sheriff to the Sheriff Principal. Before the Sheriff Principal, the education authority were successful. The Sheriff Principal decided that a placing request could seek a placing only in a school in Scotland, and not in a school outside Scotland. By then the child was already 15. The parents did not appeal the matter further.

On the basis of interpretation of the existing legislation, the Sheriff Principal's decision could not be faulted. He decided the matter by looking at the definitions section of the Education (Scotland) Act 1980 (as amended by the Education (Scotland) Act 1981). The definitions of schools, and of various categories of schools including special schools, are such that they can only refer to Scottish schools. Moreover, where education legislation permits education authorities to assist with education outside Scotland, it does so quite specifically.

Prior to this decision there was a belief in several quarters that placing requests could be made for any school in the United Kingdom (and the same applied to the equivalent English choice of school provisions). There was also a belief in some quarters that this is what was intended by the legislation. There was certainly a very powerful policy argument that if particular specialist facilities have been provided only in one part of the United Kingdom, then they should be available to pupils from anywhere in the United Kingdom. The legislation as it stood contained no specific limitation to either Scotland or the United Kingdom: if the provisions had not been interpreted as limited to Scotland, they would have applied worldwide. Some parents had argued – though not, so far as I am aware, in any formal proceedings – that education authorities should meet the cost of attending establishments abroad, where similar facilities were not available in the United Kingdom.

These issues are addressed in clause 66 of the Self-Governing Schools etc. (Scotland) Bill. These provisions seem likely to be approved by Parliament, and to become law some time in 1989.

The Bill proposes that parents of children with a Record of Needs may now make a placing request specifying a school anywhere in the United Kingdom. The special provisions in education legislation for placing requests for children with Records of Needs will accordingly cover three categories of schools. The first is the existing category of schools managed by the same education authority. The second is the existing category of private (fee-paying) special schools anywhere in Scotland – covering schools which make provision wholly or mainly for recorded children, and also special classes in primary and secondary schools, and in psychological service clinics. The third category, now proposed as a new category, covers schools in England, Wales or Northern Ireland which make provision wholly or mainly for children with pronounced, specific or complex special educational needs.

The Bill does not propose that parents should be able to request placement in establishments outside the United Kingdom. It does however propose that education authorities should be empowered to arrange for children to attend schools or other establishments abroad. The school or establishment must be one which makes provision wholly or mainly for persons with pronounced, specific or complex special educational needs. The education authority will be able to make such provision as they think fit. This will include power, at the authority's discretion, to meet some or all costs of fees, travel, maintenance, and other expenses. It will also include similar power to meet the costs of one or both parents, or some other person, if the authority think that their presence would be to the child's advantage.

It is to be hoped that education authorities will exercise this discretionary power in any cases where there is no suitable facility anywhere in the United Kingdom, but there is one abroad, and the parents are prepared to contemplate sending the child to it. The child should not be deprived of the "adequate and efficient" education which is the right of all children, merely because the child's needs happen to be unusual. If we choose not to make suitable provision here in the United Kingdom, then we should not refuse to send a child (if the parents so request) to wherever suitable provision does exist.

Failure to Educate as Provided in Records of Needs

Several parents and groups of parents have had occasion to contact lawyers with complaints that their children are not being educated in accordance with the provisions of their Records of Needs. Part V of the prescribed form of Record of Needs sets out the ways in which the

152

education authority propose to meet the child's special needs. Part V is divided into two sections, one listing provision to be made by the education authority itself, and the other listing provision to be made by other agencies. However it is the obligation of the education authority to ensure that the child receives all of the educational provision in Part V whether they have indicated an intention to provide it themselves, or through some other agency.

The most common complaint seems to concern provision of speech therapy. Many children have regular provision of speech therapy entered in the second section of Part V of their Records of Needs, as being provided by health boards. Some such children have received little or no speech therapy. Some education authorities have sought, quite wrongly, to wash their hands of the matter and refer parents to the health board, who in turn say that they have too few speech therapists.

However, it is the obligation of the education authority to ensure that the child receives the provision set out in the Record of Needs. How they achieve that is ultimately their concern. Usually, when this is drawn to the attention of education authorities, they take the necessary action to comply with their obligations. If they fail to do so, two possible courses are open to parents. They can either take the education authority to court under judicial review procedure, or make a formal complaint to the Secretary of State. They would be wise to take legal advice at that stage, if not earlier.

In this context, certain court decisions in England are sometimes referred to. The English position is different, and the English cases do not change the position under Scots law as stated above. Where Scotland has a Record of Needs, England has a "Statement of Special Educational Needs" (and, apparently, where Scottish children are "recorded", English children are "statemented"). The main sections of the English statement are a statement of the child's special educational needs; a section headed "Special Educational Provision" specifying the special educational provisions which the education authority consider appropriate to meet the needs set out in the previous section; a statement of "Appropriate School or Other Arrangements"; and a statement of "Additional Non-Educational Provision". The last category does not feature in Scottish Records of Needs. It has been held in England that education authorities are not obliged to provide something entered as a "non-educational provision". In a case concerning Oxfordshire Education Authority, speech therapy had been entered as a "non-educational provision" and the court held that the education authority were not obliged to provide it.

Matters have now been helpfully clarified by the English Court of Appeal in a decision issued on 10th March 1989, concerning Lancashire

County Council. The court held that teaching a child to communicate by speech, so that the child may be fully understood by others, is as much educational as teaching the child to communicate by writing. It is therefore the duty of the education authority to provide speech therapy to such children, even though speech therapists are employed by the National Health Service. The court pointed out that at one time education authorities employed their own speech therapists. In 1974 all speech therapists in the public service had been transferred to the NHS. However, there was still nothing to prevent education authorities from employing speech therapists if that became necessary to enable the education authority to comply with its statutory duties. Likewise, the education authority can go to other health authorities, or to private speech therapists. This part of the decision is in my view fully relevant in Scotland, though on the question of employing speech therapists directly I understand that one Scottish authority have received legal advice that it is outwith their statutory powers to do this. It may well be necessary for this point, and the consequences of it, to be resolved by the Scottish courts.

Although the Lancashire decision – and many of the cases which seem to arise here in Scotland – concern provision of speech therapy, the principles apply equally to any other provision to be made under Part V of a Record of Needs.

A pernicious practice which has emerged recently in some parts of Scotland is to qualify provisions in Part V of the Record of Needs with phrases such as "according to availability of resources" or "as available". I have even seen a provision regarding speech therapy qualified as follows: "regular speech therapy as deemed appropriate by Community Health Service to meet his/her needs". Such provisions are wholly inappropriate. The purpose of the Record of Needs is to document the way in which, despite the fact that the particular child has special needs, the education authority will ensure that the child receives an adequate and efficient education. The obligation of the education authority is to provide an adequate and efficient education, not simply to do so subject to availability of resources. While the education authority may indicate that the education authority's obligations will in part be met by provision from other services, it is most certainly not for some non-educational body such as the "Community Health Service" to determine the level of educational provision required. Although Part V of the Record of Needs is not one of the parts subject to the appeal procedure provided by education legislation, a failure by a local authority to perform its statutory duty can be challenged either by application to the Secretary of State or through the courts by judicial review procedure. There is certainly room to argue that aggrieved parents are entitled to have such provisions in

Part V of the Record of Needs subjected to judicial review. One trusts that such challenge will not become necessary, and that responsible education authorities will not seek to defeat the purpose of the legislation in this way.

Note: The Self-Governing Schools etc. (Scotland) Act 1989 received the Royal Assent on 16th November 1989. Clause 67 of the Bill, as described in this chapter, is now section 72 of the Act, and will come into force on a date to be specified by the Secretary of State. Clause 66 of the Bill, as described in this chapter, is now in force as section 71 of the Act.

XV

DISCRIMINATION, DEPRIVATION AND ABUSE

Discrimination

A family group, including a young man with a mental handicap, were turned away from a restaurant with the words: "He'll put other people off their meals". This happened recently, in a Scottish city. Such incidents are not uncommon. If we do not hear about them, it is because the victims often suffer their hurt in silence.

In Britain we have legislation against racial and sexual discrimination, but our law is deficient in that unfair discrimination on grounds of handicap is not yet outlawed. This is yet another area in which our laws for disabled people lag behind the standards of modern legal systems.

In Canada discrimination on grounds of mental or physical disability is unlawful under the Federal Human Rights Act 1977 and under provincial legislation in almost every province. Such discrimination is unlawful on the part of those who provide goods, services and accommodation, those who provide employment, education and training, and others. The definitions of mental and physical disability are very wide. Discrimination is not unlawful if it can be shown to be justified. The methods of deciding what is justified vary. The Manitoba Human Rights Act allows discrimination when it can be shown that there is "reasonable cause" for it. If there is a dispute, the person who discriminated has to prove that he had "reasonable cause", and it is for the courts to decide whether his reason amounted to a "reasonable cause". On the other hand, under the New Brunswick Human Rights code discrimination is only allowed "if based upon a *bona fide* occupational qualification as determined by the Commission". Unless the Commission on Human Rights has made such a determination, the discrimination is unfair.

In Australia, the *United Nations Declaration on the Rights of Mentally Retarded Persons* and the *United Nations Declaration of the Rights of Disabled People* are incorporated into federal law as schedules to the Federal Human Rights and Equal Opportunity Act 1986. Complaints of infringement of rights because of mental or physical disabilities are dealt with by the Federal Human Rights and Equal Opportunity Commission. Two states also have their own legislation prohibiting discrimination against mentally or physically disabled people. The New South Wales Anti-Discrimination Act 1977 prohibits discrimination on grounds of physical and intellectual impairment, and in Victoria the Equal Opportunity Act 1984 prohibits discrimination on grounds of "impairment", including physical impairment, mental illness and mental retardation.

In the United States there is a considerable amount of legislation at federal and state level outlawing disability discrimination.

In the United Kingdom there is no general prohibition of such discrimination. The law of special educational needs does attempt to ensure that pupils with special needs, including disabilities, do receive the "adequate and efficient" education to which all are entitled. In employment, the Disabled Persons (Employment) Acts 1944 and 1958 require certain employers to employ specified quotas of disabled persons – an attempt at positive discrimination – but there is criticism of the ease with which employers can obtain exemption certificates. In 1988 over three-quarters of employers within the scope of the quota scheme failed to employ the minimum quota of disabled people. We have nothing to help disabled people who are discriminated against in other ways – particularly in the provision of goods, facilities, services of all kinds, accommodation and so forth.

Legislation against disability discrimination would fit in well with existing UK legislation against racial and sexual discrimination. The Race Relations Act 1976 outlaws racial discrimination in relation to employment, education, and the provision of goods, facilities and services, training, selling or letting most premises, and (in some circumstances) private clubs. The Commission for Racial Equality has duties which include overseeing the working of the legislation, and working towards the elimination of racial discrimination.

The Sex Discrimination Act 1975 (as amended by other legislation including the Sex Discrimination Act 1986) outlaws sexual discrimination in relation to employment, education, training, and the provision of goods, facilities, services and premises. The Equal Opportunities Commission has duties which include overseeing the working of the legislation, working towards the elimination of sexual discrimination, and promoting equality of opportunity between men and women.

A similar pattern should be followed in legislation to outlaw disability discrimination.

In the meantime, is any remedy at all available to the family who were turned away from the restaurant in such a repugnant manner? It is possible that they could claim damages on grounds of verbal injury, the hurt caused to their feelings being as worthy of compensation as

157

physical injury caused by assault. In the case of licensed premises, they might seek to oppose renewal of the licence. It is not easy for people discriminated against in such ways to make public their hurt, but if they can do so, then even if they do not succeed in obtaining any specific remedy, they will draw attention to this shameful gap in our law, and the need for adequate legislation against discrimination on grounds of disability.

Deprivation and Abuse

One of the major issues of the late 1980's has been concern about child-abuse. That concern has not yet been extended adequately to other categories of people vulnerable to deprivation and abuse. In the case of people with mental handicaps, it is an equally serious issue. Some people with mental handicaps are more vulnerable even than children. They may be even less well able to tell someone what is happening, or even to comprehend what is happening, or comprehend that their circumstances could and should be improved, and that this could be achieved by trying to let someone know. Moreover, their inabilities to comprehend and communicate may be lifelong; as may be the deprivation or abuse.

For mentally handicapped people in the community, the situation is broadly similar to that for children. Most families and other carers are conscientious and loving. Indeed very many carers look after mentally handicapped people admirably and with dedication. Some are well motivated but may need a little guidance or help. But – just as with children – there are some highly unsatisfactory home situations. Deprivation does occur, as does abuse.

If this topic is discussed with staff of adult training centres, almost all will be able to give an instance of at least one case at their own centre which worries them, and where they are concerned about at least the possibility of deprivation or abuse. Professionals working with children are trained and encouraged to be alert to signs of deprivation or abuse, and are well informed about what to do in such cases. Those working with mentally handicapped people should be in the same position, but it seems that they are not. Often staff are alert to problems, but seem to feel powerless to do anything. Adequate channels for communication and action do not seem to exist. One class on an in-service course wrote case histories. These are typical:

(1) A is in her mid-twenties, and lives at home with her parents. Her parents take all of her benefit and attendance money, and she never sees a penny of it. She never has new clothes, always wearing others' cast-offs. One morning she arrived at the centre with a black eye. She told staff that her mother did it because she had broken a cup. She is

normally truthful, and staff believed her. Staff approached their manager for guidance. The manager said that as the alleged incident happened at home, nothing could be done. Staff were not aware of any procedure which they could follow to try to help A, or whom they could have contacted.

(2) B, also in her mid-twenties, lives in a household dominated by her father. She is capable of signing for her own benefit, but is not allowed to do so. Her father keeps all her benefit, and gives her 20p. per day. Most of her clothing is "hand-me-downs". At home she has to sit quietly and watch television until 8 o'clock. She is not allowed to choose any television programmes: father says they are of no value to her anyway. She is sent to bed at 8 o'clock: father says that she is a pest if allowed to stay up longer.

These are not cases where severe injuries or sexual abuse have been inflicted – though such things do sometimes occur. They are however cases where people's quality of life and potential for development and self-fulfilment, already limited by handicap, are further restricted by unsatisfactory home regimes.

The main need is not a change in the law, but greater awareness of these problems, and the will and resources to tackle them. Social work departments can intervene, informally and persuasively. As a last resort they can use statutory guardianship. Where there is evidence that crimes or offences may have been committed, that evidence can be reported to the police.

The Mental Welfare Commission have an important role in such matters. They are in a position to encourage the establishment of improved procedures. They have also asked that they be given details of any individual cases which should be investigated. The Mental Welfare Commission have a very broad remit. Their general duty is "to exercise protective functions in respect of persons who may, by reason of mental disorder, be incapable of adequately protecting their persons or their interests" (Mental Health (Scotland) Act 1984, section 3(1)). This general duty applies to mentally handicapped and mentally ill people everywhere, not just those in institutions. The Commission do have specific responsibilities in relation to people in institutions, but as the emphasis shifts from institutional care to care in the community, the Commission face an ever-growing need to exercise their protective functions in relation to people in the community.

Investigation of Non-Accidental Injury

A child arrived at school from a residential facility with injuries which were clearly non-accidental. It was very unlikely that staff at the residential facility could have failed to see the injuries in the course of dressing and getting ready for school. The injuries could have been caused by another child in the residential facility, but adequate supervision should have prevented such an incident. Those responsible for the facility attempted to dispose of the matter at a low-key case conference, at which the parents' desire for a proper investigation to try to establish what had happened was dismissed. Eventually senior local authority personnel were appointed to investigate. The parents co-operated on the basis of a verbal assurance that they would see the eventual report. They were shown selected extracts from the report only, and refused sight of a full copy. They had wanted to avoid causing unnecessary damage to the confidence of other parents in the residential facility, but they did want to find out what had happened to their child. They wanted to be sure that any criminal conduct or fault on the part of staff was identified, and that any organisational deficiencies were remedied. They were left knowing some of the results of the investigation, and knowing that other results had been withheld from them. They were left without sufficient information to have confidence that the investigation had been full and adequate. They were left with unanswered questions in their minds.

Advice to any parents who face such a situation in the future has to be clearcut. If there is evidence that a crime or offence may have been committed, insist that the matter be reported to the police promptly. Report it yourselves, if no-one else does so. Unless it is clear that a police investigation will dispose of the matter satisfactorily, report the matter to the Mental Welfare Commission. The Commission has a duty to make enquiry into any case of apparent ill-treatment of a mentally handicapped or mentally ill person. They must also make enquiry into any case of apparent deficiency in care or treatment, or of improper detention (or of risk of loss or damage to property because of the owner's mental handicap or mental illness). Such an enquiry can be carried out by an individual member of the Commission, or a committee of members, or an experienced lawyer appointed for the purpose, or a committee of members of the Commission chaired by an experienced lawyer. Such enquiries can exercise the powers and privileges of a court of law: witnesses can be compelled to attend and give evidence, and can be put on oath.

The Mental Welfare Commission's duty to enquire, and the provisions in relation to enquiries, are not limited to people in institutions. They apply in all cases of apparent ill-treatment, deficient care or treatment, and so forth. This is one of the jobs which the Commission exists to do, just as it is the function of the police to investigate crimes and offences. Parents should be suspicious of suggestions that some other method of enquiry should be used. It is unlikely that the purpose of such a suggestion is to ensure that a rigorous and independent investigation takes place. When serious complaints arise, there is a strong tendency for those close to the situation – whether implicated or not – to react defensively, and anyone else in the same organisation, or even the same profession, may tend to identify with colleagues rather than with handicapped people and their families.

Involvement of lawyers in such matters is sometimes resented. Lawyers can indeed be uncomfortable people to have around, but they do have an important function. When others are moving comfortably towards a consensus, lawyers have an awkward habit of highlighting facts inconsistent with the consensus view. They tend to take nothing for granted, to challenge assertions which may seem reasonable enough to others, and to pursue rigorously any questions which they feel have not been fully and adequately answered. Lawyers are trained and encouraged in these characteristics: they are a major safeguard against injustice. It was in the absence of any adequate legal input into decision-making that in Cleveland major decisions with serious impact on whole families could be made on the basis of no more than a doctor's "diagnosis".

XVI

SCOTS LAW AND THE MENTALLY HANDICAPPED
– UPDATE

There have been relatively few significant changes in the existing law as it was described in *Scots Law and the Mentally Handicapped*. More noteworthy has been the development of new areas of law – such as tutor-dative procedure and the Disabled Persons Act. However, there have been some changes, and this chapter mentions the main ones. It also cross-references to *Scots Law and the Mentally Handicapped* developments described elsewhere in this book. In addition, I have mentioned some areas where reform may take place. Headings refer to chapters, and numbers in the lefthand margin to pages, in *Scots Law and the Mentally Handicapped*. References in the body of the text are to this book.

Chapter I

p5 para 11   The Mental Health (Scotland) Act 1984 is now in force. It comprises the Mental Health (Scotland) Act 1960, as amended by the Mental Health (Amendment) (Scotland) Act 1983.

Chapter II

p6   The trend of reforms proposed by the Scottish Law Commission is towards a two-tier system of age categories, namely those below and above 16, with some special provisions for young people aged 16 to 18.

Chapter IV

pp10-12   In general, the status of legitimacy or illegitimacy no longer has legal significance, under the Law Reform (Parent and Child) (Scotland) Act 1986. However, while a mother has parental rights regardless of whether she is married to the father, the father only has parental rights if he was married to the mother at the time of conception, or if he marries her subsequently, or if he obtains a court order granting him parental rights.

p12   Under the same Act of 1986, the court can be asked to make an order about custody and access in relation to children up to age 16, and other parental rights in relation to children up to age 18. The court can be asked to do this by anyone "claiming interest" – not limited to parents or even to other relatives. The court has power to make "such order relating to parental rights as it thinks fit". The whole range of matters coming within the ambit of parental rights is covered. (The Court of Session can deal with custody up to age 18.)

These provisions of the 1986 Act apply to all children, handicapped or not.

Chapter V

pp22-23 The common law procedure to appoint a tutor has been revived. See Chapters III-VI.

Chapter VI

There has been no change in the statutory provisions described in this chapter, but on 25th May 1988 the House of Lords made an important decision about whether doctors have a common law power to detain mentally handicapped people, over and above the statutory powers under mental health legislation. The case is reported as *B -v- Forsey*. After a violent
p29 incident Mr B was detained under 72-hour emergency
p30 detention procedure, and then under 28-day short-term detention. Towards the end of the 28 days, he seemed to be much improved. It was decided to transfer him to an open ward. It seemed unnecessary to proceed
p30 to detention under the "normal procedure". His condition then deteriorated suddenly and he became potentially very dangerous. "Normal procedure" was initiated, but there was a gap of some three weeks between expiry of the short-term detention and approval by the Sheriff of the application under normal procedure.

The doctors tried to cover the three-week gap by making a further emergency recommendation followed by further short-term detention, but that was clearly
p30 incompetent. Short-term detention cannot be followed by either 72-hour emergency detention or another 28-day short-term detention.

The argument centred on whether in the circumstances the doctors and health board were entitled at common law to have detained Mr B during the three-week gap in statutory cover for his detention. The decision of the court was this. At common law a private individual can in a situation of necessity detain a person of unsound mind who is a danger to himself or others. The private individual can only do this for as long as is necessary to hand over the mentally disordered person to a proper authority. However, in the case of health boards (and doctors acting as their officers) this common law power is replaced by the statutory provisions. Health boards and their doctors have only the statutory powers described in Chapter VI of *Scots Law and the Mentally Handicapped*, and not the common law powers of a private individual to act in an emergency.

Chapter VIII

In a case reported in 1986, the court confirmed that only a single individual can be a curator bonis. A limited company cannot. See pages 109-110.

p42   The current limit is £3,000 for total value of money and valuables held by hospital management, beyond which limit approval of the Mental Welfare Commission must be sought.

On management of affairs generally, see Chapters X and XI.

Chapter IX

p51   Section 96 of the 1960 Act is now replaced by Section 106 of the Mental Health (Scotland) Act 1984. The new definition of women protected is given on page 78, and this section is discussed in detail in Chapter IX.

p54   The section numbers in the righthand column correctly identify the relevant sections in the Mental Health (Scotland) Act 1984.

Chapter XII

pp59-60   The common law maintenance obligations of relatives, as described here, have been replaced by the provisions of the Family Law (Scotland) Act 1985. Husbands and wives now have an equal obligation to aliment each other. They must provide such support as is reasonable in the circumstances.

Fathers and mothers – whether married to each other or not – have an obligation to aliment their children. A person such as a step-parent who accepts a child as a child of the family also has an obligation to aliment that child. The obligation covers all children up to the age of 18. It also extends to children up to 25 who are reasonably and appropriately undergoing instruction at an educational establishment, or training for employment or for a trade, profession or vocation. These provisions may be difficult to interpret in relation to some mentally handicapped people in the 18-25 age group. Unless they do come within the definition – probably, most will not – the parents' obligation to aliment will cease at 18.

All other common law obligations to aliment are swept away. The obligation no longer goes up (or down) the family tree. The parental obligation ceases at 18, except for the special provisions for some 18-25 year olds.

p60   Court actions regulating aliment are now governed by the same Act of 1985. A parent with custody can now claim aliment for children up to 18.

Chapter XIII

For changes in the law of special educational needs, see Chapter XIV

Chapter XV

Generally, see Chapter XI.

p79   The Scottish Law Commission are likely to recommend changes in the law of succession.

Chapter XVI

pp83-86   Legal rights: These may be changed as the result of recommendations by the Scottish Law Commission (see above).

The new rules for Income Support, which has replaced Supplementary Benefit, remove some of the problems with discretionary trusts. See pages 117-118.

Inheritance Tax replaced Capital Transfer Tax in 1986. This tax is charged on death. Lifetime gifts are not charged unless the donor dies within seven years. Gifts during the period of seven years prior to death are aggregated with the estate passing on death. Gifts within three years of death are charged at the same rate as on death, and there is a sliding scale of rates for gifts from three to seven years prior to death. The minimum figure below which tax is not payable is £118,000 for the tax year 1989-90. On cumulative transfers above that level, there is a single flat rate charge of 40% on death, subject to various exemptions and reliefs.

Chapter XVIII

Legal Aid and Legal Advice and Assistance

p105   Civil Legal Aid, Criminal Legal Aid and Legal Advice and Assistance are now administered by the Scottish Legal Aid Board. In many types of criminal case it is now granted by the Board, rather than by the court. Assistance by way of representation ("ABWOR") has been introduced to give limited representation in summary criminal proceedings, though it could be extended to other courts and tribunals. It is granted in the same simple way as Legal Advice and Assistance – the solicitor and client complete a form together, and the solicitor makes the assessment there and then.

p106   The £5 diagnostic interview has been discontinued, but some solicitors will give a free initial interview (or may quote a reduced fixed cost for an initial interview).

p106   Due to problems and restrictions with the administration of Legal Aid and Legal Advice and Assistance, they are not quite so fully available from so many solicitors as was the case when *Scots Law and the Mentally Handicapped* was written.

Appendix I

p129   See up-to-date information in Appendix II.

XVII

DEVELOPMENT AND REFORM OF SCOTS LAW

I have sought to trace the development of selected areas of law of major importance for people with mental handicaps. I have sought also to describe how the law now stands in those areas, and to identify directions of likely and possible future development.

So long as Scotland has its own legal system, the story of development will never come to a close. It is a well-known technique of writers of serials to end an episode with much unresolved, but with strong hints that the story is at the threshold of major and exciting developments, which could provide a resolution of the major tensions and problems which have developed. Only a brave or foolish writer would take his readers to such a point, then lay down his pen and tell them that they themselves must create the next episode. That however is what I must do. Significant development of existing law by our lawyers and judges is already under way. Major statutory reform by Parliament is, I believe, now a realistic prospect ahead. If the process of development and reform is to respond accurately and successfully to the needs of people with mental handicaps, one ingredient above all others is essential in that process. That vital ingredient is the accumulated experience, opinions and wisdom of everyone in our society with experience of mental handicap and concerned with the welfare of people with mental handicaps; particularly those whose interest and concern is such as to lead them to read a book such as this. If the opportunities of the next episode in the development of our law are not to be squandered or lost, then you, reader, must help to write it.

Parents, carers, voluntary workers and professionals are already articulating the needs and providing the impetus for the recent development of tutor-dative procedure as a way of meeting modern needs for personal guardianship of adults with mental handicaps. They must continue to contribute to this process. They have the best knowledge of the needs which require to be met, and are therefore best placed to ensure that future developments are attuned to those needs. Likewise, the growing chorus of protest at the lack of suitable provision in our law in the area of management of affairs is creating a growing pressure for improvement. I have suggested that it may be possible to achieve some improvement by development and modernisation of curator bonis procedure similar to recent developments in relation to tutors-dative. I have also suggested the revival and modernisation of the tutor-dative as a manager of affairs as well as a personal guardian. Existing law may provide some remedies in some cases of discrimination on grounds of handicap: only those who encounter such discrimination can initiate possible development of remedies. Only substantial public pressure is likely to cause the remaining provisions of the Disabled Persons Act to be brought into force, and there should be wide involvement in the formulation of regulations and the development of the practical working of the Act's provisions. In the particular areas of medical consent and sexuality, there has been development and clarification of the law, and further development is likely. Public pressure is likely to be required to achieve an adequate response to the problems of deprivation and abuse, within the framework of existing legal provision. It is no help to the victims of such problems if protection exists only on the printed page of statute, and is not translated into effective procedures and action.

The further development of these themes is of course a predictable sequel to the story which I have already told. However, it cannot be stressed too often that even if the courts were to permit inventive development of the existing law to the maximum possible extent, that is in no way a substitute for comprehensive law reform. Such development of existing law is at best a stop-gap to ameliorate some of the serious problems of the present situation; and it does give us some limited experience of the application in Scottish conditions of some of the principles which one would wish to see embodied in any new statutory code.

At last, the prospect of such major law reform is on the horizon. The Scottish Law Commission is likely in the near future to institute the process of consultation which could lead to major law reform by Parliament in most of the main areas of law considered in this book. This is likely to be the dominant theme of the next episode of our story. It is in this process of discussion and consultation that the contributions of parents, carers, voluntary workers, professionals and others is likely to be of even more vital importance.

Such law reform will not deal only with people with mental handicaps. It will deal with the whole area of mental disability. It will seek to establish suitable provision not only for those whose legal capacity is impaired by reason of mental handicaps, but also those whose disabilities are a result of all forms of mental illness, conditions associated with ageing, multiple sensory handicap and inability to communicate, and so forth. The common factor will be the impairment of legal capacity. The causes will vary largely – just as within individual general categories such as mental handicap and mental illness there is also large variation. It will not be easy for such a statutory code to meet fully and adequately the needs of all the various situations which it will seek to cover. Those concerned with each category of disability will require to participate in consultation and to scrutinise proposals, to ensure that any eventual legislation does provide a fully satisfactory solution to needs within that category. Those concerned with mental handicap, and all the many types and degrees of mental handicap, must do this. Otherwise, there is a significant risk that legislation will again treat mental handicap as if it is substantially akin to mental illness, or – perhaps – as if it is simply a form of life-long senility.

Pressure for reform of mental disability law has been growing, even while this book has been in course of preparation. In December 1988, the Rights and Legal Protection Sub-Committee of Scottish Action on Dementia published a discussion paper entitled *Dementia and the Law: The Challenge Ahead*. In January 1989, the English Law Society's Mental Health Sub-Committee produced a discussion document on *Decision-making and Mental Incapacity*. The Law Society of Scotland is contemplating a similar review.

The Scottish Action on Dementia Proposals

The Scottish Action on Dementia document should be read by anyone seriously interested in other areas of mental disability law. For those concerned with mental handicap, it contains much that is familiar, though its viewpoint is of course the different one of people suffering from dementia. In just forty clearly written pages it summarises relevant areas of existing law and outlines specific proposals for a possible statutory code. The proposals take as their model the existing system of Children's Hearings (which I described briefly on pages 14 and 15 of *Scots Law and the Mentally Handicapped*). They suggest the parallel establishment of Mental Health Panels of members of the public selected and trained for service on Mental Health Hearings. They suggest that the skills of persons with legal, medical or social work qualifications would not necessarily be required. Cases would be brought before the Panels by a Reporter.

It is suggested that the Mental Health Hearings should have a wide range of powers, including ordering supervision by social work departments; consenting to medical treatment; ordering that a person should reside in a residential home, hospital or other specified place; making necessary orders in relation to the management of affairs; powers to order detention; powers to appoint a curator, who would preferably be a relative or carer; and powers to appoint a "welfare guardian" who would normally be a relative or social worker, and who could also be curator.

Some parents of mentally handicapped people may be alarmed by some of the proposed powers, but the proposals do contain many essential ingredients, including a code for personal guardianship and management of affairs. It must be remembered that the starting point for these proposals is the situation of elderly people whose legal capacity has been impaired by age. Accordingly, they do not address concerns such as those of parents worrying about what regime may be imposed upon their mentally handicapped child after they themselves have gone, or are no longer able to cope. Many people concerned with mental handicap will be more interested in provision of social work facilities – such as places at adult training centres – rather than the ordering of social work supervision, yet we discussed in Chapter XV (under "Deprivation and Abuse", pages 158-159) situations where the ability to order social work supervision could be a valuable power. Problems of decision-making in relation to sexuality will require to be addressed in any comprehensive law reform, but it is understandable that this topic was not addressed by those concerned with the elderly. Moreover, one trusts that the inappropriate words "mental health" will at last be excised from statutory use in relation to intellectual disabilities other than mental illness.

Given that law reform will almost certainly seek to cover the whole field of mental disability, it is important that those whose main interest is mental handicap should understand the concerns and views of those representing other types of disability, should form a picture of the areas of common concern, and should be alert to the particular requirements of mental handicap which may be less significant, or not significant, in other areas, and which may therefore require to be particularly explained and safeguarded.

Any law reform will require to deal with the mechanism by which remedies are delivered, as well as the remedies themselves. From the point of view of mental handicap, the use of a system akin to Children's Hearings may at first sight seem rather inappropriate. There is perhaps a symmetry in having Children's Hearings to deal with problems in childhood, and a similar system to deal with problems of old age. Mentally handicapped people do sometimes require crisis-management, but the fundamental need is not for a system of intervention in crisis, but for adequate ongoing – often lifelong – provision. I pointed out in Chapter II ("Fundamental Issues") that even if the law's special treatment of an individual is accurately matched to his needs and capacity, such differentiation is nevertheless a form of discrimination, depriving him of some of the rights and legal status which the rest of us have. These are major steps, with lifelong significance. Most jurisdictions find it appropriate to entrust such decisions to courts of law, albeit courts with special jurisdiction and experience in family and personal matters. Those concerned with mentally handicapped people would probably require a degree of persuasion that such decisions should not be taken with the authority, legal expertise and independence of a court of law.

Moreover, I have already expressed my reservations about the tendency to try to meet needs in relation to adult mentally disabled people by importing provisions from child law. As we have seen, this has already happened in legislation as far apart as 1585 and 1913. One must question whether such a step betrays inappropriate paternalism, and a denial of adulthood, taking us away from rather than towards normalisation.

On the other hand, it is better if possible to base reform upon experience, rather than upon untested theory. That is why I point to the value, for these purposes, of developing our existing common law as best we can, rather than simply waiting for reform. We do have experience of the operation in Scottish conditions of the Children's Hearing system: it works well. Of more direct relevance is the expertise and experience which is being built up by mental health officers, but they are not mentioned in the Scottish Action on Dementia paper. If one is to look to child law, then perhaps the most relevant area of experience is that which has been built up in relation to special educational needs, where we have an assessment system designed to ensure that individual needs are identified and met, so that children with special needs do not fail to receive the overall standard of provision to which all children are entitled, namely an adequate and efficient education. This is a system closer in its basic principles to the long-term needs of adults with permanent mental disabilities, than are the principles governing the Children's Hearings structure.

An interesting point, not mentioned in the Scottish Action on Dementia paper, is that if children who are alleged to have committed offences are brought before Children's Hearings, that takes them out of the criminal law system. If a system of Hearings for the mentally disabled was established, should they in the same way take out of the normal criminal system mentally disabled people who get into trouble with the police? In some cases, that may resolve problems of inappropriate use of criminal law procedures. In other cases, it may be better in the long term for some mentally handicapped people to know that they will have to face up to the consequences of their actions in the same way as anyone else.

One fears that, in practice, a system akin to Children's Hearings would prove to be unworkable, in that it would run into the same resistance from families as did old-style statutory guardianship. A

171

Reporter with the function of bringing cases before special Hearings would find it difficult to avoid an interventionist image which would be the antithesis of normalisation. There would be a risk that the provisions would be seen as removing mentally handicapped people into some special category, rather than fulfilling the fundamental requirement of making the minimum necessary adjustments to allow them to live as normally as possible, and to give a legal basis to such adjustments as are necessary.

These objectives are not easy to achieve. In Chapter XII, I described the new regime in New Zealand as being eminently worthy of serious consideration in the context of reform of our law. However, even supporters of this well thought out, modern statutory code have expressed reservations, such as the following comment from a member of New Zealand's Task Force on Mental Health Law Reform:

> This type of legislation is always a two-edged thing. It can be used to "enable" people to live to the full; but it may also be used too widely, or with too much paternalism, or oppressively.

This is strongly reminiscent of the criticisms of our modern use of tutor-dative procedure here in Scotland, as I described them on pages 53-54. If such concerns are to be minimised, then in my view we must do more than simply translate the Children's Hearings model into adult mental disability law. We must also do more than simply import uncritically the best foreign model which we can find.

Law Reform — Provision for People with a Mental Handicap

My purpose in this chapter is to stimulate input into the process of law reform from all who read it. The formulation of detailed proposals should follow such input, not precede it. Accordingly, I have not attempted to play the role of architect or draftsman of a possible code of law. So far as law reform is concerned, my contribution in this book is closer to that of the builder's merchant. I have set out a range of materials, which should be considered in preparing the brief, and from which the architects and draftsmen may care to select. Some have been quarried from our own common law, and others have been imported. They should not be used simply because they exist, or simply because others have used them, but only if they meet our needs. They may require to be adapted. They must certainly be integrated into a cohesive structure.

The structure must be planned and built with care. Not only will it serve a very important function, but also we and our descendants will probably have to live within it for a very long time. In the key areas of personal guardianship and management of affairs the last significant law reforms by Parliament were the introduction of statutory guardianship in 1913 and the reform of the law in relation to curators bonis (and other judicial factors) in 1849. The reforms now needed will be wider-ranging than either of those. If we create a new code in the 1990's, we must think in terms of a century or more. We simply cannot afford to get it wrong. We cannot afford to omit anything or overlook anything. We must meet all present needs and any predictable future needs. We must try to give room to adapt to future needs which cannot be exactly predicted, without having to dismantle and rebuild.

The Nature of Legal Incapacity

So far as I can ascertain, there has been little or no adequate research into one question which is of considerable significance in relation to any reform of mental disability law. What are the skills and abilities which are needed to have full legal capacity? What is the nature of the impairment of those skills which impairs legal capacity? How can we best assess such impairment, and relate the results to specific modifications in legal capacity?

It is interesting to note that it has been considered possible to review child law without such information in relation to children. Discussion of the age at which children should have full legal capacity, or the ages at which they should have lesser degrees of legal capacity, has proceeded without any data as to how and when children develop the skills and abilities needed for such levels of legal capacity. Even if we knew that the "average" or "normal" child of a given age has a particular level of such skills and abilities, we would also need to know the degree of divergence from that norm.

I am told that these questions would open up a large and mostly untrodden field for psychological and statistical research. However, projects to assess statistically the abilities, disabilities, problems and other characteristics of people identified as having mental handicaps have included study of characteristics which lawyers would identify as relevant to legal capacity. Notably, in 1987 the Information Services Division of the Scottish Health Service produced a report entitled *The Balance of Care for Adults with a Mental Handicap in Scotland*, by Nicki Baker and James Urquhart. Their research instrument included the questions set out overleaf. Such questions would elicit information about certain everyday situations in which legal capacity would be relevant, at levels of skill and ability which would be at the borderline of their capacity for many mentally handicapped people.

A study of legal capacity from a psychological and statistical point of view would provide useful hard information relevant to the reform of the law. It would also provide methods of assessment for future use in

MONEY HANDLING

11.	Is able to use money **and** knows approximately what change to expect from £1 when buying a single item	1.	Yes
		2.	No

SHOPPING

12.	When wanting to buy simple items such as a packet of biscuits or cigarettes. . . .	1. . could manage this unaided
		2. . could manage with help/direction
		3. . could not manage at all

"Managing unaided" means someone who would be able to go to an appropriate shop, where he/she is <u>not</u> known, would be able to make his/her wants known (without a note), and tender appropriate money. Assume that getting to the shop is not a problem.

BUDGETING

13.	Is able to plan expenditure so that, for example: money normally lasts until the end of the week or he/she will put money aside towards a special item such as clothes, an outing or a holiday	1. . unaided
		2. . with help or direction
		3. . not at all

Fig. 2: From *The Balance of Care* (pp 124-125)

individual cases. Legal provision and procedures would then be based on a better knowledge of need, and would be geared to the assessment procedures which would be used. If it is not practicable for such research to be carried out for the purposes of law reform, then any new code must be designed to accommodate progressive development and improvement of assessment techniques.

Fundamental Principles

As to the fundamental principles which should underlie any new statutory code, these were set out in the last paragraph of Chapter II. The law must not deal with mentally handicapped people on the basis that they *are* problems. They may *have* problems, or particular needs. They are a normal group in any population. They are not some separate and distinct group. Their individual capabilities range through imperceptible degrees from those who have no significant handicap at all to those who are most profoundly handicapped. At some point along that continuum impairment of legal capacity begins to become significant. The entitlement of 'all, however handicapped, to human dignity and to basic human rights is no less than anyone else's. The care with which that dignity and those rights must be safeguarded increases with the degree of incapacity. The purpose of special legal provision is not to shunt them off into some separate category of citizens. The purpose is to make the minimum adjustments necessitated by their handicaps to bring the effective level and quality of their status, dignity and rights back to that of other citizens, so far as ever possible.

In seeking input in the process of law reform from parents, carers, voluntary workers, professionals, and so on, one seeks to hear what would be the voice of mentally handicapped people themselves, if they could formulate and communicate their own needs and views. Sometimes, some of them can do this. We may not hear ideas for specific statutory provisions, but we may be reminded of their basic purpose.

It is fitting that the last words of this book should be not mine, but those of a person with a mental handicap. They remind us of the human significance of our concern that to protect is also to restrict. From the point of view of mentally handicapped people, they are relevant to every topic considered in this book. I was talking to a young lady who had a curator bonis. Using her own words, and with no prompting other than general discussion of the management of her affairs, she said this: "I think it hurts inside you, not to be independent".

175

GLOSSARY

The definitions and explanations given below are simplified. They are designed to aid understanding of these terms as they are used in this book.

Terms which appear in quotation marks are the author's own terms, as used in this book, and do not necessarily have general currency.

Legal terms are terms of Scots law unless otherwise indicated.

For references to text, see Index.

The 1913 Act:	The Mental Deficiency and Lunacy (Scotland) Act, 1913.
The 1960 Act:	The Mental Health (Scotland) Act, 1960.
The 1984 Act:	The Mental Health (Scotland) Act 1984.
Accountant of Court:	An official whose duties include the supervision of curators bonis.
Acts of Sederunt:	Regulations made by the Court of Session governing court business and civil procedure.
Adult:	A person aged 18 or over.
Agnate:	Father or other male relative on father's side.
Alternate Guardian:	(Canada) Someone who takes over automatically upon resignation, incapacity or death of a personal guardian.
Child, Children:	Person under the age of 18. In places, "child" and "children" refer to offspring of any age.
Children's Hearing:	Children up to age 16 may be brought before a Children's Hearing if one of a list of "grounds of referral" exists. Children put under supervision before they are 16 remain under the jurisdiction of the Children's Hearing until they are 18. In cases of dispute, the Sheriff decides whether there is a ground of referral, and if so sends the case back to the Children's Hearing to

deal with it. The powers of a Children's Hearing include: sending the child to an assessment centre; putting the child under the supervision of a social worker; putting the child into certain kinds of homes and schools; making other voluntary arrangements; or simply taking no action. If a Children's Hearing thinks that the child is seriously mentally disturbed or handicapped, it is possible for the child to be sent to hospital, but this must be done by the Sheriff, rather than by the Children's Hearing itself.

Choses in action:

(England, and some North American jurisdictions) Property rights of an intangible nature, such as shares, claims under insurance policies, entitlements under wills and trusts, and so forth.

Civil Law:

All areas of law other than criminal law.

Common Law:

Law from sources other than Acts of Parliament. The main such source comprises principles of long standing as developed, explained and applied by the courts in their decisions.

Conservator:

(United States) A manager of affairs.

Court of Protection:

(England) A court which deals with the property of mentally disabled people.

Court of Session:

The supreme civil court in Scotland. The court is divided into an Outer House and an Inner House. Judges sit singly in the Outer House, hearing almost all kinds of civil cases. A bench of at least three judges sits in the Inner House. The Inner House is mainly an appeal court, hearing appeals from the Outer House, the Sheriff Courts, and elsewhere. Under certain conditions, there is a further appeal from the Inner House of the Court of Session to the House of Lords. The Inner House of the Court of Session is also the first court to hear certain special cases and

177

	petitions. The Court of Session sits only in Edinburgh.
Criminal Law:	The area of law concerned with crimes.
Criminal Responsibility:	Responsibility for commission of a crime, established by prosecution before a criminal court, and liable to result in punishment by the state. This phrase can also mean the mental capacity to have such responsibility.
Crown Office:	The office of the Lord Advocate (q.v.).
Curator:	One who looks after the property, business and affairs of minor children or of adults who lack legal capacity. May be appointed to look after affairs generally, or with a specific remit limited to one particular matter (such as a civil court action).
Curator Bonis:	Person appointed by the court to manage all the property, business and affairs of an adult who is unable to do so.
Developmentally Disabled:	(United States) Mentally handicapped.
Disabled Person:	A chronically sick or disabled person, or a person suffering from a mental disorder who comes within the provisions of social work legislation.
"Disabled Persons Act":	The Disabled Persons (Services, Consultation and Representation) Act 1986.
Discretionary Trust:	(a) A trust in which the trustees have a discretion to make payments from the capital of the trust funds.
	(b) A trust in which the trustees have a discretion as to how income should be allocated.
Executor:	The person responsible for winding up the estate and affairs of a person who has died. If the deceased left a Will, the executor (or executors) will usually be appointed in the Will. Failing an executor appointed by Will, the court has power to appoint an executor.

Facility and Circumvention:	Taking unfair advantage of someone in order to cause them to take detrimental action or enter some detrimental transaction. The person must have some condition making him liable to be intimidated, misled or imposed upon. In such circumstances, the action or transaction may be declared invalid.
Fatuous:	(Historical) Having a serious mental handicap, probably equating to severe or profound mental handicap.
"Full Guardian":	A guardian whose powers are not limited.
Furious:	(Historical) Suffering from serious mental illness, generally including propensity to violence.
Future Needs Assessment:	An assessment of school children who have a Record of Needs, carried out in about the second-last year of compulsory schooling. The assessment is carried out by the education authority, but includes an input from the social work department as to whether the child is a "disabled person" (q.v.). The assessment results in a recommendation as to whether the child should stay on at school until 18. If the child is a "disabled person", the social work authority must carry out a further assessment as to the child's needs under the "welfare enactments" (q.v.).
Guardian:	In relation to children, the person having care and control of a child under 16. Otherwise, see "Personal Guardian" and "Statutory Guardian".
House of Lords:	The final court of appeal for civil cases from both Scottish and English courts (and for criminal cases from the English courts).
Idiot:	(Historical) Person with a mental handicap.
Incapax (plural Incapaces):	Person(s) with less than full legal capacity; person(s) whose affairs are managed by a curator bonis; adjective with same meaning.

179

Inheritance Tax:	A tax on capital passing on death, or within seven years prior to death. Also chargeable on certain trusts.
Insane:	An historical term for persons suffering from certain forms of serious mental illness, but in law used inaccurately (and still in use) for people with mental disabilities resulting from mental illness or mental handicap.
Insanity:	(In criminal law) Insanity in bar of trial means that the accused's mental condition at time of trial is such that the trial cannot proceed. Insanity as a defence means that the accused's mental state at the time of the alleged crime was such that he is not guilty even though he may have done what is alleged. A wholly inappropriate and outdated term still in legal use in relation to consequences of both mental illness and mental handicap.
Judicial Factor:	Person appointed by a court to manage fund(s) or asset(s).
Legal Advice and Assistance:	A form of legal aid for most matters other than court proceedings.
Legal Aid:	State assistance with the costs of court proceedings.
Legal Capacity:	The possession of full legal status, with personal freedom, ability to make personal decisions, ability to take and undertake legally valid actions and transactions, and having legal responsibility for obligations and wrongdoing. The adult with full capacity is the norm in our law.
Legal Incapacity:	Legal capacity (q.v.) can be reduced for several reasons, such as youth or mental disability. Anyone with less than full legal capacity has some degree of legal incapacity. The legal capacity to make personal decisions or to manage affairs may be reduced. Some actions and transactions may not have full legal validity. The person's level of legal responsibility may be reduced. Legal

180

incapacities may also be imposed by law on people such as bankrupts, prisoners and certain other offenders, aliens, and others. This book is not concerned with legal incapacities which are unrelated to personal capability.

Legal Rights: The entitlement of certain close relatives (husband, wife, children or their descendants) to share in the estates of persons who have died.

Limited Conservator: (United States) A manager of affairs with limited powers.

"Limited Guardian":   A personal guardian with limited powers.

Lord Advocate: The head of the system of public prosecution in Scotland. Also the senior adviser to the Government on all matters of Scots law, and the person who sues and is sued on behalf of the Crown and all Government departments and agencies.

Manager: (New Zealand) A person appointed to manage affairs (also used in this book as a general term with same meaning).

"Mental Disability":   A mental handicap, mental illness, or serious communication difficulty which impairs legal capacity.

"Mental Disability Law":   All law which applies or arises by reason of mental disability (comprising for the most part modifications of the general law, and special provisions, protections, responsibilities, restrictions, and so forth).

Mental Handicap: A handicap characterised by both intellectual functioning which is significantly below average and also marked impairment in ability to adapt to the cultural demands of society.

Mental Health: The converse of mental illness, but misleadingly used in the law in relation to mental handicap as well as mental illness.

181

Mental Health Officer:	An official employed by the local authority social work department (usually an experienced psychiatric social worker). He or she has various duties and functions under mental health legislation in relation to detention and statutory guardianship. These duties include a responsibility to set in motion detention or statutory guardianship proceedings when necessary, if the patient's nearest relative does not do so. The Mental Health Officer also has functions in relation to application, renewal, and discharge procedures; but no functions in relation to curator bonis and tutor-dative procedures.
Mental Illness:	A disturbance affecting emotional, social or cognitive functioning and behaviour.
Mental Welfare Commission:	The Mental Welfare Commission for Scotland, which protects the interests of those who are not able to protect themselves adequately because of mental handicap or mental illness. The Commission has supervisory duties and powers in relation to those in detention and statutory guardianship. It can set up official enquiries. It has several other functions in relation to the welfare and protection of mentally handicapped and mentally ill people.
Minor:	Girls from twelfth to eighteenth birthdays, boys from fourteenth to eighteenth birthdays.
Mitigation:	(Criminal Law) Where the accused is guilty, a plea in mitigation sets out extenuating circumstances and, if successful, will result in a reduced penalty.
Named Person:	The person to whom application may be made for advice and information about the special educational needs of a child who has a Record of Needs.

182

Natural Fool:	(Historical) Person with a mental handicap from birth.
Partial Guardian:	(Canada) A personal guardian with limited powers.
Partial Legal Capacity:	The possession of some legal capacity (q.v.), but not full legal capacity.
Patient:	A person receiving or needing medical or similar provision or treatment; but in legislation misleadingly applied to persons for whom special provision is made by reason of mental disability, even when such provision is not of a specifically medical nature.
"Personal Guardian":	A person appointed to act in a supervisory and decision-making role in relation to personal matters (as opposed to management of affairs). Personal guardians may have comprehensive powers or only specified limited powers.
Plenary Guardian:	(Canada) A personal guardian whose powers are not limited.
Private Law:	Most areas of law other than criminal law and the law governing the official actings of the state and public bodies.
Procurator Fiscal:	Each Sheriff Court district has a Procurator Fiscal. With his assistants and deputes, he is responsible for investigations which may result in criminal charges, for preparing cases for prosecution, and for conducting prosecutions in the Sheriff Court. Procurators Fiscal are appointed by the Lord Advocate (q.v.), and are subject to the Lord Advocate's instructions.
Public Law:	The law governing the official actings of the state and public bodies.
Pupil:	Girls from birth to twelfth birthday, boys from birth to fourteenth birthday.

Record of Needs:	A document prepared by an Education Authority about a child who has special educational needs which are pronounced, specific, or complex. Contains information including details of impairments, needs, and ways in which needs are to be met.
Retardation/ Retarded:	(United States and elsewhere) Mental handicap/mentally handicapped. Not used in United Kingdom.
Scottish Law Commission:	The body responsible for keeping the law under review, and for preparing programmes for systematic revision and reform of the law.
Security:	In relation to manager of affairs, a financial guarantee against loss caused by failure to act properly.
Sheriff:	The judge in a Sheriff Court (q.v.).
Sheriff Court:	The main court in Scotland below the Court of Session, dealing with a wide range of civil and criminal cases. Scotland is divided into six sheriffdoms, most of which are sub-divided into Sheriff Court districts, each served by its own Sheriff Court. Each sheriffdom has a Sheriff Principal, who can hear appeals in civil cases against the decisions of the other sheriffs in his sheriffdom.
Sheriff Principal:	(See "Sheriff Court")
Stand-by Guardian:	(United States) Someone who takes over automatically upon resignation, incapacity or death of a personal guardian.
Statement of Needs:	English equivalent (approximately) of Scottish Record of Needs (q.v.).
Statute Law:	Law created by Act of Parliament.
Statutory:	Adjective from statute law (q.v.).
"Statutory Guardian":	A guardian under the 1984 Act (q.v.), having certain powers to control place of residence, medical treatment and examination, training, etc.

Trust:	An arrangement in which the creator of the trust transfers assets or funds to one or more trustees. The trustees hold and administer those assets and funds, not for their own benefit, but for the benefit of one or more beneficiaries. The way in which the trustees do this is normally set out in the trust deed, but is also subject to various rules of law. The creator of the trust may create a trust to commence during his lifetime, or he may in his Will create a trust to commence on his death.
Trust Deed:	The document creating a trust.
Trust Fund:	The funds and assets held and administered by the trustees under a trust.
Trustee:	A person who holds and administers the trust fund under a trust. (Alberta) A manager of affairs appointed by the court.
Tutor:	(a) Person with physical care and control, and managing property, business and affairs, of a "pupil" child. (b) Person appointed by a court to act in a similar role for a mentally disabled adult. See also "tutor-dative" and "tutor-at-law".
Tutor-at-law:	The nearest agnate (father or nearest male relative on the father's side) appointed by a court to act as tutor (q.v.), under a procedure more cumbersome than that for appointing tutors-dative.
Tutor-dative:	A tutor (q.v.) appointed by a court (other than a "tutor-at-law"). May be appointed to act as personal guardian only, and may be appointed with limited powers. Two persons may be appointed to act as joint tutors-dative.
Unborn:	A child who has been conceived but not yet born.
Ward:	Person subject to guardianship.

185

Ward of Court:	(England) A child may be made a ward of court by court order. The court then exercises parental and administrative jurisdiction and control over the child's person and property.
Welfare Enactments:	Various provisions under health, social work, chronically sick and disabled persons, and national assistance legislation.
Welfare Guardian:	(New Zealand) A personal guardian.
Young Person:	In education law, a child over school leaving age (about 16) but under 18.

APPENDIX I
Selected references and further reading

Constraints of time and space do not permit full listing of references and authorities. Most of those given here in turn quote further relevant authorities. Generally, I have not listed standard modern legal texts with which Scots lawyers will already be familiar, and I have listed only a few selected case authorities. I have not repeated references which are adequately identified in the text. I have designated * references of general relevance to a chapter or section, recommended for further reading by lawyers and non-lawyers alike. Readers requiring assistance in tracing material for further study are recommended to consult SSMH's Information Service (see Appendix II).

In the left hand margin I refer to page numbers in this book. Where numbers appear in brackets, those before the comma (or the only numbers, if there is no comma) refer to paragraphs, or parts of paragraphs, counting from the top of that page. Numbers after the comma refer to lines, counting from the top of the paragraph in question.

Chapter I

* A.D. Ward *Scots Law and the Mentally Handicapped,* SSMH, Glasgow, 1984.

* Annual Reports of the Mental Welfare Commission for Scotland.

p 1 (3,2) Now the Disabled Persons (Services, Consultation and Representation) Act 1986.

(3,6) *See* Chapter VIII.

p 4 Scottish Health Education Group *Finding out about Mental Handicap,* Edinburgh.

p 4 H.V. Cobb and P. Mittler *Significant Differences Between Retardation And Mental Illness,* International League of Societies for Persons with Mental Handicap, 1980.

Chapter III

p 12 (6,7) *See* A.D. Ward "Revival of Tutors Dative", 1987 SLT (News) 69.

Chapter IV

* Fraser on *Parent and Child, and Guardian and Ward*. For historical study I recommend the 3rd edition, 1906, by James Clark, as it comprises the entire text of the 1866 2nd edition, issued under Lord Fraser's supervision, with Clark's additional passages marked by brackets.

* J.E. Graham *The Mental Deficiency and Lunacy (Scotland) Act, 1913*, W. Hodge & Co., Edinburgh and Glasgow, 1914.

* Scottish Law Commission *Report on the Legal Capacity and Responsibility of Minors and Pupils*, published 16th December 1987.

p 18	(5)	Justinian, Institutes, I, XXIII.
	(5,11)	Buckland *Manual of Roman Private Law* 2nd edition p104.
p 19	(2,1)	The Guardianship of Children (Scotland) Acts 1886-1973.
	(3,6)	The Age of Majority (Scotland) Act 1969.
	(5 et seq)	Fraser, *op. cit.,* pp651 et seq.
p 20	(2,5)	Statute 1585, c 18.
	(4,4)	*See,* e.g., Fraser, *op. cit.,* p652.
	(6)	Stair *Institutions of the Law of Scotland* I, 6, 25.
p 21	(3)	Fraser, *op. cit.,* pp662, 663.
	(4)	*Ibid.,* p660.
	(7,3)	*Bryce v Graham* (1826) 6 S 425, (1828) 3W&S 323.
	(7 et seq)	Stair, *op. cit.,* IV, 3, 7-9.
p 22	(2)	Fraser, *op. cit.,* pp659, 660 and authorities there cited.
	(5,2 & 3)	*Ibid.,* p654.
p 23	(2,8 & 10)	Judicial Factors (Scotland) Act 1880 s4, amended by the Law Reform (Miscellaneous Provisions) (Scotland) Act 1980 s6.
	(3,4)	*See* Fraser, *op. cit.,* p668 footnote 5.
	(5,6)	*Graham* (1881) 8 R 996.

p 24 (4,2-5)   *Graham (supra).*

      (6,7)   *Dick v Douglas* 1924 SC 787, 1924 SLT 576.

p 25 (1)   *See* Fraser, *op. cit.,* p292.

      (3,14-18) D.A. Primrose "Changing Sociological and Clinical
                 Patterns in Mental Handicap", The 1983 Blake
                 Marsh Lecture, *Brit. J. Psychiat.,* 1984, 144, 1-8.

      (4,8)   The Lunacy (Scotland) Act, 1857 s49.

      (5,4)   The Lunacy (Scotland) Act, 1862 s1.

p 26 (1)   Report of the Royal Commission on the Care and
                 Control of the Feeble-Minded, 1908, cd. 4202. The
                 Report is difficult to obtain: extracts are quoted in
                 Graham, *op. cit.*

      (3,10-12) 1913 Act, s11(2).

      (3,15-16) 1960 Act, s29(4).

p 27 (2,2-4)   The Mental Deficiency and Lunacy (Scotland) Act
                 (Secretary for Scotland's) Regulations, 1914, S.R.O.
                 No 706/S.60, regulation 4.

p 27 (4)   ) The various provisions are conveniently
p 28 (1)   ) gathered together in Graham, *op. cit.,* pp67, 68 & 72.

      (2,2)   *Dick v Douglas* [*see* p24 (6,7) *supra*].

      (4 & 5)   Scottish Home and Health Department and Scottish
                 Education Department, Social Work Services Group
                 Review of the Mental Health (Scotland) Act 1960, April 1982,
                 page 6.

p 30 (3,1)   Ward *Scots Law and the Mentally Handicapped (supra)*
                 pp22-23.

      (3)   *See* A.D. Ward "Revival of Tutors Dative," 1987 SLT
                 (News) 69.

Chapter V

                 *   *Guardianship for Persons who are Mentally Retarded, A
                 Manual by the New York State Commission on Quality of Care
                 for the Mentally Disabled,* October 1982.

                 * S.S. Herr "Rights into Action: Protecting Human
                 Rights of the Mentally Handicapped", *Catholic University
                 Law Review* Vol 26 Winter 1977, Number 2 (an article

189

based on a survey of rights of mentally handicapped people in Sweden, Denmark, the Netherlands and Britain).

p 31	(1,4)	U.N. General Assembly, 26th Session 1971, resolution 2856.
	(1,10)	Declaration dated 24th October 1968.
	(1,10)	*Guardianship for Mentally Retarded Persons, Position Papers of the American Association on Mental Deficiency*, approved by AAMD Council, 1973-1975.
p 34	(7,12-15)	B.D. Sales, D.M. Powell, R. Van Duizend et al. *Disabled Persons and the Law - State Legislative Issues*, Plenum Press, New York, 1982, pp532-649.
p 36	(9,2)	Dependent Adults Acts, Chapter D-32.
p 39	(4)	*See* letter from M.G. Baron, member of Guardianship Working Party, (English) Law Society's Group for the Welfare of People with a Mental Handicap, *The Times* 21 March 1987.

Chapter VI

p 43	(1,1)	[*See* p12 (6,7) *supra*].
	(2,1-2)	[*See* p24 (6,7) *supra*].
p 50	(4,6)	*B,* 1989, unreported.
p 53	(1,2)	1988 SLT (News) 4.

Chapter VII

		* J.M. Thomson *Family Law in Scotland*, Butterworths, London, 1987.
p 55	(2,2-5)	Fraser, *op. cit.,* p662.
p 56	(1,6-14)	Memorandum referred to, pp48-49.
p 56	(2)	Thomson, *op. cit.,* Chapter X; Norrie, 1985 SLT (News) 157; Thomson, 1985 SLT (News) 223; Thomson, 1986, *Scottish Law Gazette*, Vol 54, No 3, 60.
p 57	(4,5)	Thomson "Sterilisation of Mentally Handicapped Children" 1988 SLT (News) 1, at pp3 & 4.

Chapter VIII

* J.K. Mason & R.A. McCall Smith *Law and Medical Ethics*, Butterworths, London, 1987.

* (England) *Competency and Consent to Medical Treatment* Report of a Mencap Working Party, March 1989.

* (England) M. Gunn "Consent to Treatment and People with Mental Handicaps", *Mental Handicap*, December 1987, Vol 15.

p 59 (1,4)   *In re B* [1987] 2 All E.R. 206.

       (2,3)   *F v West Berkshire Health Authority.*

p 62 (3,6-9)   J.K. Mason & R.A. McCall Smith, *op. cit,* p142.

p 63 (4,4)   [1957] 2 All E.R. 118.

      (5 & 6)   D. Carson "Why the law lords said yes to sterilisation" *Health Service Journal*, 8th June 1989, pp690-691.

S.J. Gibson "Sterilising the handicapped", *Independent*, 31st May 1989.

p 67   For discussion and historical perspective on subject of sterilisation *see* Roy and Roy "Sterilisation for girls and women with mental handicaps: some ethical and moral considerations", *Mental Handicap*, 16th September 1988, Vol 16, p97.

Chapter IX

* (England) H. Dixon & M. Gunn *Sex and the Law,* Family Planning Association Education Unit, November 1985.

* (Australia) W. McCarthy & L. Fegan *Sex Education and the Intellectually Handicapped,* ADIS Press, Sydney etc., 1984.

p 78 (1,6)   *X and Y v The Netherlands*, decision dated 26th March 1985, Application No 16/1983/72/110.

p 80 (2)   *See* Bright and others *The Law and Persons with Intellectual Handicaps*, Report dated March 1981 of the Committee on the Rights of Persons with Handicaps to the Attorney General of South Australia, Chapter V.

p 83 (4,7-8)   On Community Charge generally *see* SSMH *People with mental handicap and the poll tax,* 1989 (leaflet).

p 85 (3 & 4)   *Gillick v West Norfolk and Wisbech Area Health Authority* [1986] AC 112, [1985] 3 All E.R. 402, HL.

Chapter X

p 91 (2,7)   Court of Session Act 1868.

   (2,10)   Judicial Factors (Scotland) Act 1880.

p 94 (3,5-16)   *Fraser v Paterson (No 2),* 1988 SLT 124.

p 95 (2,6-9)   E.g. *see* N. Barry "Who looks after the guardians?", *Scotsman,* 18 March 1989.

p 99 (3,2)   *Fraser v Paterson,* 1987 SLT 562.

p109 (last para, 2) *McFarlane v Donaldson,* (1835) 13 S 725.

p110 (1,1)   *Brogan, Petitioner,* 1986 SLT 420.

Chapter XI

   * (England) A.B. Quinn *A Guide to families wishing to make legal provision for a mentally handicapped member,* Anthony Quinn & Co., London, 1989.

p112 (2)   Application No. 12567/86.

Chapter XII

   * *Towards Mental Health Law Reform,* the report of the Legal Information Service/Mental Health Foundation Task Force On Revision Of Mental Health Legislation, December 1983.

   * *Legal and Consumer Issues in Mental Health Law,* Vol One of the Proceedings of Conference 1987, Mental Health Foundation of New Zealand.

p121 (4,2-4)   *Towards Mental Health Law Reform (supra)* p175.

Chapter XIII

p141 (4)   * (United States) S.S. Herr *Rights and Advocacy for Retarded People,* Lexington Books, Lexington and Toronto, 1983.

p141 (4)   *See* (1) P. Morris "Making the right match", *Community Living,* 1987; Sept/Oct, pp8-9 (reprinted in

Mental Handicap Bulletin 70/9, BIMH Publications Sales).

(2) (Australia) J. O'Brien "Citizen advocacy is important because . . . ", *Interaction* (the Australian magazine on intellectual disability), August 1987, pp32-34.

(3) J. Hadley "Speaking for One and All", *Community Care*, 1st September 1988, pp14-15.

Chapter XIV

* SSMH *Information for the Named Person*, 1987.

* Scottish Consumer Council *In Special Need: A handbook for parents and young people in Scotland with special educational needs*, HMSO, 1989.

* Scottish Consumer Council *The Law of the School: A Parent's Guide to Education Law in Scotland*, HMSO, 1987.

* (England) B. Cox *The Law of Special Educational Needs, A Guide to the Education Act, 1981*, Croom Helm, 1986.

p148 (2,4) p150 (5)	) *See* note on page 155.)
p151 (2)	*Lamont v Strathclyde Regional Council* 1988 SLT (Sh. Ct.) 9.
p153 (4,15-18)	*R. v Oxfordshire County Council, ex parte W.* [1987] 2 F.L.R. 193, D.C.
p154 (1)	*Regina v Lancashire County Council, ex parte CM.*

Chapter XV

p156 (4)   (Australia) *see* J. Anderson "Anti-discimination laws for people with intellectual disabilities", *Interaction* (the Australian magazine on intellectual disability), November 1987, pp19-22.

Chapter XVI

p163 (3,7)   *B v Forsey* (H.L.), 1988 SLT 572

Chapter XVII

p172 (3)   J. Dawson, quoted by S. Bell in paper on "The Protection of Personal and Property Rights Act: Does it achieve what it sets out to?" to World Mental Health Congress, Auckland, August 1989.

Glossary

* D.M. Walker *The Oxford Companion to Law,* Clarendon Press, Oxford, 1980.

APPENDIX II

Useful Addresses

Accountant of Court
Meldrum House, 15 Drumsheugh Gdns, Edinburgh EH3 7QG
031-220 1898

British Institute of Mental Handicap
Wolverhampton Road, Kidderminster DY10 3PP   0562-850251

Citizen's Advice Scotland
26 George Square, Edinburgh EH8 9LD   031-667 0156

The (English) Law Society's Group for the Welfare of People with a Mental Handicap
c/o A.B. Quinn, 112-114 Finchley Road, London NW3 5HT

Family Planning Association - Information, Education, Resources
4 Clifton Street, Glasgow G3 7LA   041-333 9696

Law Society of Scotland
26 Drumsheugh Gdns, Edinburgh EH3 7YR   031-226 7411

Lay Observer for Scotland
30 Castle Street, Edinburgh EH2   031-226 2503

Mental Welfare Commission for Scotland
25 Drumsheugh Gdns., Edinburgh EH3 7RB   031-225 7034

Scottish Action on Dementia
33 Castle Street, Edinburgh EH2 3DN   031-220 4886

Scottish Association for Mental Health
38 Gardner's Cres., Edinburgh EH3 8DQ   031-229 9687

Scottish Child Law Centre
1 Melrose Street, off Queen's Cres., Glasgow G4 9BJ   041-333 9305

Scottish Consumer Council
314 St. Vincent Street, Glasgow G3 8XW   041-226 5261

Scottish Down's Syndrome Association
54 Shandwick Place, Edinburgh EH2 4RT   031-226 2420

Scottish Law Commission
140 Causewayside, Edinburgh EH9 1PR   031-668 2131

Scottish Legal Aid Board
44 Drumsheugh Gdns, Edinburgh EH3 7SW   031-226 7061

Scottish Society for the Mentally Handicapped
13 Elmbank Street, Glasgow G2 4QA   041-226 4541

INDEX

abortion, consent to, 36, 70, 71
abuse,
  generally, 158-161
  public pressure, 168
Accountant of Court, 92-97, 101, 106
  110, 112, 116
adult training centres, 158, 170
age,
  children, of, relevance of, 11, 18, 19,
    60, 140, 148, 162
  conditions associated with, 168, 170
  trend towards 2-tier system, 19, 162
Age of Majority (Scotland) Act 1969, 22
agnate, nearest male, appointment of,
  13, 19-25
Alberta, *see* management of affairs
  (Alberta);
  personal guardian (Alberta).
aliment, obligation to, 164, 165
Allanbridge, Lord, 110, 115
annuities, and Income Support, 118
assessment of needs, *see* children;
  mentally handicapped.

Baker, Nicki, 173
Balance of Care for Adults with a
  Mental Handicap in Scotland,
  The (Baker and Urquhart), 173
bank accounts, operation of, 105
Bolam v Friern Hospital Management
  Committee (1957), 63
Brandon, Lord, 63, 64
brieves of "furiosity", "idiotry", 21
B v Forsey, 163

Capital Transfer Tax, 165
carers,
  abilities, 136, 137
  definition, 134, 135
  generally, 47, 51, 77, 95-97, 105, 106,
    123, 140, 158 et seq., 167-169
  local authorities' responsibilities,
    134-137

Caring for People: Community Care
  in the Next Decade and Beyond
  White Paper, 3, 5, 118, 132, 135
certified houses/institutions, 27
Child Abduction and Custody Act 1985,
  57
Child Abduction, Convention on the
  Civil Aspects of International, 57
child guidance service, 150
children,
  abuse and deprivation, 158-161, 168
  age, relevance of, 11, 18, 19, 60, 140,
    148, 162
  aliment, obligation to, 164, 165
  assessment of needs,
    educational needs, 132-134, 148 et
      seq.
    education authority, duties of, 133,
      148 et seq.
    health boards, role of, 134
    "observation and assessment"
      introduced, 148, 149
    recording from age 2, 148
    review, 134, 149
    social work authority, duties of,
      133, 134
    special needs, *see* education
      (special needs).
    teachers' reports, 148, 150
    welfare needs, 133, 134
  curator and dealings of, 18, 19
  custody,
    access, and, up to 16, 162
    definition and relevance of, 56, 57
  detention, improper, 160
  law of, influence of, 17, 20
  management of affairs, 55
  medical consent, and, 56, 57, 61
  parental rights,
    generally, 36, 56-58, 68, 148, 149,
      160, 162, 163
    order relating to, 57, 58, 62, 67, 163
  personal guardian of, extent of
    power, 55 et seq.
  pupil, 19, 55, 60
  residence, control of, 55, 57

197

medical consent,
court authorisation (continued),
where advisable, 66, 68, 72, 75
detained patients, certain,
unnecessary for, 73
drug-testing of sportsmen, 75, 76
examination/treatment, medical
evidence of need of (Alberta),
74
generally, 12, 30, 38, 40, 56, 59, 60,
125, 168
implied, 60, 62, 63
legal capacity for, based on
reasonable understanding, 61
life-saving procedures (USA), 36
medical/dental examinations/
treatment, 47, 71-75, 169
medication, 3 months and over, 73
necessity, based on,
abortion, 36, 70, 71
"best interests of patient", as,
63- 66, 68, 70-72, 74, 75
F case authoritative in Scotland, 62
generally, 60, 62, 74, 75, 168
Jeanette case, lesson of, *see*
Jeanette case.
treatment, appropriateness of, 64
NZ provisions, 125, 126
partial capacity, where, 71
pupil children, 60, 67
statutory,
guardian, power lacking, 47, 61
provision, 74, 75
sterilisation cases, 36, 59, 65-72, 75
treatment, irreversible, where, 74
tutor-dative, by, 47, 64, 66, 67, 71, 72,
76
tutor with health care powers, 61, 64,
72
unconscious patient, 60, 72
violent behaviour, excluded where,
74
medical evidence,
detention, supporting, 163, 164
generally, 23, 27, 29, 37, 40, 43-45, 48-
50, 64, 82-85, 98-100, 102 et seq.,
106, 111, 113, 114, 140
medical negligence, 63 et seq.
medical practitioner, access of, 29, 47
medical/psychological advice/
examinations, 82, 148, 150
meningitis, 4

men, protection of, 78, 87
mental defectives, 26
Mental Deficiency, American
Association on, 33
Mental Deficiency and Lunacy
(Scotland) Act (1913), 26, 27, 29,
47, 53
mental disability law,
Alberta, statutory guardianship,
36-39
American developments, 34 et seq.
definitions, 3, 5
English proposals, 39-42
exclusions from, 5
reform, pressure for, 167 et seq.
see also children; disabled persons;
mentally handicapped; mental
illness.
Mental Handicap, British Institute of,
147
*Mental Handicap in Scotland, The
Balance of Care for Adults with
a,* (1987) Baker and Urquhart, 173
Mental Handicap, International League
of Societies for Persons with, 32
mental health law, *see* mental disability
law
mental health officer,
access of, 29, 47
lacking, where role, 45, 53, 98
role of, 29, 45, 47, 53, 98, 171
Mental Health Panels/Hearings
suggested, 169
Mental Health (Scotland) Act (1960), 26,
27, 53, 77, 162, 164
Mental Health (Scotland) Act (1984),
generally, 28-30, 53, 159, 162, 164
Part X, 73-75
s. 41(2), 29, 45-47
s. 44(1)(2), 46, 47
s. 94, 100, 111-113
s. 106, 77-88
mental illness,
definition, 4
early provision for, 13
impairment, degree and nature of,
variability, 5
mental handicap, and, distinction, 4,
169
Mentally Disabled, Commission on the,
(American Bar Association), 34
mentally disordered/impaired, 3

204

205

tutor-at-law (continued),
  removal of, 21
  security for performance of duties,
    21, 22
  single court petition, 114
  tutor-dative, and, 13, 21, 24, 52
tutor-dative,
  adult, mentally disabled, as legal
    relationship with, 27
  advantages of, 23, 24, 52
  agnate, nearest male, as, 23, 50
  appointment,
    alternate excluded, 45
    automatic transfer, 50, 115
    competition for, 52
    health care consent, with, 72
    individual, of, 53
    joint, 30, 43, 45, 50, 52, 114, 115
    local authority, of, considered, 53
    mental health officer, absence of
      role, 45, 53
    minor children, tutor of, 57, 58
    petition for, *see* petition for
      appointment *(infra)*; cognition.
    remuneration, relatives and others
      without, 114
    temporary, pending tutor-at-law, 24
    younger person, jointly with, 50
  carer as, 49, 51
  criticisms of procedure, 53, 54
  curator-dative becomes, 13, 20, 23
  definition, 12
  deinstitutionalisation, and 50, 51
  drug-testing, authority to consent to,
    76
  history, 23 et seq., 52
  home away from family home,
    where, 50, 51
  legal aid related to means of
    handicapped, 48, 67
  limited duration, 30, 43, 44, 101
  medical,
    certification, model, 48, 49
    consent by, 47, 64, 66, 67, 71, 72, 76
    evidence, 23, 43-45, 48-50, 98, 102,
      114
    treatment, consent to, 47
  Morris petitioner (1986) 12, 30, 43-45,
    48, 52, 53, 105
  parents and professionals divergence,
    53, 54

tutor-dative (continued),
  personal guardian,
    extension to management, 115
    manager, and, as, 14, 16, 114, 168
    solely as, 14, 43 et seq., 113, 114
    "stop gap", as, 64
  petition for appointment,
    cognition as earlier prerequisite, 23
    Court of Session, to, 30, 48, 57
    generally, 23, 30, 44, 45, 48-50, 114,
      115
    opposed, 50, 52
    service requirements, 49
    see also appointment *(supra)*;
      cognition.
  powers,
    "Alberta" and English proposals in
      Morris case, 43, 44
    limited, 30, 43, 44
    need, tailored to, 14, 30, 44, 48
    personal guardian, as, 27, 126
    restraint and recall, 47, 48
    statutory guardian's powers
      compared, 27, 28, 30, 45 et seq.
  review/variation of order, 43
  revival of, 10, 12-14, 23, 24, 28, 30, 43,
    50, 53, 64, 101, 163, 167
  social work reports, lack of, 45
  statutory code, integrated, inferior to,
    54
  tutor-at-law, and, 13, 21, 24, 52
  see also personal guardian.

UN Declarations on the Rights of,
  Disabled Persons, 156
  Mentally Retarded Persons, 31, 156
United States of America,
  Disabilities, Developmental and Bill
    of Rights Act, 142
  Disabled, Bureau of Protection and
    Advocacy for the
    Developmentally (New York), 142
  Protection and Advocacy System, 142
    see also management of
    affairs (USA); personal
    guardian (USA).
unsound mind, person of, 22, 25, 91,
  99, 102
Urquhart, James, 173

209